Parent to Parent

PARENT TO PARENT
Working Together for Ourselves and Our Children

Peggy Pizzo

Foreword by Benjamin Spock, M.D.

BEACON PRESS   BOSTON

Copyright ©1983 by Peggy Pizzo

Beacon Press books are published under the auspices
of the Unitarian Universalist Association of Congregations in North America,
25 Beacon Street, Boston, Massachusetts 02108
Published simultaneously in Canada by
Fitzhenry & Whiteside Limited, Toronto

All rights reserved

Printed in the United States of America

(hardcover)   9   8   7   6   5   4   3   2   1
(paperback)   9   8   7   6   5   4   3   2   1

Library of Congress Cataloging in Publication Data

> Pizzo, Peggy Daly.
>   Parent to parent
>
>   Bibliography, p.
>   Includes index.
>   1. Parenting — United States. 2. Self-help groups —
> United States. 3. Child welfare — United States.
> I. Title.
> HQ755.8.P572   1983   306.8'74   82-72505
> ISBN 0-8070-2300-0
> ISBN 0-8070-2301-9

TO CARA AND TRACY

Work contributing to this book was supported by the Carnegie Corporation of New York; however, the author is solely responsible for the views and opinions expressed in this book.

Acknowledgments

In developing both the organizing concepts for this report and the manuscript itself, I shared ideas with and listened to comments and perspectives from many supportive and thoughtful people. In addition, several people read through parts of this manuscript in various drafts and critiqued them for me.

At the Carnegie Corporation of New York, Barbara Finberg has always offered patient, thoughtful guidance. I deeply appreciate her support. Avery Russell has given sound, professional editorial and publishing advice. When he was a project officer at Carnegie, Mark Geier first encouraged this undertaking and was always enormously helpful in reading early drafts. Gloria Brown has been a warm and sensitive analyst and supporter. Adelina Diamond provided solid, enthusiastic comments on the manuscript.

I am particularly indebted to Rochelle Beck, Jack Calhoun, Fran Eizenstat, Dana Friedman, Ellen Galinsky, Edith Grotberg, Judith Hagopian, Nicholas Hobbs, Patricia Ireland, Lynn Kagan, Geraldine Jackson, Juel Janis, Jim Levine, Laura Miller, Susan Muenchow, Bambi Cardenas Ramirez, and Barbara Warden. During part of this book's preparation, Charito Kruvant generously offered me what a writer needs most — space, time, and someone to answer the telephone.

Gil Steiner was a continual, steady, analytical, and supportive luncheon companion, critic, and reader of early drafts. The lively interest of Marian Wright Edelman in several chapters helped recharge me for the last stretch needed to complete this book. Ed Zigler has been a generous adviser, friend, and colleague.

Stuart Eizenstat, who supervised my policy work at the White House, not only gave me helpful encouragement but challenged me to see national domestic policy in broad and fresh perspectives. Jo Ann Miller, a perceptive, sensitive editor, helped me with good advice. Erwin Glikes extended to me both his valuable candor and his incisive, good-humored insights. Leona Schecter, my agent, was an invaluable support throughout.

Mildred Foxx Prioleau and Ed Green helped me prepare and conduct interviews with Black parent leaders of self-help and advocacy organizations, and Mildred Prioleau conducted interviews with the leaders of several organizations. The most sensitive, honest, and open interviews that parent advocates gave me were due to her considerable talent.

Elsa Dixler provided me with competent, and often salutary, editorial advice and assistance. Finally, at Beacon Press, Joanne Wyckoff, my editor, has always shown a perceptive appreciation of the significance of parent advocacy and a skilled and sensitive use of the editor's pencil.

These colleagues — and the Carnegie Corporation of New York — are not responsible, of course, for what is written in *Parent to Parent*. I assume sole responsibility for this book.

Several typists — Stephanie Spiesman, Dorothy O'Callaghan, Liz Howell, Dot Foust, and Sandy Maryman — have invaluably assisted me.

I am also deeply appreciative of the many parents who gave me hours of time in order to share their experiences with me.

Within my own personal social system of "supportive services," my sisters and brothers, parents and parents-in-law have all helped to make this effort possible. My husband has marshaled numerous practical and philosophical services to encourage me. As for my children, they accompanied me to interviews, wrote numerous essays, stories, and books of their own, and cheered me on. Most of all, they have taught me the most important part of what parent self-help and advocacy is about: protectiveness, caring, and energy originating in a powerful, very old, and enduring human commitment.

Foreword

BENJAMIN SPOCK, M.D.

Why is it that in recent years parents have had to make such mighty efforts to organize themselves, join forces for strength and comfort, and go forth to battle for elementary rights for their children? They've had to struggle for such causes as better public schools for all, special education and medical services for the handicapped, and more humane care in hospitals and in residential institutions.

Partly it's because for so long parents, like everybody else, depended on science to find the answers to all problems, and on professionals, technicians, institutions, and government to provide the means. But they've found — in too many cases — that the services they expected were callous or belittling or inadequate or beyond their means or simply nonexistent in their locality. Their children, especially handicapped children, were being shortchanged.

It's almost impossible for us inhabitants of the twentieth century to realize how much science, technology, institutions, and government have changed — supposedly for the better. But in the process they have taken control of our lives and left us subtly dependent, lacking in the degree of initiative that our ancestors had to show, because these new ways have been much too complex for us to carry out as individuals.

In earlier times, when most Americans lived on farms or in small communities, they expected to be responsible for their own needs. They took the initiative in town meetings to secure the kinds of schools and other services they decided they wanted. Medical care was primitive by our standards but very personal. When a family in a crisis needed practical and emotional support, their neighbors pitched in, out of affectionate feelings. If a child with a disability was able to attend a one-room school, the teacher expected to adapt the work to this individual's ability, just as he or she did with all the other pupils. If the child couldn't attend, a parent was often able to give the same lessons in the three R's as the teacher did, for there were no special facilities such as science and language laboratories or even school libraries.

In modern times, services have become increasingly technical, institutionalized, and impersonal, especially in cities. Their availability has varied shamefully in different localities, depending on the economic level and the vagaries of politics. The professionals, elaborately trained, have too often kept a cool and supercilious distance between themselves and their clients, which intimidates and undermines the self-confidence of the latter. To make matters worse, many families have lacked the back-up security that comes from having relatives nearby or from being long-time residents of a closely knit neighborhood. Citizens in cities have commonly felt impotent to change conditions in their schools, institutions, and health facilities through the political process. "My vote doesn't count — it's only one in a million!" they explain.

No wonder it has taken a long time, remarkable initiative, and great courage for small groups of ordinary parents to set out to get for their children what was not forthcoming from the system. Part of the inspiration came from the examples of the civil-rights, natural-childbirth, and women's movements.

The parents of children with disabilities realized that as much as anything else they desperately needed the companionship of other parents with similar problems, in order not only to share knowledge of how to help their children but to overcome the painful sense of inferiority and isolation, of "being different." The blessed sense of acceptance they received gave them the optimism and energy necessary to tackle the other problems.

A small core would recruit other parents of children with the same problem, through acquaintanceships formed in clinics or through newspaper advertisements. They would offer a variety of benefits through one-to-one and group conferences, sharing information about how to care at home for children with a particular handicap and knowledge about where and how to secure better services and schooling. Parents would get a boost in morale and self-image through coming to know and respect each other. Sometimes great emotional comfort would come from sharing criticism of tactless or pompous professionals and other staff people. Such activities can be grouped under the heading of self-help.

The other broad area of activity is called advocacy. Parents work together to secure better services for children. They raise funds for research and services. They lobby legislators for funds and for changes in the law. They put pressure — polite or aggressive — on officials of the state, municipality, school district, agencies, and institutions, even organizing demonstrations when professionals prove recalcitrant. They mobilize public support for reforms. They keep watch, after improvements are made, to see that they are continued.

Peggy Pizzo, whom I've known and admired for years, has written an indispensable book for all who want to improve services for children. She is not telling parents, "Do this, don't do that." Instead, she has traveled all over the country to listen to the people who've played crucial roles in organizing groups and let them tell their stories in their own revealing, dramatic words: Grace Monaco of the Candlelighters, who are parents of children with cancer; Jolly K and Lee Lapicki of Parents Anonymous, who befriend and counsel other parents who've abused or fear they will abuse their children; Sophia Harris of the Federation of Community Controlled Child Care Centers of Alabama, who wants to provide good facilities without the prying of officials or the condescension of professionals; Daphne Busby of the Sisterhood of Black Single Mothers, which fosters sound parenting by fostering self-respect. Peggy has also interviewed organizers of the National Association for Retarded Citizens, Parents Concerned for Hospitalized Children, Fathers United for Equal Justice, the North American Council for Adoptable Children, and Mothers Against Drunk Drivers (MADD).

The clear conclusion that comes out of these many interviews is that there are distinctly different philosophies about how close or far away to keep from professionals, whether to go national or stay local, whether to hire full-time staff when they can be afforded or to insist that volunteer parents continue to do the work, whether to keep groups small or let them expand, how far the original group or national organization should try to control new branches.

Well, this is an inspiring story of how ordinary American people without previous political or organized experience can rise to the occasion and find the inner and mutual resources to persuade or force our society to grant justice to its children. It is indispensable reading for anyone who wants to do likewise. But it will also impart understanding to nurses, teachers, technicians, physicians, administrators, legislators, lawyers, and judges throughout the field of services for children.

Contents

Acknowledgments   ix

Foreword   Benjamin Spock, M.D.   xi

Introduction   1

1. The Shared Experience   10
    Bonding: A Powerful Force for Change   19
    Parent Stress: A Special Kind   21

2. A History of Parent Activism   33
    Pivotal Victories for the Handicapped and Blacks   35
    Health: A Perennial Issue for Self-Help   38
    Parents and Schools   42
    The Sixties Activists   46

3. Images of Parents   48
    The Incompetent Parent   50
    The Victimized Parent   56
    Consequences of Negative Parent Images   61
    A New Image: The Resourceful Parent   69

4. What Parent Groups Provide   79
    New Communities   82
    New Confidence, New Self-Image   89

5. Shaking Up Institutions   103
    Personal Pain and Institutional Reform   104
    What Gets Parents Started   108
    What Works   113

6. Working for Laws that Work for Children   128

   Getting Legislation Passed   131
   Implementation: Making the Law Work   142
   The Battle to Keep What We've Won   148

7. Parent Groups: Common Problems,
      Common Practices   150

   Getting Organized   150
   Projecting a Serious Image   153
   The Home Base   156
   Funding   157
   Expansion to a Statewide or National Organization   159
   Coalition Politics   169
   Case vs. Class Advocacy   170
   Alternative Services vs. Advocacy   172
   Sustaining a Group   173
   The New Pioneers   174

8. A Look Toward the Future   177

Appendix: Parent Self-Help and Advocacy
  Organizations   195

Notes   203

Bibiliography   217

Index   223

Parent to Parent

INTRODUCTION

This book is about the refusal of parents to accept suffering or blunted opportunity for their children.

And this book is about parents rebuilding a stronger sense of self-worth by turning to other parents — people like themselves — for help.

It's terrible to watch children suffer — especially your own. The prolonged suffering of a child spurs a desire to do something to stop it. When a parent can't "make things right," he or she feels powerless and angry. Over time, many parents feel pulled toward a resigned belief that they are inevitably impotent in the face of this suffering.

Perhaps this is why our society often shuts out people whose children suffer. We don't want to see. It's not that we don't mobilize resources, especially money, to help — all of the endless fund-raising campaigns, mothers' marches, walkathons, bike trips, charity benefits attest to compassion for children who suffer, or for at least some of them. But we don't want to *feel* what parents feel when a child suffers. So we reconcile the conflicts between the need to push away and the need to respond by building institutions and filling them with "the best that money can buy" in equipment, staff, and technology. Then we close the door. All too often we close the door in the face of the parents whose children are to be helped. This book reflects the response of parents in different parts of our country to that unacceptable closed door and to the very un-American squeeze on opportunity that so many institutions seem to tolerate for children.

It's also wrong that so many of us struggle to be "good" parents in an anxious fog of self-doubt. The help extended to us by the experts and professionals who so much want us to be good parents — even when their efforts *are* helpful — influences our sense of ourselves as people who need to be helped. Too often, it doesn't matter enough to the helpers that eager experts raise more parental self-doubt and diminish self-esteem. This book describes a new and growing response: parent-to-parent support groups, in which parents are both helpers and helped, in which promoting parental self-esteem matters as much as the exchange of information useful to good child-rearing.

In writing this book, I set out to document organized parent self-help and advocacy in a personal way. I have gone directly to a core source of knowledge: parents themselves. With the support of the Carnegie Corporation of New York, I found and interviewed members of almost two dozen national, state, and local parent organizations.

Parents who engage in self-help and advocacy have chosen to do several things: define *for themselves* what they need to do a better job; organize or join a group with other parents who have either made or are making a similar definition; expressly (but not exclusively) depend on one another for emotional support and practical guidance; and, in most cases, unite with each other to challenge institutional and political decisions that harm or threaten their children and to direct the development of new public policies and practices.

In writing this book, I have focused on organizations developed primarily by parents for other parents, and now directed by them. Every month dozens of newsletters from these organizations came into my home. Reading them, as well as stacks of congressional testimony, manuals on organizing effective advocacy, and books and articles describing how our institutions respond to parents and children during childbirth, divorce, hospitalization, and death, led me to a better understanding of parent activism. I have spent months talking to dozens of parents in urban, suburban, and rural communities about their experiences in parent groups. I have tried to reflect the thoughts, feelings, and perspectives of these parents as much as possible. I have tried to show what parent activists do and why, how and when they succeed, and what they think are effective strategies for change. I believe that many readers can profit from their story.

In part I decided to write this book because I grew very tired of the way the media depict parents. Books, movies, and magazines that discuss children and families today all employ images of parents that deeply influence our attitudes about the needs of children, the value of families, the operation of programs, the fashioning of public policy. So often the images used are "deficit" ones, highlighting parental weaknesses or incapacities. I wanted to present another view; the resourcefulness that so many parents in self-help and advocacy groups share. This book highlights new choices and options used by parent activists for confronting powerful feelings of incompetence as well as for confronting injustice or suffering.

This book doesn't *tell* parents to do anything. As parents, we all experience times when we need to listen to knowledgeable people telling us what to do. But we often expect experts or authorities to furnish too many answers for us.

I think we benefit from listening to other parents describe how they've met the challenges of child-rearing, and then building the approaches that make the most sense for our lives and our families. We need more books that bring us the actual experiences of ordinary people meeting the extraordinary task of raising children. We need more books that deliberately overlook the opportunity to tell parents what to do in order to describe and discuss how parents are doing for themselves, and what happens as a result.

Parents face lots of problems; we grope, fumble, and make mistakes. But there is a great deal of problem-solving strength, such deep resourcefulness, in so many of us. We need to hear our stories; we need to learn from each other.

Furthermore, professionals, experts, and scholars need to hear about and understand the ways in which parents are tackling the challenges of child-rearing on their own, in fresh new ways.

So readers will not find here a manual on organizing a parent group in ten, twelve, or even twenty easy steps. Instead, they will find many ideas about parent groups, how they get started, when they are successful, and how other parents locate them.

Other readers too can gain from learning about parent activism.

- Scholars and researchers who shape professional and public opinion and members of the academic community who prepare the new generation of professionals to work in courts, schools, hospitals, and adoption and foster-care agencies will find in

this book new ideas about connections between parents and government, parents and institutions, and parents and professionals when benefits and services for children are the aim. The rising generation of professionals will work with activist parents who reject dependence on experts. They need to understand this parent movement, its origins, and its implications for effective help to children and parents.
• Advocates for children and families will find practical, successful ideas and strategies and both present and potential allies for the redress of unfair social conditions that harm children.
• Policy makers will find parents' perspectives on policies and programs that are effective — and on how these policies can meet children's needs better.
• Physicians, nurses, teachers, lawyers, social workers, and mental-health workers will find in this book old friends and new allies, together with some successful strategies for the continued struggle to improve services for children and families.

Professionals, experts, and scholars may find this book tough on their performance. Parent activists are often angry and hard in their judgments. Bitter rifts sometimes develop between professionals and leaders of self-help groups; some professionals fear that self-help leaders unwittingly support the movement to dismiss all human services professionals as unnecessary. I have reported parent anger as I heard it. I have also reported the compassion that parent activists often expressed toward professionals as a group, and their understanding of the system's role in constricting professionals' actions. I believe both responses are justified.

I have tried to keep my personal experiences if not out of the book entirely, then at least in its margins. In the Introduction, I think it useful to do otherwise. I am a parent. I am also a professional, by training a specialist in child development. In both capacities I have seen plenty of what can only be termed abusive behavior toward parents. On one of my stays in a maternity ward, I saw a tiny young woman, with freshly plaited braids hanging down her back, eagerly waiting by the hospital elevator for her new baby to be brought up. (Babies were kept on a different floor and brought up only for feeding, which gives you some idea of that institution's understanding of parent-child bonding and of the vulnerability of new parents.) The doors opened and the nurses briskly distributed the babies and reentered the elevator. The young mother waited, then, voice quavering slightly, asked where her baby was. "Your baby's too sick to be moved right now," called out a nurse as the doors shut. "The pediatrician will explain it to you tomorrow." This little person, who couldn't have been more than twenty, quietly crumbled. "No one," she said, "told me my baby was sick." Not one word of support came from behind the desk where the nurses sat chatting during feeding time. No word of explanation was offered for hours.

Other incidents come to mind: a "learning-disability specialist" rattling off a list of the "deficiencies" she had detected in the extraordinarily bright nine-year-old son of a construction worker and his wife — a boy who had not yet mastered addition and subtraction and could barely read. "Minimal brain dysfunction, some aphasia [loss of power to express or comprehend language], poor eye-hand and other sensory motor coordination, possibly related to slight ptosis [drooping of the upper eyelid, sometimes from paralysis of facial nerve] of the right eye, could have been a birth injury..." She chatted on, shook hands, and left. The father turned to me (I was his boy's teacher, barely twenty-two). Embarrassed, terrified, struggling to conceal his emotions, he wanted to know, "What's going to happen to him? Will he be all right?"

I've witnessed many other incidents like these two. Years later, I'm still angry about them. This book has some roots in that anger.

But I have also experienced the stresses of working in the "helping services." At the age of sixteen, I began working as a nurse's aide at a local hospital. I put in eight-hour shifts on weekends and forty-hour weeks during the summer. By the time I was twenty-one I had seen a substantial amount of human suffering. I had seen just as much compassionate human service — caring sustained through overpowering strain and demands. Since then I have worked in Head Start, in early childhood education programs, as a tutor in a mental institution, as a day-care-center administrator, as a public schoolteacher in a special education center, as a research analyst of children's services, and in government, including the United States Children's Bureau and the

White House staff. Numerous statistics describe children's needs and the value of services that meet those needs. I know those statistics, and some of them will appear in this book. But for the moment I want to note that from nineteen years of personal experience, I know how much these services are needed; I know they can make a positive difference for children and families.

In addition to these memories, I had some immediate reminders to help me maintain perspective while writing this book. Mornings I awaken to a radio alarm clock that was pressed upon my husband by a family whose baby had been brought near death by meningitis. As a young intern in a children's hospital, my husband had waged an aggressive, calculated, and finally successful attack on the meningitis by working for sixty hours, with few breaks for food and none for sleep. This expression of parental celebration of a baby's recovery reminded me each day that professionals and institutions are welcome to many families. At night, as I wrote at my desk, I could hear the shrill beeper summoning my husband back into a ward where children suffer and caring adults routinely forgo comfort and sleep to help.

So sometimes, in reading the works of those who find so much evil and so little good in human services — and especially in services for children — I am grateful that I have personal evidence from both past and present of the system's contribution to children's lives. One reason we have been so disappointed in professionals may be that we expect far too much, far too quickly. We expect enormous devotion and commitment from people not bonded to us by birth and common lineage, shared childhood or intimate daily associations. And in great measure we *do* receive considerable devotion.

As we move through the 1980s, economic troubles make the tax-paying population more hostile to the expenditure of public dollars on all but the most essential programs. A small but highly vocal minority among parents opposes any new proposal for publicly supported children's services on the grounds of intrusion into family privacy and infringement of parents' rights. And an increasingly large segment of the population wonders how effective the public schools — America's major experiment in allocating general public resources to benefit children — really are.

This policy climate does not favor government funding of children's services, unless evidence can be marshaled to show minimal costs and substantial benefits.

Self-help clearly attracts the approval of the public and of some policy makers because it holds out the promise of high benefit for virtually no public expenditures. If Alcoholics Anonymous can effectively ensure that even a small percentage of American alcoholics break loose from their dependence on a drug through private efforts, then at the very least (in fiscal terms) fewer people will be using the nation's publicly supported detoxification and alcohol-abuse programs. A similar appeal exists for Parents Anonymous. The protective-services system for children is strained by the rapidly increasing number of cases of child abuse and neglect. Government-funded social services cannot possibly provide supportive counseling to all families under stress. When abusive and potentially abusive parents in a group such as Parents Anonymous help each other prevent harm to their children, at minimal cost, they lighten the load for workers in child-protection services and free resources badly needed by publicly funded child-welfare services.

Still, proponents worry that the popularity of self-help could cause the scarce dollars of the 1980s to be withdrawn from human services. This is not what most parents in the self-help groups described here want. To them, the important policy question is not withdrawal of funds but effectiveness of service. To this end parent activists have labored, with some distinct success. To name three examples: Education of handicapped children is far more effective today than it was twenty years ago, in no small measure because of the activism of parents in promoting research and teacher training, in changing public schools, and in securing judicial and legislative protection for their children's rights. Second, because of parent self-help, children who a decade ago would have spent their childhoods in juvenile institutions are growing up successfully in adoptive homes in New York City, San Francisco, and Washington, D. C. Finally, an increasing body of medical literature indicates that babies and young children benefit both physically and psychologically from new hospital practices for handling childbirth and overnight stays of children —

practices that parents in self-help groups have helped to achieve. I don't believe the American public will completely jettison public support for children's services even in harsh economic times, *if* the evidence shows that children and families do benefit. In assuring those benefits, parent self-help and advocacy will be a valuable resource.

Not every parent activist who reads this book will find his or her organization discussed or even listed. (A list of parent groups appears in the appendix.) This book retains a deliberate focus. I chose to look at groups engaged in both self-help *and* advocacy. Within the context of historical and social forces influencing parent activism, it describes and discusses activities of parents in over two dozen organizations. These activities center on three objectives: promulgation of new laws that work well to promote fairer, more effective services and protections for children; reform of institutions whose practices are harmful; and mutual support among parents.

I have chosen, primarily because of constraints on my time, not to write about parents whose advocacy is directed at winning withdrawal of public funding for services designed to help children. I respect but do not agree with their belief that government support of services ultimately harms their children. This book is about parents who advocate *for* government involvement (including federal involvement) in children's services, but only on terms that parents can accept.

In addition, some organizations that are highly regarded for their child-advocacy work and known for their support of parent advocacy are not discussed at length. These groups, such as the International Childbirth Education Association, the National Association for Retarded Citizens, the Head Start Association, and the Children's Defense Fund, simply fall outside the scope of this study because they are not now primarily composed of or run by parents.

Finally, parent groups involved exclusively in self-help but not in advocacy, such as the La Leche League, also could not be fully discussed here. Limitations of time prevented me from considering purely self-help groups.

No doubt limitations of awareness also prevented me from

writing about many parent activist groups whose experiences would have been valuable to readers. Readers' indulgence in this matter is sought; this book is meant to give an overview and a sense of the dimensions of the very interesting phenomenon of self-help and advocacy among parents. It is not an encyclopedic compilation of all the groups in existence today.

In this book I have written about parent organizations in the present tense, although I am aware that when this book is read by a particular parent, professional, or academician, some of these organizations will have changed their activities to a degree. One or two, perhaps, will no longer exist, or will exist under different names. No organization is ever static; changes will occur. Yet I believe that the activities of parent organizations as I have observed them and reported them will have value for readers, even if some are slightly different when this book is read.

In discussing parent activism, I have also deliberately chosen to present the positive features. No reader should imagine that the world of these parents and children is upbeat most of the time. Nor is everything rosy within the world of self-help and child advocacy. Finally, not all parents of children who suffer, or of children who have been excluded from a fair share of the nation's resources, engage in or plan to engage in self-help and child-advocacy organizations. Many of us effectively protect and rear our children with personal, individual activity and with resources we or immediate members of our families possess. Some of us neither need nor presently want the unique support that parent organizations offer. But at some point in our lives, we might. And for growing numbers of parents, self-help and child-advocacy groups are an important, new, valuable child-rearing resource — and a phenomenon with implications for culture and policy which this society would do well to reflect and act on.

The Shared Experience

1

> I had created in my mind a very detailed picture of the ideal mother I would be and the ideal child my baby would be.
>
> The day the baby came into our home I wanted out! I didn't know what to do when he cried. Nothing I did pleased him. I started to panic. He was not at all the bubbling, bouncing, Gerber baby I'd planned on.
>
> I felt enclosed and alone in this panic... I recall how desperately I needed someone to show me that I was not alone. That there were several solutions to my problems... If it's possible for me to reach one person who feels as alone as I did, who wants help as much as I did, I want them to know we are here.
>
> —Participant in a parent support group[1]

"We have consistently observed desperate anxiety in the mothers of the newborn, especially the new mother," write two women associated with a parent-to-parent support center for hundreds of suburban mothers. "She has a fear of the newborn, and a fear of damaging the newborn, and a fear of being alone with the infant."

Fear of being alone and enclosed in our anxieties about our children, doubts about our competence as parents, intermittent forebodings about ultimate helplessness given the powerful challenges of raising children in our time: the women at the Mothers' Center rightfully recognize these as widespread, normal emotions among new parents.

Profound emotions like these, however, are not confined to the uncertain years with a new infant or toddler. Consider how this parent, a literary historian from DeKalb County, Georgia, describes her community's discovery of drug use in adolescent children:

> ...we had to learn the hard way — through the shocked discovery that our own child or a friend's child or a neighbor's child was using drugs...For most parents, regardless of their sophistication about drugs or their political liberalism or conservatism, such a discovery comes like a sudden kick in the stomach. It's a sickening feeling — compounded of a protective fear for their children, of a bewildered fear of an alien drug culture, and of a sorrowful fear about their own apparent helplessness and loss of control.[2]

This parent knows. She not only experienced fear for her own children; she helped to build a nationwide parent campaign against teenage drug use, the National Federation of Parents for Drug-Free Youth, discovering in the process that millions of us dread drug-induced damage to our children, and dread most of all our own helplessness to do anything about it.

Like the new mother quoted above, parents in revolt against drug abuse have endured, and overcome, a disabling sense of themselves as impotent. The parent groups they organize are a way of saying, we unashamedly acknowledge the fears and self-doubt of parents. We know these emotions touch millions. We've been there. Now we want other parents to know we are here.

There is in America an ever-widening grass-roots movement of parent-initiated organizations which, whatever their particular pursuits, share a belief that with mutual support and action, parents can effectively confront and reduce many of the anxieties and risks of raising children well. As parents know, some anxiety is an inevitable occupational hazard of parenthood. But helplessness, say parent advocates, particularly if our children are being hurt, is not inevitable. Neither, they argue, is the quenching of self-esteem that so many parents experience, not just in facing the personal challenges of child-rearing but in the search for help and in encounters with the powerful helping institutions that we Americans have built to protect and educate our children.

A mother writes of her experience in a hospital where her one-and-a-half-year-old daughter is undergoing surgery:

> She was given a shot of something in her room that was to make her drowsy so she would not be conscious when taken to surgery. Well, they did not wait for it to take effect, some-

thing to do with a schedule to keep, and took her awake. If I had been allowed to hold her in my arms while this took effect, I'm sure it would not have taken very long. Instead we rode with her in the elevator with her wide awake and as the elevator opened, other nurses in green with masks took her from me. This really scared her. It really hurt to see her taken from me, to watch her go, to have the elevator doors close between us, and to have her left, still wide awake, with a lot of strangers taking her to the operating room. I can imagine what went through her little mind. I didn't see her again until they brought her back into the room. I did not know then that I should have requested — demanded — to be with her in the recovery room. When she was given to me she shook for three solid hours, and cried when anyone came near her. When we got home, she hung on to me, wouldn't let me out of her sight for a good three months...[3]

The painful experience of this mother seems a symbol of parental impotence and institutional and professional dominance. But it's not. This mother is writing to Children in Hospitals, a Massachusetts-based self-help and advocacy group which has helped to reverse the policies of some of the most prestigious and powerful hospitals in the world.

Children in Hospitals was organized by parents. So was the Candlelighters, an organization of parents who would seem likely candidates for the role of helpless, hand-wringing bystanders to professional and technological expertise. The parents who belong to the Candlelighters all have children who have (or have had) cancer. Slightly more than a decade ago, children with acute leukemia were dead within months. Now, more than 50 percent of children with this kind of leukemia may be cured. But survival depends on access to radiation and drug treatments which constitute for many children and parents ordeals of endurance through years of uncertainty.

Candlelighter parents contend with the experience that all parents dread most: the death (or life-threatening illness) of one of our children. Many people thus expect the Candlelighters to be dispirited, immobilized, grateful for whatever is provided by the scientific and medical establishment. But their newsletter, which does contain poignant accounts of pain, is also replete with crisp articles reporting the latest evaluations of chemotherapy, analyzing the national cancer care system, critiquing undesirable attitudes among some professionals, and offering suggestions about coping with the side effects of cancer treatment in children. "Most of the stories that are written about us," says Grace Monaco, president of the Candlelighters Foundation, "make it sound impossible for a family to survive when they meet a catastrophe like this. That is a bunch of crap. Parents, we all want to survive, and given the opportunity, we have survived."

Deepening their power to nurture their offspring, to stave off harm and to fight for their children, the Mothers' Center originated in 1975 in suburban Long Island when a group of new mothers came together to share their experiences of childbirth. They ended up sharing a common awareness that liberated them from feelings of shame, inadequacy, and failure in ways that no other experience and no other movement had been able to do. They then used that new-found awareness to persuade the administrator of a local hospital that a fairly radical departure from his hospital's ways of treating parents and their families would help fill his sagging obstetrical unit. By 1982, other Mothers' Centers, modeled on the original Long Island center, were being established in places as far away as Missouri, Georgia, and Florida.

In New York City, the Sisterhood of Black Single Mothers spreads out from its storefront in Bedford-Stuyvesant over the city's five boroughs in a network of empathetic telephone accessibility and mutual support. Its members appear at professional meetings, in public forums, and on radio and TV shows to educate both professionals and the general public as to the strengths and pride of Black single mothers. Confronting negative attitudes about them and their children, "We let them know how we feel about it," says Daphne Busby, founder of the Sisterhood, "so that there won't be an excuse about 'I've never heard from a Black single mother that it bothered her, I didn't know she thought that way.'"

Like so many parents in the 1970s, Philadelphia parents had had enough of fifty-day teacher strikes, teaching and school promotion practices that awarded high-school diplomas to students barely able to read, and mounting costs in a system that seemed unable (or unwilling) to inform parents fully about the procedures by which the schools were run. In 1972, a small group of parents in the City of Brotherly Love formed a Parents' Union for Public Schools. Such a union was needed, they said, because the growing power of the teachers' unions meant higher salaries and costs to the taxpayer, more decisions influencing their children's education made behind closed doors, and less accountability to the people who pay the bill — the public. Less than ten years later, the Philadelphia Parents' Union had a staff of twenty-five and an impressive contribution of over a thousand hours of personal time monthly from parents and other citizens all over the city.

In Washington, D. C., the National Parents' Center is run by the National Coalition of Title I Parents. With its active membership of low-income parents whose children are eligible for federal funds for the educationally disadvantaged, this group reaches out to thousands of parents in central cities, backwoods, and barrios across the country.

Another self-help and advocacy group, the National Society for Autistic Children (NSAC), also now has its headquarters in Washington, after organizing and winning many a legislative battle from the kitchens and living rooms of its members. For years parents of autistic children were held as the cause of their children's strange, sometimes self-destructive behavior; prolonged parental and child therapy was offered as the only cure. In the late 1960s, a handful of parents put together a national organization and helped to blaze new and more accurate paths of understanding about autism. Now, when Congress considers the federal budget for the research institutes that fund scientific studies of the causes of autism, NSAC's advice is almost always sought.

Also in the nation's capital is the North American Council on Adoptable Children (NACAC), which encourages its several hundred local groups to develop parent-to-parent support and counseling for adoptive parents and to work for laws that assure permanent homes for the hundreds of thousands of children needlessly growing up in institutions or foster homes. NACAC is widely respected for its participation in the successful passage of the Opportunities for Adoption Act and the Adoption Assistance and Child Welfare Reform Act, recent national laws that help homeless children.

Finally, a few blocks away from the White House is the Parents' Campaign for Handicapped Children and Youth, founded by parents of disabled children who believe that "parents are the leading experts on their child's needs...they must be involved every step of the way in working with professionals on educational and health plans that affect their child's future." Since its inception, the Parents' Campaign has worked to help both parents and professionals learn about and enforce the 1975 landmark legislation assuring a free, appropriate education for every handicapped child: the Education for All Handicapped Children Act.

Just across the border, in Silver Spring, Maryland, another organization, the National Federation of Parents for Drug-Free Youth (NFP), has its headquarters. In 1980, nearly four hundred local groups established a nationwide organization of parents determined to use "parent peer pressure" to prevent drug use by their children. In 1982, representatives of more than two thousand groups met at the White House to discuss this parent movement. NFP strongly encourages parent-to-parent support both to prevent drug use and to free teenagers from drug addiction. "In a time of powerful adolescent peer pressures, parents need peer pressure too," says its pamphlet. "In working together with other parents, you become many." Some of the NFP's most successful advocacy campaigns have resulted in the banning of "head shops" which sell children items such as candy Quaaludes and comic books showing how to snort cocaine.

Also in Silver Spring is the International Association of Parents of the Deaf, emphasizing "parents reaching out to other parents, sharing their frustrations and hopes,...showing younger parents that deaf children *do* grow into happy independent adults."These parents work hard for equal opportunities for education and for corporate and public policies that provide amplified telephones, sign-language interpreters, and services that remove barriers which once kept too many deaf people isolated.

An international organization, Parents Without Partners, is based in nearby Bethesda, Maryland. From twenty-five people in 1957, PWP grew in two decades to 150,000 members with chapters in every state of the union and in Canada. Their aim: to use their shared experience of single parenting to help each other function "confidently and comfortably both inside the family and outside in the community." When the new federal Parental Kidnapping Prevention Act was being debated in the Congress in 1980, Parents Without Partners was one of the organizations that successfully worked for passage of federal remedies to child-snatching.

The heartland also has its activists. In the "steel city" west of the Appalachians, Pittsburgh, a parent-run organization has in less than two decades helped transform public and professional understanding of learning disability. In the early 1960s, children with average or above-average ability who couldn't sit still in school, couldn't learn to read, had short attention spans, and confused or reversed letters and numbers were censured (along with their parents) as "lazy," "uneducable," or "discipline problems." In 1964, a handful of parents founded the Association for Children with Learning Disabilities (ACLD). By 1981, ACLD had 80,000 members, offered more than six hundred publications on learning disability, and was capable of pouring thousands of letters into congressional offices urging the funding of special education for children with learning disabilities. By the early 1980s, teachers, physicians, and policy makers agreed that children (and adults) with learning disabilities *can* learn, but they learn differently from other people.

In Minnesota, OURS, a group of five thousand adoptive families, many of whom have adopted children from around the world, meets regularly. These parents share practical information about raising children from a variety of cultures and work for changes facilitating international adoptions.

In California is the headquarters of Parents Anonymous. Beginning in the early 1970s with a group of three abusive mothers and a supportive social worker, it has grown into a nationwide self-help movement among abusive parents.

Finally, in a city with the peaceful name of Fair Oaks, California, is a mothers' movement whose initials spell MADD. These are parents with good cause for anger: their children have been killed or crippled by drunk drivers. Mothers Against Drunk Drivers, founded in 1980 by a woman whose thirteen-year-old daughter was hit and killed while walking to church, counsels other stricken parents, refers them to bereavement groups, and crusades for stiffer federal and state legislation against intoxicated drivers. Between 1980 and 1982, MADD inspired remarkable changes, including the passage of major legislation in both House and Senate and consideration of legislative and enforcement changes by nearly half of the nation's governors and state legislators.

Not every parent, of course, chooses advocacy and mutual help. But there are hundreds of such groups criss-crossing the country. Local parent action groups have sprung up around many school systems; in several states divorced fathers are coming together to help each other and to argue for changes in child custody laws; and all over the country, parents whose children's mental, emotional, or physical health has been impaired in some way keep a watchful eye on special education, on private and public residential institutions, and on the health-care system.

Many of us associate self-help groups with disability, illness, or chronic problems: Alcoholics Anonymous, Make Today Count (cancer), Reach to Recovery (mental illness), Overeaters Anonymous. Or we think of mutual support groups as a response to a sudden crisis shared by the group's participants. But self-help — the popular name for what is actually *mutual* provision of support, guidance, and practical services — is a burgeoning American movement. The National Self-Help Clearinghouse estimated in 1981 that there were then 500,000 self-help groups in the United States, reaching 10 to 15 million members.

Despite the diversity of stressful concerns addressed by hundreds of thousands of self-help organizations, one of the most characteristic features of any such group is a unifying shared experience. This experience — whether it's difficulties with obesity, alcohol, or smoking, harsh life in an impoverished urban neighborhood, or the death of a loved one, attracts the group's members to one another and braces their common belief that they can use their own resources to help in ways most "outside" people cannot, since they have not participated in the shared experience. Group members shift their images of themselves from resourceless victims to troubled but resourceful people able to offer and use each other's strengths to build confidence and competence. To a large degree, members of very different self-help groups have all shared a deeper unifying experience than the obvious one: impairment of their sense of self-worth. Disability, injuries or illnesses, and stressful life transitions sometimes diminish self-esteem precisely because they threaten an established, reassuring sense of self. A large part of the value of mutual-help groups is the discovery that a diminished sense of self-worth is shared. So, too, the very activities of mutual-support organizations reinforce the bonds of the group by establishing another, special, shared experience — a conscious (and often successful) endeavor to help each other.

One of the first things that parents and family members of the hostages taken in Iran did, for example, was to form a mutual-support group. Similarly, the devastated parents of the children slain in Atlanta came together, founded a group, and pressed city authorities to take a more serious view of linkages among the apparently random killings.

Like mutual help, all advocacy emerges from an experience of stress, either one's own or someone else's. All advocacy is fueled by feelings of caring and commitment. The knowledge of the suffering of children, of their exclusion from a fair opportunity for normal development, is a special motivation. There have always been caring human beings who have advocated for homeless or sick children and for the children of the poor.

Self-advocacy, the assertion of one's own rights in a sustained effort to systematically improve unfair, fundamental social and economic conditions, is also a long-standing American tradition. The exploitation of industrial laborers by factory owners, the prohibition directed at Blacks of the free exercise of the right to vote, the denial to women of equal pay for equal work: the history of organized self-advocacy in America illustrates that here, as in self-help, the shared experience is a basis for concerted action. Here too, the shared experience is the experience of stress, but of stress that originates in painful injustice.

But why are *parents* turning to self-help and advocacy? Parents are surely one of the most helped groups in America. Public libraries stock shelves of books with child-rearing advice; scores of magazine articles tell us how to solve our children's problems; millions of professionals help educate and care for our children in schools, pediatrician's offices, hospitals, child guidance clinics, and social-service agencies.

Then, too, self-help and advocacy demand commitments of time, energy, and often financial resources. Certainly the day-to-day work of raising children is already time-consuming and expensive. So why are parent activists taking money out of their personal savings to support organizations? Why do they spend hours of their leisure time in meeting, telephoning, organizing conferences, buttonholing legislators, and testifying before legislative committees? Is there a unifying shared experience fueling parent self-help and advocacy organizations?

The most universal shared experience we have as parents is the struggle to protect children and to get for them the resources they need to develop well. Listening to parent activists describe their work, one soon learns that their organizational activities are not radically different from the basic tasks we undertake as parents. In self-help and advocacy, parents take the intimate, nurturing vigilance needed for effective child-rearing into a social and political domain.

Why? Parents turn those powerful protective and nurturing energies outward for two reasons. First, when it takes more than personal efforts to protect children or to acquire the resources basic to a fair chance at life, the passionate commitment of the parent-child bond propels parents into connection with others. Second, the help presently available for sometimes excruciating parental stress is often unhelpful or just not helpful enough.

BONDING:
A POWERFUL FORCE FOR CHANGE

Specialists in child development agree that the fundamental bond between parent and child profoundly influences not just individual children or their families but whole societies. That powerful bond energizes parent advocacy as well.

Bonding is the emergence of a deep, unique attachment between parent and child, and typically occurs with tremendous force around the time of birth. Touch, interaction, and eye and skin contact are necessary to bonding. Being close to the baby is essential. Studies show that in the early days of life, institutional barriers to proximity, such as prolonged separation of the baby from the parents, interfere with and may even impair the process.

Psychological proximity — a feeling of intimacy, of understanding the baby's needs and behavior — matters too. Physical contact over the course of a child's development is crucial to psychological closeness. But confidence in our own worth and competence as parents also influences how much psychological proximity to our children we develop and sustain. When parents experience life crises, such as the birth of an ill or handicapped infant, divorce, the death of a loved one, or the loss of a job, our sense of ourselves as capable parents can be impaired. With that can come impairment to the sense of closeness — psychological and physical — to our children. If professionals approach or work with parents undergoing stress in ways that strongly diminish parental self-esteem, they can impede psychological proximity between parent and child. If institutional practices make us doubt ourselves as parents or fail to help us interpret our child's behavior, they build barriers between parent and child.

I do not mean that physical proximity is always desirable. As children grow and develop, there are many times when some physical distance is a good thing. Nursery schools, summer camps, and our school system offer parents and children opportunities to meet challenges on their own, to learn more about themselves, and often to develop a better understanding of each other. In fact, it is often parents with strong psychological proximity to their children who feel most at ease letting their children move out into the unique worlds of childhood and adolescence.

When a child's health, safety, or well-being is threatened, however, or when permanent (or apparently permanent) barriers seem to thrust the child out of the parents' reach, then a primary parental impulse is often to narrow his or her physical and psychological distance from the child. Much has been written about "proximity-seeking" behavior in children, who try to come close to their parents when danger threatens. Much less has been written about "proximity-seeking" by *parents* when they sense danger to the child. Yet that healthy parental impulse, which has served children well for thousands of years in evolutionary history, is in modern society often grossly misunderstood, or even ignored, by professionals and institutions — and sometimes by parents.

Parent advocacy confronts personal and institutional barriers to proximity. Some groups do this in a literal sense, focusing their efforts on changing hospital practices such as isolation of the newborn or ill child from its parents. Divorced fathers struggle to break down the judicial prejudices that interrupt their contact with their children. Parents of institutionalized children have at times literally broken through the walls of state hospitals to discover and expose what has been happening.

In a more symbolic sense, parent advocacy groups seek to lower institutional barriers to proximity to their children. Whether demanding a say in the ways schools are run or speaking out against social-service practices that decrease their self-respect, parent activists are declaring themselves in favor of maintaining proximity. Consequently, parent advocates are not simply campaigning for a fairer share of services, nor are they concentrating solely on protecting the children from harmful institutional practices. The power of bonding shows itself in their conviction that proximity, closeness, comfortableness with children is so important that it must be a built-in feature of any new services or ongoing attempts at institutional reform.

PARENT STRESS: A SPECIAL KIND

Threatened loss of a child, a sense that powerful forces can deny the child what it needs, a feeling of distance that interferes with effective understanding of the child — for anybody caring for children, these create stress. But bonding makes parents feel we must mobilize life-supporting resources for our children. When a child's health or chance to survive is impaired by forces too imposing for one parent to combat, that person feels a burden unlike any other. This is the experience of helplessness in a person driven by powerful impulses to help — a profound special stress.

Both the newsletters of parent advocacy groups and the

personal interviews I conducted reveal that their members live with, or have struggled through, such parent stresses. In an interview, for example, a mother who had been shocked to discover that she was capable of child abuse and in response had helped to organize a chapter of Parents Anonymous explains:

> ...I moved here and my kids were all sick. My husband was out of work because the place where he had been working went bankrupt and he decided to open up his own business. My sister left her husband and moved here and was leaning on me, and then I turned to my father to make things better, but he was dying... He's leaning on me and my sister is leaning on me, and I couldn't take it. All of a sudden I was faced with the reality of how alone I really was and that there isn't someone here to protect you — going to protect me like my father did.
> I had an awful lot of reality coming down on me, and it came out in my feelings toward my children. I could not cope with my children. There was no way that I could put out, and my feelings were that of "just please leave me alone." I wanted to run away. I really wanted to pack a bag and just leave this whole thing behind, but I had no place to go.

The mother of a girl with learning disabilities describes in *ACLD Newsbriefs* experiences recognizable to many parents of children with serious learning difficulties:

> [My daughter] did not begin to put words together until she was nearly four. She could not use the telephone independently until she was eleven. It was a good thing that we changed our residence a couple of times because in each new city we quickly ran out of schools and community programs for her to be kicked out of. She did not pass the second, the seventh, or the eighth grade.

A parent activist in the North American Council on Adoptable Children describes what it's like to develop psychological proximity with children who have had little stability and a lot of hurt in their lives:

> [Most adoptive parents] see through some of what's thought to be retardation or severe trauma, and discover that there is a human being in that shell who will respond to loving and

caring...sometimes it is a very difficult task, a very trying task. I have witnessed several of these adoptions which I think would try the patience of Christ. And yet the parents involved have survived and survived well, and much good has been done because of that.

And a Candlelighter writes in a newsletter:

Kristine is strong now and appears healthy in every respect. Her hair is growing back in and she is happy and active...I know that there is no known cure for a neuroblastoma and that her...survival chance is only thirteen percent, but I am happy for every day that she is with us.

Note: Since this letter, another tumor in abdomen...[she is] on chemotherapy, same four drugs. I believe most parents of cancer patients realize that this road we walk is one of mountain tops and valleys and that as long as we continue to hope and believe and do what is in our power to do, someday this disease will be conquered.

Materials provided by the National Society for Autistic Children explain:

At eighteen months, he would not let his mother touch him. No hugging. No talking. Only the uncontrolled screaming, the eternal staring. Monty slipped in and out of reality.

Monty has autism, a neurological disorder that victimizes thousands...To an autistic child, life is often a violent and painful jumble of sensations.

Other parents have written or spoken of the struggles involved in raising chronically ill children, of what it's like to be a Black parent whose children are denied a basic education, of the strain involved in being the only parent, of the pain when their child has died. Threaded through all these special experiences is parent stress — the feeling that one is helpless, or powerfully impeded, when one's children need help.

Parent stress is not only painful; it also has the unfortunate result of complicating child-rearing. As parents become more constricted, our sense of distance from our children increases and raising them becomes more difficult. Yet the dynamics of bonding propel us to narrow that distance and to nurture our children well. Parent advocacy has its origins in a strong belief that if parents are to live up to the powerful demands of the bonds that tie us to our children, we must know that we are cared for and must be supported and encouraged. Daphne Busby, of the Sisterhood of Black Single Mothers, describes this conviction:

> ...It is our philosophy that when you do feel good about what you are doing or who you are, everything that you do as a result of that is going to be positive...your kids sort of feed on those vibes...So we try to start from that place and say to the sisters, let's start feeling good about who we are and the organization. What we do is always an attempt to sort of lift each other up...

"Lifting each other up," nurturing a stronger sense of self-respect, is one of the most fundamental shared responses to the shared experience of impairment or immobilization of the "parent self."

Cultural conditions, too, are shared among parent advocates. In listening to many different parents, I heard widespread agreement that three such conditions make many different stresses worse: the loneliness of parents in today's society; help that is unhelpful, inaccessible, or (at times) harmful in schools, hospitals, courts, social agencies; and parent-professional relationships that damage parental feelings of competence and confidence.

Together with an impaired sense of self-worth, these problems form the basis for the three fundamental objectives of parent organizations. These are mutual support among parents, work for professional or institutional change, and enactment and enforcement of new or improved laws.

Loneliness

I am struck, from the interviews I conducted for this book, from the reading I've done, and from personal experience, by how much isolation is a fundamental experience of parenthood now. In our sprawling suburban and rural communities, and in urban neighborhoods inhabited by transient strangers, mothers at home with infants and young children experience loneliness in ways that few other occupational groups do. Most housework is done alone; most mothering is done alone. In contrast, almost all other work in our society is done in groups, where the workers share feedback about performance, ideas for better approaches, and gripes about the job.[4]

Parents' concerns about effectiveness also separate us from one another. Worrying about possible failures, many parents isolate themselves through a sense of shame or fears of being inadequate. This loneliness is particularly acute for mothers and for parents of "different" children — children who have "problems." When these problems are frightening to others in the community, parents of "different" children, and their parents, can find themselves ostracized.

Writes one parent of a child who was diagnosed at three as seriously handicapped:

> Family and friends fell by the wayside in a fantastic pattern of despair...like a chain of dominoes. Many of these friends were professionals that I had the utmost confidence in. Pillars of strength and guidance drifted away like straws in the wind ...I knew then that from that day forward my whole life must change if Matthew were to survive. His vulnerability frightened me. I knew what I must do. I could no longer go it alone. I needed other mothers, other fathers to relate to.[5]

Such abandonment is experienced by many parents undergoing other life transitions which make them "different" — divorce, unemployment, adoption of ethnically different or troubled children.

Finally, isolation can result simply because many parents face challenges that are particular to this generation of families and that grandparents, relatives, or friends have not experienced and don't understand. Adolescent drug abuse, single and shared parenthood, child-custody disputes, and repeated encounters with school systems unfamiliar with learning disabilities or mental retardation are new primarily for this generation of parents.

Unhelpful Help: Unavailable, Ineffective, or Harmful Services

Impelled by loneliness and the demands of bonding to protect our children and seek the resources they need, we look for help in the schools, hospitals, courts, and social-service agencies that have emerged from a three-hundred-year tradition in America.

Some of us find precisely the help we need, but many parents do not. There are an estimated 10 million handicapped and chronically ill children in the United States; millions of their parents have painfully experienced long, fruitless searches for educational or medical help that just didn't (or doesn't) exist. For example, parents seeking to adopt children labeled "unadoptable" by virtue of age, race, or handicap have felt rejected by child-welfare agencies that do not publicize the availability of homeless children, distribute their photos, or offer information about adoption processes.

For parents who are able to obtain schooling, counseling, or medical care, these services are sometimes not helpful, or not helpful enough. Parent activists often speak movingly of services that *have* helped them, but they also describe encounters that clearly fall outside the definition of "help."

The mother of a learning-disabled child quoted earlier writes about her daughter:

> She needed *appropriate* attention — i.e., recognition of and acceptance of the fact that she *really* had difficulty learning, expressing herself, and understanding certain things. How many times did I hear, "If she is so smart, then how come she can't do this?" or "What she needs is a little discipline...."[6]

An Atlanta mother concerned about marijuana use by preteens describes what happened when a group of parents sought information on marijuana from drug-abuse centers and clinics. The parents, she says, were

> surprised by the attitude of many counselors and professionals in the field, who admonished them for "getting all uptight" about pot... [They] were also shocked to learn that, despite a large complex of drug and alcohol treatment facilities, there were no centers or resources for dealing with young marijuana users who were not yet multidrug abusers or addicts.[7]

Finally, for other parents, the unhelpfulness of the system becomes actual harm. No one likes to believe that children are hurt by the institutional and professional practices designed to serve them. But in recent years, a new activist literature has pointed out that marijuana use, once dismissed by experts as relatively harmless, can result in long-term serious health impairments; that there are thousands of children who don't learn because they're not allowed in school, or because federal money sent to improve their schools never reaches the school district; that babies born under professionally prescribed general anesthesia in hospitals may be vulnerable to all kinds of deficiencies, including brain damage; that children in professionally supervised state and mental hospitals such as Willowbrook in New York are subject to vile abuse; that children who could be adopted are maintained for years in foster care because some child-welfare specialists find it is financially more rewarding to keep them there; and that the courts routinely permit drunk drivers who have killed children in alcohol-related car crashes to return to the roads — and to repeat crashes.

Parents, Professionals, and Painful Encounters

A big part of "unhelpful help," say parent advocates, is the stress generated by relationships between parents and professionals. Many of us feel that professionals and their services are somehow omnipotent. Our desire to believe that professionals have a kind of magical power to solve human problems puts a terrible strain on the people to whom we assign that power. But nearly all of the parents I interviewed spoke of the painful inequality that parents feel in their relationships with professionals. Some said that they feel they are seen as objects which must be attended to if the child is to be helped, or as barriers to the help professionals want to give to children. In these kinds of relationships, they say, parents are not perceived as distinctive people with unique histories, ideas, and feelings, even when professionals are sensitive to the individual uniqueness of children. Rather, parents are referred to as "mother figure" or "father figure" or sometimes just "Mother," someone without even a name, as in "Mother has been having problems for quite some time now." At its extreme, mothers on the delivery-room table feel, in the words of one Mothers' Center participant, like "just another piece of meat."

What most angered parents with whom I talked, however,

was the professionals' use (or misuse) of judgment. The necessity of submitting to such judgment is felt by parents seeking help for children who use drugs, whose "family deficiencies" are quickly assumed to be the cause of the drug problem, and by parents wanting to adopt, whose character and competence are assessed in extensive and sometimes rigid "home studies." Fathers seeking custody must have their fitness evaluated by the courts. Parents of handicapped children feel tremendously vulnerable to the judgments of educators and social workers, physicians and nurses, and most especially, the administrators of tests.

The mother described earlier, whose family stresses had brought her to the brink of child abuse, describes difficulties with professionals:

> It's a really human kind of job when you're dealing with another person, and what gives you the right to judge me? You don't know what's going on, you don't know what I'm feeling. What right do you have to judge me?

This sentiment is echoed by Daphne Busby, who describes an unwillingness to accept negative, stereotypical judgments as one motivation behind the formation of the Sisterhood of Black Single Mothers:

> It is important for a parent to have a place where she can feel she can get some real concrete help... and not have to tell everything about herself, every intricate detail about her financial, personal, whatever, life, in order to get something immediate that she needs.

Many of the parents felt that even the first parental experience, giving birth, is all too frequently made stressful by the disparaging judgments of professionals. The women who founded the Mothers' Center say that in conducting hundreds of interviews with postpartum mothers, they discovered how vulnerable women felt to negative judgments by the health professionals they encountered during childbirth. Those interviews show what happens when new mothers feel they've been judged as "failing to measure up" during this most sensitive time. Contrary to all our romanticized notions of childbirth as a wonderful boost to female self-confidence, the founders of the Mothers' Center report that the women they surveyed commonly emerged from childbirth with lowered self-esteem.

In fact, so powerful are the forces contributing to stress between parents and professionals that even respected professionals who must interact with their peers as *parents* feel that they are suddenly treated as inferiors. Dr. Philip Roos, a psychologist expert in mental retardation, writes about taking his own toddler, whom he sensed (correctly) to be profoundly retarded, to a neurologist:

> Since this worthy [man] was a consultant to the large state institution for the retarded of which I was the superintendent, I felt confident that he would immediately recognize the obvious signs of severe retardation in our child. Imagine my consternation when, after failing to accomplish even a funduscopic [vision] examination on Val due to her extreme hyperactivity, the learned consultant cast a baleful eye on my wife and me and informed us that the child was quite normal. On the other hand, he continued, her parents were obviously neurotically anxious, and he would prescribe tranquilizers for us.[8]

When parents organize their own help, however, it is not simply because of individual disenchantment with an individual human-service worker. Rather, parent self-help originates in the conviction that some fundamental assumptions around which human services are organized make those services distinctly unhelpful, at least in some respects. Chief among these are indifference to knowledge and compassion gained in direct personal experience, apparent professional tolerance of unhelpful or harmful behavior toward children and parents, and a pervasive image of parents that denigrates parental competence and resourcefulness.

The parent activists I interviewed do not seek to abolish schools, hospitals, courts, or mental-health centers. As parents, we want our children to be well educated, and for the most part we want schools to accomplish that objective. Low-income parents active in school reform have a particularly ardent belief that schools are one route by which their children will leave poverty behind. Consequently, dependence on the schools to do their part is a necessary aspect of parental lives. Most of us still want our babies born in environments that are highly professionally supervised. Parents of handicapped or chronically ill children know they will spend years leaning on health professionals, depending on hospitals. But those parents are quite sure that their children ultimately have a better chance for normal lives if they are entrusted to good health-care professionals.

The solution? Some American parents experiencing the deeply stressful inner paradox of feeling helpless and feeling strongly pulled to help eventually damage or dull themselves or their children. Parent activists emphatically reject that "solution." When dependence on institutions is and will continue to be necessary, they choose a different response: mutual support; persistent, assertive advocacy for reform of those practices that they know are hurting or will hurt their children; and enactment of the laws that authorize and fund needed change.

Acting in concert with sympathetic professionals, parent activists in the 1970s revolutionized hospitalized childbirth practices, special educational opportunities for handicapped children, hospital policies regarding parental presence during a child's hospital stay, and opportunities for adoption of older, minority, or handicapped children. Consider that:

In 1973, more than a third of all hospitals in a national Childbirth Education Association survey flatly prohibited fathers' presence in delivery rooms. The remaining two-thirds conditionally permitted fathers.[9] By 1980, four out of five hospitals permitted — and many encouraged — fathers' participation in childbirth.[10] A 1982 *Parents Magazine* poll, to which more than 64,000 parents responded, found that almost 93 percent of the husbands were with their wives during labor, with 85 percent present at delivery.[11]

In 1970, almost all fifty states had laws exempting handicapped children from public education.[12] By 1977, a nearly total reversal of policy had been accomplished: forty-nine states had laws *mandating* publicly provided education for at least most handicapped children.[13] In 1966, between 1.2 to 1.8 million handicapped children were receiving a free appropriate public education; by 1979, this number had more than doubled, to 3.9 million.[14] These gains are attributed to both changes in state law and enactment of the 1975 Education for All Handicapped Children Act, which was strongly adovcated by parents, who have occupied a critical place in translating this new federal law into real local and state change. Exemption of some children and inadequate state resources to carry out the new laws persist as problems. But without a doubt, parent activists have won major new opportunities for their handicapped children.

In 1969, only three states provided financial adoption assistance, despite the extraordinary and often inevitable medical and other expenses of adopting troubled or handicapped foster children who were waiting by the thousands for homes.[15] Throughout the 1970s, parent advocacy for homeless children grew; by 1979, parents had helped enact forty-six state laws mandating at least some type of state adoption assistance.[16] And in 1980, for the first time, a federal law authorizing national adoption assistance was passed. Here too problems still remain, but parents have helped make once unresponsive governments respond.

In the 1950s and 1960s, most parents of sick children were expected simply to leave their child at the hospital and visit only at rigidly prescribed times. Even as late as 1973, more than half the hospitals in the metropolitan Boston area did not permit parents to "room in" with a hospitalized child.[17] By 1981, however, a national survey of hospitals in the United States and Canada showed that 97 percent of all hospitals permit parental rooming in with sick children.[18] Parent advocates and concerned professionals are responsible for this dramatic reversal, achieved in less than two decades.

Other accomplishments are under way for the 1980s. Parents active in the antidrug movement are credited by experts with helping to reduce daily use of marijuana by high-school seniors from 11 percent in 1978 (when the first parent groups formed) to 7 percent in 1981.[19] Mothers Against Drunk Drivers helped to reduce alcohol-related fatal auto accidents in Maryland, California, and Virginia.[20]

The subsequent chapters of this book examine how parents have accomplished some of these successes, how mutual support builds parental self-confidence, and how parent activism evolved in the United States. Other chapters discuss the roots of this movement in deficit cultural images of parents and the organizational problems and solutions that parent groups have in common.

As individuals, we may experience little, if any, need to know about, sustain, or improve the activist parents' response to parent stress. But this stress is something we *must* respond to, in the manner that best suits us. As parents, the need to help and to reject helplessness is one of our most deeply shared experiences. In that sense, learning about the work of parent advocates is useful to us all. The help that parents in these organizations give one another helps us all, for it shows that we are anything but helpless. The struggle may be hard; the victories may take years — but we are not helpless.

A History of Parent Activism

2

"They are our children, not theirs!" cried angry Jewish parents as they demonstrated in the New York streets in October 1917. These parents were protesting the introduction into the public schools of the Gary Plan, which stressed vocational training over academic preparation. Jewish and other immigrant parents saw the Gary Plan as a way to deny upward mobility to their children. Anti-Gary Leagues were formed by parents in many poor and working-class neighborhoods, and representatives of parent and community groups expressed their opposition at public hearings. One representative said: "There is no parent who is not absolutely opposed to the Gary system. Most of the people of the city believe that it does not fit in with *their* ideals of education"[1] (emphasis mine). Parents took the issue to the polls. In the 1917 municipal election, despite support for this educational approach from the city's political, business, and social leaders, parents soundly defeated the Gary Plan.

New York City parents' interest in education had been considerable for some time before the Gary Plan was introduced. So great was their demand for education, for example, that when children were turned away from the New York City schools in 1894 because of overcrowding, the groups of angry parents at some schools were so large that the police had to be called in.[2]

The determination of New Yorkers to wield some influence over significant decisions about their children's education did not diminish with the defeat of the Gary Plan. Shortly after World War I, parents seeking improvements in the schools founded the United Parents' Associations of Greater New York Schools (later called the United Parents' Associations of New York City, or UPA). "The time is ripe," they declared in a 1922 statement, "for the parent to...study the educational problems of the school, to learn something of child schoolroom psychology, to hear the views of acknowledged educators, and to take concerted action when they are convinced that changes should be made."[3] Their early objectives included some that would not seem foreign to parents today: adequate dental care for schoolchildren; a school budget that would increase the numbers of teachers; no appointments of unqualified people; community use of school buildings. Over the past six decades, according to a listing prepared by the organization's members for UPA's sixtieth anniversary, the UPA's victories have meant state aid to kindergartens, increased funds for dental services in the elementary schools, a $7.5 million budget increase in the immediate post-World War II years when teachers were very scarce, and schools opened and maintained by parents when teachers were on strike.[4]

In other parts of the country, as early as the first decades of the nineteenth century, Black parents also acted as advocates for their children. When Black children were barred from public education, parents established mutual-aid societies and financed their own schools, despite severe economic hardships. In 1807, for example, the first school for the education of Blacks in the District of Columbia was founded by three illiterate ex-slaves, who built the school with their own hands. By 1898, at least twenty schools had been founded under the sponsorship of the African Methodist Episcopal Church alone, with an annual income of $150,000 contributed by 300,000 people.[5] In the interim Black parents also repeatedly sought to have their children admitted to segregated schools. For example, in the mid-1800s, Boston excluded Black children from white schools. Black parents in 1849 petitioned the courts for integration; the Massachusetts State Supreme Court upheld segregation. Undaunted, Black parents pursued other approaches, until in 1855 the state legislature prohibited segregated schools in Massachusetts.[6]

Education was not the only focus of early organized parent activism. In the Progressive era, roughly from the end of the nineteenth century through about 1920, mothers banded together under the aegis of "Organized Motherhood" in order to lobby for pure food and drug laws, equal rights for mothers in custody decisions affecting children,[7] foster-care homes, "mother's aid" for widowed or abandoned mothers, and kindergartens and preventive child-health services. In 1897, a group of several thousand mothers, headed by Alice Birney and Phoebe Hearst, founded the National Congress of Mothers. The Parent-Teachers Association (PTA) evolved in the first two decades of this century out of this national network of mothers' clubs.[8]

Despite these early examples, widespread parent activism seems to be primarily a post-World War II and even perhaps a post-1960s occurrence. The burgeoning of parent groups in the 1970s has historical roots in four postwar phenomena: (1) the successes of such efforts as the pursuit of desegregation by Black parents and of improved opportunities for the retarded by the parents of these handicapped children, as well as those of the more general self-help organizations of the fifties and sixties; (2) alarming reports of the inadequacies of two major institutions that touch virtually every American parent — hospital maternity wards and the public schools; (3) technological breakthroughs which have meant new frontiers in our knowledge about what's good for children; and (4) the special formative experiences of those who became parents during the 1970s: the sixties generation.

PIVOTAL VICTORIES FOR THE HANDICAPPED AND BLACKS

After the nineteenth century, retarded children were often institutionalized in state hospitals and schools set up for that purpose. Nothing could be done, specialists believed, to alter the dismal futures of the severely "feeble-minded." Further, retarded children often aroused fear in some communities, who attributed this affliction to some disease or parental wrongdoing. Conditions in these publicly funded institutions were sometimes grossly inferior and abusive. But the parents of shut-away children were often still bound to their children by strong ties of love. As they were forced to see their children subjected to substandard care, they began to agitate for better conditions.

In the 1930s and 1940s, parents of retarded children began forming grass-roots organizations, either to demand changes in public education and in residential institutions for the retarded or to set up alternative, more acceptable services for their children.⁹ These local groups slowly became known to each other, and in 1950 confederated into the National Association for Retarded Citizens (NARC) to lobby for federal involvement in mental retardation. By fiscal year 1957, Congress had earmarked $1 million, which it added to the appropriations of the Children's Bureau, for special projects designed to aid in the diagnosis and treatment of retarded children.¹⁰ NARC maintained steady national pressure, and in the 1960s hundreds of federal policy decisions provided preventive, diagnostic, treatment, and education services to the mentally retarded, including legislation for comprehensive planning, grants to promote preventive health and other services, and grants to improve institutions. In much of the other Great Society legislation as well, the special needs of the retarded were emphasized. This virtual revolution in policy reflected new concepts, both about the possibilities for fuller lives for all handicapped children and about the federal government's responsibility for aiding such children. This lesson was not lost on the parents of millions of other handicapped children in America.

Nearly thirty years of grass-roots advocacy and organization had preceded this surge of federal efforts to aid mentally retarded children. Of course, the Kennedy family interest in mental retardation and subsequent presidential initiatives were extremely helpful. But it was the combined impact of presidential concern *and* effective grass-roots ability to marshal congressional support that made the U.S. Congress respond. The significance of good organization at the local level was noted carefully by other parents of handicapped children, who began establishing or improving their own national networks.

Black parents too were becoming increasingly dissatisfied with the relegation of their children to separate and distinctly unequal schools. Beginning in the 1940s and 1950s, parents of Black children courageously and quietly organized in small rural communities, mostly in the South, to bring lawsuits for desegregation — sometimes risking life-threatening reprisals from the Ku Klux Klan or other white supremacists. Their courage made possible the 1954 Supreme Court decision that segregation in public schools is unconstitutional and sustained the parents whose children walked through howling, violent mobs in Little Rock, Arkansas, and elsewhere to attend integrated schools. These efforts, aided by the civil-rights movement in general, slowly began to result in increased integration. By 1958, over one-fourth of the school districts in the South had desegregated, at least to some degree.[11]

Black and other minority parents then turned their attention both to desegregation in the northern schools and to the abysmal quality of education their children were receiving in so many inner-city schools. By the mid-1960s, parents had begun working for community control of schools and decentralization of decision making that affected their children's education. Partly as a result of these efforts, schools became an increasing focal point for parent activism. Some parent activists fought hard for racial integration of schools; others just as forcefully opposed desegregation, especially involving the busing of schoolchildren. Increasing parent demands for more say in the running of the schools may not have been an anticipated consequence of the movement for racial integration, but it was.

During the 1970s, parents of handicapped children — not just of the mentally retarded — refined their skills in legislative and other kinds of advocacy for their children and added a new activity to their efforts: precedent-setting class-action lawsuits. In 1971, the PARC case *(Pennsylvania Association for the Retarded* vs. *the Commonwealth of Pennsylvania)* established the right of retarded children to free public education; Pennsylvania was ordered to provide retarded children with access to education. This decision gave Pennsylvania parents a directive to the public schools which years of persistent, plodding work with school boards and school superintendents had not achieved.[12] In 1972, *Mills* vs. *Board of Education for the District of Columbia* broadened this victory, resulting in a court decree that every school-aged child in the District of Columbia, regardless of handicap, was entitled to receive a free public education. By 1976, at least thirty-six lawsuits designed to establish similar rights had been filed in twenty-five states.[13]

Parents of handicapped children also began to form coalitions in the 1970s. Parents of children with cerebral palsy, the learning disabled, the blind, and the deaf began to be aware that their separate efforts could be far more effective if they combined in coalition. Using coalition and the threat of lawsuits, parents renewed their efforts to obtain state legislation mandating public school education for handicapped children and — something the courts could not do — authorizing and appropriating state funds to establish the educational services they needed. Massachusetts provided the most publicized breakthrough with the passage of Chapter 766, a law mandating publicly funded educational services to all handicapped children. Other states passed similar legislation; buoyed by their success, parents from all over the country worked together to obtain the first federal law in this area, the Education for All Handicapped Children Act (1975).

The successful advocacy of parents of handicapped children, particularly in the area of public education, was most often referred to by people interviewed for this book as a prototype of parent activism. Some people even think of it as the only example of parent advocacy; no other kind of activism seems as widely known.

Both Black parents and the parents of retarded and other handicapped children brought home to many American parents during the sixties and seventies the fact that inadequate, unjust, and unfair conditions for children do not have to be quietly and painfuly tolerated. While educational conditions for both these groups of children are far from perfect now, they have improved since the 1950s. Both these movements, it should be noted, quickly broadened their ranks with lawyers, educators, and sympathetic, civic-minded citizens. But the unrelenting parental dream of better opportunities for children undoubtedly provided much of the fuel for the victories. And these successes inspired other parents to become activists.

HEALTH: A PERENNIAL ISSUE FOR SELF-HELP

During the 1930s, organizations reaching out to troubled people with health problems such as mental illness or alcoholism were formed. These problems were experienced by a significant proportion, but not a majority, of the American population. Alcoholics Anonymous, Reach to Recovery, and the later self-help groups for drug abusers gained a reputation for being successful — far more successful, some said, than the hospitals and clinics which were being supported by public and private funds. As the seventies unfolded, the self-help movement spread, and people founded organizations to help themselves combat health problems that were quite common: mild to moderate obesity, for example, or cigarette smoking. From these experiences came a new awareness, especially among women, about the contributions of nutrition and life-style to good health.

The movement for increasing reliance on self and less reliance on hospitals, doctors, and institutions to promote good health converged with the women's movements, and the emphasis on discovery and mastery of one's body reflected in the best-selling *Our Bodies, Our Selves* proved a fertile ground for all kinds of efforts aimed at helping women maintain good physical and mental health. Chief among the female experiences that attracted the attention of self-help groups was reproduction. In increasing numbers, such groups helped women master the experience of giving birth. To broaden these efforts into a national movement, all that was needed was a spark — real evidence that parents and children would benefit from increased self-reliance and decreased dependence on professionals and experts. That spark was supplied by scientific research.

The sixties were a decade of explosion into the public arena of knowledge about child development. Researchers began to document the intricate processes that develop a baby's brain cells or that mark the emergence of language in toddlers. Suddenly this information was translated from scholarly journals into thousands of magazine articles, diaper-service handouts, popular how-to manuals, and appearances on TV talk shows by pediatric and other child-development experts. Striking new possibilities for public policy emerged as the literature indicated that IQs could be raised by a significant number of points if children were led to the right programs or parents did the right things. It was a time of tremendous excitement and hope for a new approach to raising children — healthier, brighter, more energetic children than America had ever produced before. Furthermore, expectations rose that these new breakthroughs would guarantee improved health and development, especially intellectual development, for the millions of children that Americans "uncovered" in the sixties — those badly hurt by poverty and harmful physical and social conditions. Thus, while all children benefited, American society would also be able to knock away the obstacles that kept poor and retarded or handicapped children from equal opportunity. Possibilities seemed to widen with every new finding. The prosperous economy clearly permitted dreams of public policies that would expand services. Even the economic downturn of the early seventies seemed a temporary pause in the American record of "making things happen."

The newfound awareness of infant development in the early 1960s also led to greater interest in technological and scientifically intricate management of childbirth. Between 1900 and 1970, hospitalized childbirth had contributed to the decline of infant and maternal mortality and helped to make possible the reduction or elimination of childbirth pain. By 1970, 99.4 percent of all births occurred in hospitals, a big jump from 1950, when 60 percent of white births and 27 percent of nonwhite births occurred in hospitals.[14] Heavily anesthesized childbirth was now routine; hospital childbirth procedures had been firmly (some said rigidly) established; and new technology like fetal monitoring seemed to promise greater safety for mothers and infants. Parents and professionals alike generally assumed that childbirth must be guided by medical experts, who would make the decisions.

However, toward the end of the sixties, disturbing reports appeared. Researchers were finding links between the routine application of general anesthesia and fetal damage, mental retardation, and learning disabilities. Increasingly, the professional literature documented that medication which entered the mother's bloodstream crossed the placenta with unfortunate results for the baby: depressed rates of respiration and a greater inability to shake off the effects of the anesthesia in the early hours and days of life.[15] Much speculation took place about anesthesia's harmful effects on the infant brain.

Mothers who during the 1950s and 1960s discovered and used the European method of prepared or coached childbirth, often with little or no anesthesia (some of whom later joined the self-help group for breastfeeding mothers, La Leche League) published books and pamphlets describing these new methods and their benefits to the health of mothers *and* babies.[16] Armed with both professional findings and the successes of the methods of Drs. Dick-Read, Bradley, and Lamaze, women's groups and prepared-childbirth advocates spoke out against hospital procedures that denied choices to parents.

But hospitals were slow to abandon their routine procedures in favor of unanesthesized labor and delivery — "natural childbirth." Parental involvement in decisions about what kind of anesthesia to use and when to use it was generally unwelcome. Physicians were shocked by the sudden demand by "mere mothers" to be given a choice between, for example, one injection of a painkiller as the baby's head began to crown or local anesthesia, spinally administered midway through labor. How could mothers demand involvement in decisions that were clearly the prerogative of the medical profession?

Mothers (and fathers) in turn asked how they could trust the medical profession's claim that hospitalized childbirth was the safest possible type of birth when doctors were unwilling to let parents really understand, participate in, or even be awake for the procedures they used. Faced with the formidable task of persuading hospitals and physicians individually, small groups of parents and professionals began to press their concerns. These groups evolved into a major social and economic force, rooted in several national organizations, advocating natural childbirth, father participation in labor and delivery, and in general less technological interference with childbirth. "At the present time," write Drs. Marshall Klaus and John Kennell, "sweeping and fundamental changes in maternity practices relating to labor, birth, and the early postnatal period are under way."[17] Calling these changes a "revolution in maternity care," they list eight childbirth practices undergoing change, ranging from the mother's position during labor to the birth environment to parents' general control of the birth.[18] The easy access of present parents to all kinds of choices about where and how their babies will be born owes much to the earlier movement for increased self-reliance in childbirth.

PARENTS AND SCHOOLS

During the 1970s some cracks also began to appear in the great hope of most American parents: universal public education for children. The recessions of the seventies meant rising unemployment. The idea that one's child could have a chance at college and the professions no longer seemed as real when Ph.D.'s couldn't find jobs. Other occurrences increased parental dissatisfaction with public schools. For one thing, despite the explosion of knowledge about learning and child development, tests revealed that children were being graduated from high school, certified as fully literate, knowledgeable citizens, when they couldn't even read or do simple sums.[19] The April 1977 newsletter of the National Coalition of Title I Parents cited the results of one such battery of tests, the National Assessment of Educational Progress. This nationwide evaluation of seventeen-year-olds compared reading levels in 1971, 1974, and 1975 and found that 20 percent of those in disadvantaged urban areas and 42 percent of the Black students were functionally illiterate. Further, between 1967 and 1978, the average verbal score of both male and female students taking the College Board's Scholastic Aptitude Test (SAT) declined by thirty points. Average math scores went down by twenty points for males, twenty-three points for females.[20] International tests on fourteen-year-olds in 1970 showed American students ranking far behind their peers in France, the Netherlands, Germany, Japan, and England in math and science, although they did rank equally well or better in reading comprehension and literature. American students in their last year of high school fell far below those in these five countries, plus Italy and Sweden, on all measures.[21]

Schools also seemed to be moving beyond their original narrow mandate into sensitive areas such as sex education, sometimes with apparent disrespect for the values that some parents were striving to instill in their children. Parents were frequently prohibited from viewing written records kept on their children. Further, schools were becoming increasingly unsafe places, where drug dealing and muggings took place.

These problems occurred against a backdrop of rising costs and increasing teacher organization to achieve higher salaries.

Between 1970 and 1980, the cost of public elementary and secondary education more than doubled, from $41 billion to an estimated $95.4 billion.[22] The federal government's funds for such education, mostly targeted toward handicapped and low-income children, account for about $5.7 billion of that $54.4 billion increase; state expenditures rose by $27.1 billion; local funding, by $21.4 billion. Teacher salary increases influenced this dramatic upswing in public school costs. Not that those increases were undeserved: the average annual salary of the elementary school teacher in 1960 was $4815. By 1970, this had climbed to $8412, and by 1979, to $15,474[23] — still no princely sum for an occupation that in 1976 boasted virtually all college-educated members, with more than one-third of that group having achieved advanced degrees.[24] The tactics teachers used to raise their wages, however — collective bargaining and walkouts — disturbed the public. From a single action in 1961–1962, strikes rose to 114 in 1967–1968, pulling more than 163,000 teachers out of the schools. In 1975–1976, 203 strikes meant disruption of services from over 218,000 teachers.[25] Furthermore, school systems became top-heavy. Two close observers of the nation's schools commented in 1976 that the typical school district had an administrator for every twelve and a half classroom teachers and a classroom teacher for every twenty-two students.[26]

Furthermore, the power centers, where central decisions about schooling were made, became increasingly remote from the typical parent. School districts had consolidated into larger, more bureaucratic systems, reducing the number of districts from almost 84,000 in 1950 to 16,200 in 1977.[27] In 1946, the enrollment per school district was approximately 230 children. By 1980, more than four-fifths of all American pupils were enrolled in school systems of more than 2500 pupils each.[28] Proportional representation by school boards rose enormously. In 1900, one school-board member represented roughly 138 citizens; by 1976, that figure had risen to 2470 citizens. And in a large urban center, each school-board member might represent a quarter of a million people.[29] This increasing remoteness of the entity that is supposed to represent public (and parent) control of the schools was reflected in a 1975 survey disclosing that about half of all parents could not name a single thing accomplished by their school boards in the previous year, and did not even know how many individuals sat on their local school boards.[30]

Consequently, during the 1960s and 1970s, American parents began to feel that they were paying more into public schools and getting less — much less — in what mattered to them. Most were unwelcome at the collective bargaining table where next year's salaries and a good many policies affecting their children were decided. So many parents expressed their dissatisfaction with two things they could control; they withheld their approval of local bonds financing the schools, and in increasing numbers they withheld their children, transferring them to private schools. Between 1962 and 1976, the public approval rate for public school-board elections fell from 72.4 percent to 55.6 percent.[31] Between 1969 and 1979, nonsectarian private-school enrollment, despite the high tuitions associated with such schools, rose from 366,157 to 722,318 students.[32] Only about one in ten American children now attends private school, but many analysts believe that the proportion will grow, particularly if such measures as tuition tax credits or educational vouchers are legislated to assist parents in meeting the increased costs of private education.

American parents reacted to the distressing events in public education by expecting the PTA to take on these issues. The Parent-Teachers Association had, after all, emerged from an activist mothers' movement, and in the first decade of its national existence had fought for many reforms needed by children. However, accustomed to a now rather complacent role in bake sales and raffles, the PTA was slow to adapt to this rising parent demand. In 1972, the national organization did change its by-laws so it could be involved in the decision making that resulted in school policy. The PTA nevertheless had substantial problems associated with simply maintaining membership, which dropped from 12 million in 1963 to about half that in 1979,[33] with most of the decline occurring in slightly more than a decade, from 1964 to 1975.[34]

Parent activists are divided about the continuing value of the PTA. One said: "They always shy away from anything activist. Even when we wanted to take a position and lobby the state legislature on a bill banning head shops [stores that sell drug-use paraphernalia] that was coming up very soon, the PTA explained we'd have to wait until next month, till the regular meeting." Others felt that local PTAs were going ahead on their own and speaking up against school-board policies or positions that seemed unfavorable to children. But PTAs are, after all, parent-teacher organizations, and the polarization resulting from increased teacher militancy, strikes, and closed collective bargaining does not augur well for an organization struggling to combine parent activism with a firm, longstanding identification with having, as one parent expressed it, "feet on both sides of the fence."

Perhaps as a consequence, organizations with names such as the Parents' Union, Parents United for Full Funding, Parent Representatives on Better Education, and Parents' Action Network began to emerge in different parts of the country. Two national organizations developed to offer support, publications, and information in the cause of increased parent and citizen participation in the schools. One was the National Committee for Citizens in Education (NCCE), founded in 1973 by several school administrators who believe deeply in parent involvement in public school policy making. Advocacy for passage of the Family Educational Rights and Privacy Act of 1974, which assured parental access to children's school records, was one of the first activities undertaken by NCEE. A special project, called the Parents' Network, was developed shortly thereafter. The network links several hundred local parent-citizen groups into a loosely federated national group.

Also in 1973, the Institute for Responsive Education (IRE), a Boston-based national organization, was formed to "advocate and assist citizen participation in education decision-making."[35] IRE is also connected to an informal network of parents' groups throughout the country working for basic change in the school system. Finally, the National Coalition of Elementary and Secondary Education Act Title I Parents was also founded in the early seventies to give a concerted parent voice to support of federal programs that fund local school districts to improve opportunities for educationally disadvantaged children.

Unlike the movement to change policies and practices in hospital maternity wards, the movement to improve the effectiveness and openness of public schools cannot yet be said to have produced large-scale national change. Parents do now have access to their children's school records, an important change. As of 1979, almost half the states had laws requiring testing to establish "minimum competency" in students seeking promotion or graduation, or were considering passage of such laws.[36] Many observers attribute these laws to parental demand, although some parent activists are chary of the standardized testing involved in minimum-competency assessment. In any event, the new exactitude in expecting at least minimal performance from the publicly funded school system undoubtedly reflects, at least in part, the efforts of advocates to bring public schools under an increased measure of parental control.

THE SIXTIES ACTIVISTS

Many well-publicized flaws that appeared in schools and hospitals also appeared in institutions that affect smaller populations of parents — adoption agencies, foster-care and child-welfare services, mental hospitals, divorce courts. But the history of these institutions in America shows that parents are often blamed when such services are inadequate. These institutions serve parents traditionally perceived as having failed in some way. Cracks in their performances don't engender the same distrust among parents in general that revelations of deficiencies in more universal services do. Over the past decade, however, the pattern of troublesome findings in the more "special" services melded with the pattern of problems in public education and hospitalized childbirth and augmented feelings that the experts couldn't be trusted to have the kind of control over decisions affecting children that they apparently had — and apparently wanted to keep. Of course, skepticism about institutions was in the spirit that characterized the whole generation that grew up in the 1960s and became parents in the 1970s.

Many parents insisting on fundamental changes in hospitals, schools, and other services during the seventies were probably not engaging in activities that felt utterly alien. These parents had been shaped by years of political consciousness and principled activism. In the 1960s, this generation challenged white supremacy and won laws guaranteeing rights to equal opportunity, organized a national movement to end American involvement in the war in Vietnam, entered into consciousness-raising and mutual support about women's issues, and developed a national women's movement. Even those who did not directly participate in these efforts reacted to them and felt their force during formative adolescent years. Consequently, many parents of the seventies had already developed political consciousness, skills, and inclination to look beyond an incident of harm to a pattern of unfairness and ask why it occurred. They had acquired the habit of asking whether something about the system that encompasses an individual life causes individual harm.

Beyond such political consciousness, some of the sixties generation developed the courage to confront and to uphold their convictions even in a climate hostile to those beliefs. They made many hard decisions in the 1960s: whether to go to war, go to jail, or leave the country; whether to join a civil-rights march and risk a beating from hostile police or stay at home; whether to give their energies to antipoverty work or to the safer, better-paid professions. Would a young man who had been willing to defy the American selective service system accept the obstetric ward's policy of "fathers aren't allowed"? Would the young woman who had been willing to confront the Birmingham or Chicago police or the Texas Rangers be cowed by her daughter's school principal? Many of the parents of the seventies and eighties were prepared for making decisions of conscience and acting on those decisions.

Today, grass-roots advocacy organizations, comprised of citizens who band together to demand legislation or institutional changes, flourish. Having absorbed lessons from the labor-union and civil-rights movements of earlier decades, particularly the lesson that even the powerless can achieve power, groups of everday people are organizing like-minded others. The members of these many organizations have learned how to build political strength, lobby, draft legislation, bring lawsuits, and penetrate the structure of government to ensure a place for themselves in governmental decision making.

Images of Parents

3

We all develop self-images that mirror our judgments of ourselves as effective parents. Many parents undoubtedly view themselves as competent, quiet, rather private individuals who are quite capable of rearing their children with little help from anyone outside their immediate families. Sometimes this self-image may be jarred in moments of crisis or in unpleasant encounters with schoolteachers or medical professionals who view parents in a negative light. But this disagreeable dissonance may only temporarily alter parents' self-perceptions, and the individuals involved are able eventually to return to a more peaceful self-image.

For many parents in contemporary American society, however, self-images are regularly displeasing and painful. Contemporary magazines and books abound with "confessions" of parents who see themselves as failures or who live in fear that they are moving inexorably toward failure. In this sadder experience, the self-image consistently reveals incompetence, ineffectiveness, and helplessness, pulling one inevitably toward dependence on others who are (or must be) wise, good, and utterly successful.

We are all aware in this post-Freud era of the influence that our own family environment has had on shaping self-images, but we pay less attention to the way in which cultural images — mental conceptions evidenced in the language or literature used to describe a group — influence, and sometimes warp, developing self-images. Over the past two decades, of course, scholars have begun to analyze the power that negative cultural images exert on the self-images of minorities and women.[1] Similarly, negative cultural images of parents can have regrettable and sometimes injurious effects on the way in which parents think of themselves;

they siphon off the confidence and thus the adaptability that positive self-image fuels in human relationships — qualities that are essential to the well-grounded and authentic human caring that is essential to raising children.

Since self-image is the source of much energy, self-help and advocacy groups often concentrate on helping parents reshape or develop a positive view of themselves. For that reason, I want to analyze here the roots of several cultural images of parents which recur continually in the literature describing policies and programs established to help children. Fundamental and sometimes unconscious beliefs about the relationship between parents and "experts" often emerge in the language and writing of policy makers, professionals, and scholars who concern themselves with children and families. In particular, three images — the Incompetent Parent, the Victimized Parent, and the Resourceful Parent — reflect sentiments that guide the assumptions upon which services to children have been and continue to be built. These images reveal attitudes that have influenced the perspectives professionals are taught (subtly or overtly) to have about parents. Finally, these images shape our feelings about ourselves as parents, our interactions with each other, and our fundamental relationships with our children. Thus, they are strong currents in the headstream of parent activism.

The image of the Incompetent Parent portrays a person who is incapable of meeting essential needs of child-rearing. In this imagery, moral defects, ignorance, emotional inadequacies, and deficient skills cause incompetence. Parental incompetence in turn "results" in misfortune and harm to children, or thwarts some basic right of the child, such as the right to equal opportunity. Typically, the Incompetent Parent image appears in discussions about why professionals, programs, public and private services, and government in general should do more to help children.

The Victimized Parent image portrays a person who is well-meaning but a helpless victim of powerful forces, swamped by events he or she is unable to influence or control in the rearing of his or her children. Parents here fail to raise children well because external pressures prevent them from doing so, not because of personal incapacity or moral torpor. Traditionally, the Victimized Parent is treated as a sympathetic figure, struggling with oppressive economic and social conditions which obstruct good child development. Victimized Parents are typically overwhelmed by these conditions, which can be countered chiefly by professionals, programs, and government. More recently, however, in scholarly works, legislative testimony, public statements, and advocacy brochures, parents are described as victims of the very forces that are supposed to aid them: professionals, experts, helping institutions, and government.

I want to propose a third image: the Resourceful Parent. This is the image that the parents interviewed for this book have constructed for themselves. The Resourceful Parent is first of all a decision maker who works hard to discover what resources are available for rearing children well and what choices can be made, often in defiance of powerful forces. When few options for children exist, the Resourceful Parent generates new choices by combining with other parents to establish halfway houses, peer counseling, support groups, or preschool programs. Parents also generate alternatives through advocacy for institutional change or for a law that provides fairer, more effective services and protections for children. Resourceful Parents want help that is more accessible, more responsive, and more humane.

The most central shared characteristic of the Incompetent Parent image and the Victimized Parent image is passivity. In contrast, Resourceful Parents are contributors to public policy, not just recipients of it; they are valued partners with professionals in the delivery of public services to children; they are mediators, protective buffers between vulnerable children and powerful institutions; and they are the final arbiters (or at least the parties with the most rights to that position) of all decisions about the child.

Let's look at how these three images appear in the literature about parents and children and the programs and policies constructed for them.

THE INCOMPETENT PARENT

The Incompetent Parent image pervades nineteenth- and twentieth-century policy and professional literature about children and services for them. Incompetence and poverty, historical studies show, have long been associated in the public mind.[2] In our early history, moral defects and personal failings were thought to be the chief causes of poverty, which in turn caused even greater incompetence; hence the development of the workhouse and almshouse to reform the poor — children as well as adults — through virtuous training and hard work. In the early nineteenth century, however, reformers began to argue that the children of the poor should not be punished because of their parents' incompetence, nor should the polity be endangered by ignorant and immoral citizens who had been reared by inadequate parents. Thus advocates established the need for services to reform and educate the children of incompetent parents, and to prepare them for responsible participation in the republic, for a more productive and moral adult life than that led by their parents.

Early advocates of public schools frequently based their case on the deficiencies of poor parents. An 1805 petition to the New York legislature for publicly funded education laments that children are "reared up by parents who are become either indifferent to the best interests of their offspring, or through intemperate lives, are rendered unable to defray the expense of their instructor." These children, says the petition, inherit "those vices which idleness and the bad example of their parents naturally produce."[3]

DeWitt Clinton, the first president of the New York Public School Society, echoes these sentiments:

> Early instruction and the fixed habits of industry, decency and order are the surest safeguards of virtuous conduct; and when parents are either unable or unwilling to bestow the necessary attention on the education of their children, it becomes the duty of the public, and of individuals who have the power, to assist them in the discharge of this important obligation.[4]

Because of the pervasive, profound racism of the times, nonwhite parents were presumed incurably incompetent — permanently, genetically inferior — by virtue of their race, so public education was presumed unnecessary for their children. Since Black, native American, and other nonwhite children were not "destined" to have the same rights as white children, even many social reformers felt there was no need to prepare them for educated citizenry.[5]

As might be expected, advocates of child-health, child-welfare, foster-care, and juvenile delinquency services also battled against what they saw as parental incompetence. The New York Society for the Reformation of Juvenile Delinquents recommended that the legislature establish a House of Refuge for

> boys...whose parents, either from vice or indolence, are careless of their minds and morals and leave them exposed in rags and filth to miserable and scanty fare, destitute of education, and liable to become the prey of criminal associates. Many of such parents would probably be willing to indenture their children to the manager of a House of Refuge; and far better would it be for these juvenile sufferers that they would be thus rescued from impending ruin."[6]

Such attitudes were exemplified in the actual practice of some child-welfare workers, notably Charles Loring Brace, leader of the Children's Aid Society. Brace and other "child savers" advocated foster care for the neglected children of impoverished parents, whom Brace termed "the dangerous classes." Between 1849 and 1929, the New York Aid Society "drained New York City," as Brace described it, of about 100,000 children of Irish and other immigrant families. They were placed in foster homes in the rural West or the South, where extra hands were needed. As in education, Black children were ignored in the arguments for foster care and excluded from publicly supported homes and orphanages in the early stages of the development of child-welfare services.[7]

The use of the Incompetent Parent image intensified as immigrants flooded into American cities during the last quarter of the nineteenth century and the first quarter of the twentieth century.[8] By 1900, more than a third of the nation's population was of foreign birth or parentage, and the flow of immigrants continued unabated.[9] White, Protestant, middle-class reformers were frequently appalled by parents who spoke foreign tongues, practiced non-Protestant religions, clung to strange folkways, and lived in crowded, dirty tenements. Consider, for example, the comment of a member of the Children's Aid Society, one of the foremost child-welfare agencies of the time: "The whole was very depressing. It seemed like the worst part of Old Europe transplanted... You felt hopeless of ever reforming such natures and under all common probabilities the children must be beggars and prostitutes and thieves."[10]

At the turn of the century, Dr. Josephine E. Baker, one of the leaders of the fight to provide pure milk, better sanitation, and preventive child-health services, described her experience as a health visitor in the Irish immigrant wards: "I had interviewed mother after mother too ignorant to know that precautions could be taken and too discouraged to bother taking them even when you tried to teach her."[11] Immigrant children died, wrote Dr. Baker, because "the babies' mothers could not afford doctors and seemed too lackadaisical to carry their babies to the nearby clinics, and too lazy or too indifferent to carry out the instructions you might give them. I do not mean they were callous when their babies died. Then they cried like mothers for a change."[12] One of the arguments typically advanced for children's hospitals was that sick children died needlessly because of incompetent or deficient parental nursing. Neglectful parenting itself was sometimes assumed to have either caused or worsened the illness.[13]

Nineteenth- and early twentieth-century reformers tended to question the competence of lower-class families only. They believed that poor children might eventually be saved from their dismal fates by mothers who had been trained to be competent. This movement for "educated motherhood" motivated many of the Progressive-era reforms directed at eliminating the hardships of the lower classes. But around the turn of the century, Incompetent Parent imagery began to appear in speeches about middle-class mothers made by educators, physicians, and child psychologists. A president of Wellesley College, explaining why women should go to college, said in 1897: "Little children under five years of age die in needless thousands because of the dull, unimaginative women on whom they depend. Such women have been satisfied with just getting along, instead of packing everything they do with brains."[14]

Among the policy results of this new application of Incompetent Parent imagery was the 1929 defeat of the first federally funded maternal and child health services legislation, the Sheppard-Towner Act. First passed in 1921, this law sought to make preventive health services for mothers and babies more accessible. A coalition of social reformers, women's groups, and Mothers' Clubs worked hard for the initial passage of Sheppard-Towner, and Incompetent Parent imagery of the type just cited from the writings of Dr. Josephine Baker animates their arguments for preventing the deaths of impoverished and ignorant mothers and babies.

In its eight years of existence, the Sheppard-Towner program did much to stimulate publicly funded maternal and child health clinics. Between 1924 and 1929, for example, 1594 permanent local child-health or prenatal centers were established.[15] However, the program was defeated in 1929, in no small part because of the effort of the medical profession, who argued that all mothers, not just impoverished ones, lacked sufficient competence to guide themselves and their babies safely through the perinatal period. All mothers needed expert oversight by a private physician — private medical care being preferable, of course, to publicly funded child-health stations, which at times were run by nurses, social workers, and other nonphysicians. The Incompetent Parent imagery used by the middle-class reformers of the Progressive era to enact Sheppard-Towner thus was applied to *them* in the defeat of the program.

In the first half of the twentieth century, as the older professions such as pediatric medicine solidified, new professions such as child psychology and psychiatry emerged from psychological and psychoanalytical theory. Additionally, the discovery by Montessori and other educators that even very young children are interested in and ripe for learning supported the growth of professions focused on parent education and on the study and promotion of good child development.

During this period, the "ideology of educated motherhood," as historian Sheila Rothman terms it, evolved into a belief that the future success of American society lay in educating mothers to increasingly higher levels of competence, in order to supply the product so eagerly sought by a new brand of reformers: the well-adjusted, bright, sociable, healthy child with just the right mixture of id, ego, and superego. The average mother, said the experts, needed quite a bit of training in order to carry out this mission. "Everyone will concede that it is the mother's hand that moulds, but she greatly needs preparation for the process," explained one educator. "She needs what many do not possess, the refinement which association brings, a broad outlook, a logical mind...qualities in which the average mother has little or no training."[16]

By the middle of the century, some social reformers deeply concerned about the misery endured by millions of children of minority groups, most of whom lived in great poverty, relied heavily on the Incompetent Parent image in advocating programs and policies to alleviate that misery. A large body of literature emerged attempting to persuade the American public that poor minority children stayed poor because their parents were deficient in deferring gratification, in leading organized family lives, in stimulating intellectual development, and in modeling good middle-class behavior. For Black children, in particular, these assumptions soon snowballed into elaborate theories about "cultural deprivation" — theories which held that Black children and youth fared poorly in school and work because they were deprived from birth of the much-touted benefits of white middle-class culture. Within the "culturally deprived" treatise lies images of Black parents as incompetent; more tempered than nineteenth-century images, they portray Blacks as caring parents who are nevertheless unable to confer on their children the cognitive, social, and emotional qualities needed for healthy development.

In the late 1960s and 1970s, Black activists increasingly attacked theories about cultural deprivation as racist. Some social reformers responded by giving up these theories in favor of deeper scrutiny into the causes of poverty and particularly Black poverty. Others responded by broadening the concept of deprivation to include all parents. By the 1970s, *all* parents, regardless of class, were frequently depicted in the professional and policy literature about children and families as weak (while paradoxically retaining the power to inflict traumatic psychological damage on children). Some experts consistently wrote about parents as if they were well-intentioned, childlike, but inferior beings in need of large amounts of guidance. Articles, books, and congressional testimony decreed the inability of American parents in general to navigate the multiple threats to their children's well-being safely. Once again, widespread general parent education was advanced as a solution. As Steven Schlossman writes in the *Harvard Education Review:*

> ...rather than concentrating almost exclusively on the needs of lower-class and minority children, interest appears to be turning equally toward the developmental needs of all youngsters, irrespective of ethnic, racial, or socioeconomic background. Parent education has, in a sense, been "democratized" as the notion of "cultural deprivation" gives way to a more generalized theory of "developmental deprivation."[17]

Once again, as in the Progressive era, the image of incompetent parenthood, enthusiastically embraced by middle-class social activists eager to help the children of the poor by "reforming" (in this period, "training") their parents, has come back and been applied to all parents, middle-class and impoverished.

THE VICTIMIZED PARENT

The viewpoint that some parents failed to rear their children well because they had been victimized by horrendous social and economic conditions, *not* because they were morally or personally incompetent, appeared at times during the Progressive era. The image of the Victimized Parent, wanting to do well but crippled by the wretched conditions of the urban slums and the exploitative industrial order, shows up in the writings of Robert Hunter and of Progressives such as Jane Addams and Florence Kelley.[18] Often, the conception that parents are victimized by forces they cannot control is linked both to the writers' protracted exposure to actual life in low-income neighborhoods (Jane Addams lived in the slums) and to their sympathies for early working-class efforts at unionization. Trade unions, these reformers believed, would inevitably improve parenting — as would the passage of significant social legislation guaranteeing workman's compensation and unemployment insurance — by raising workers' wages and improving the security and continuity of their incomes.

Underlying their support for labor unions and social legislation was the belief that these would lead to a new economic order, freeing parents from the overwhelming hardships that impaired their ability to rear children well.

The Victimized Parent image appears in the earliest successful proposals for publicly funded financial assistance to mothers raising children alone. Late nineteenth-century policies supported the removal of children from their families when widowed or deserted mothers were too poor to finance their care and education. These children were often placed in orphanages, so that they would not become vagrants while their mothers were preoccupied with caring for smaller children or so that single mothers could obtain employment and not depend on public relief. Historian Catherine Ross estimates that by the 1890s, one in every thirty-five children in New York City was living in an orphanage — an expensive public policy, from the perspective of both financial and human costs.[19]

The consequences of this policy could be bizarre, as Grace Abbott, an early chief of the United States Children's Bureau, reports in an illustrative life history supplied by the redoubtable Dr. Josephine Baker. Ms. Abbott writes of a New York City mother whose husband is blind. She has placed her entire family of six children in an institution so that she can earn income. After investigation, the Bureau of Charities requires her to take two of the children out of the institution and keep them at home. To earn the money needed to support them, she is advised to become a foster mother. Acting on this advice, this woman ends up boarding four children from an institution, while four of her own children remain in institutions.[20] Ms. Abbott remarks: "Society has almost forced the widow to earn sufficient income for her children's training at the cost of the home, or to drive from that home the children whom she should train."[21]

This depiction is light-years away from that of the parent whose vice, indolence, or immorality bred the "dangerous classes" that mid-nineteenth-century reformers felt compelled to "drain" away from the urban centers of the nation. In fact, the judge (Judge Pinckney of Illinois) who proposed the first state law authorizing what came to be known as mothers' pensions did so because he "found himself continually asked to take children from *poor but competent mothers* and commit them to institutions"[22] (emphasis mine). A separate class — impoverished but competent parents — is conceptualized in the arguments for this policy. (It should be noted, however, that mothers applying for this public assistance were required to demonstrate that they were in fact competent.[23])

In the Progressive era, some of these policy proposals, like Victimized Parent imagery itself, were slow to be accepted by the majority of American people, who apparently preferred to believe that impoverished parents failed for the same reasons they were poor — because they were incompetent. On balance, this view seemed to predominate during the first three decades of the twentieth century. Then the Great Depression threw large segments of Middle America out of work. Many formerly solid, middle-class, competent parents became impoverished; many children and families, not just of the lower classes, suffered hardships through no fault of their own. In 1932, for example, New York City's Health Department reported that 20 percent of the schoolchildren examined were suffering from malnutrition.[24] The Children's Bureau found widespread malnutrition and hunger in other parts of the country as well.

In the literature shaping the policies and programs developed during the 1930s to help children, attention is focused less on saving victimized children from their incompetent parents than on helping victimized children *and* victimized parents. The image of Victimized Parents appears frequently in arguments for unemployment insurance, survivor and disability insurance, and aid to families with dependent children. As Secretary of Labor Frances Perkins put it, it was imperative to enact children's services capable of "saving the children from the forces of attrition and decay which the Depression turned on them above all others."[25]

The Second World War, too, with its widespread disruption of normal family life, profoundly changed the experience of many parents, and advocates of children's services spoke out for new services on the grounds of war-caused hardship. Dr. Leona Baumgartner, assistant commissioner of health in New York City, expressed sympathy for women who needed special funds for infant and child care while their husbands were overseas and for "young mothers who had never been far from home, mothers with hardly enough to keep themselves and no resources for paying and even planning for the coming baby."[26]

In the postwar era, parents in the middle classes were less subject to jolting disruptions. Once again the focus turned to impoverished parents and particularly to Appalachian whites, Blacks, and ethnic minorities, who were participating in large-scale migrations from rural areas to urban centers. Americans became gradually more aware of the enormous obstacles that racial prejudice placed in the way of social and economic progress in minority populations; some traded images of minority parents as incompetent for images of victimized parents hopelessly overwhelmed by profound suffering. During the past several decades, these two images have vied as explanations for why impoverished minority families have suffered disproportionately from problems like infant mortality, poor child health, incomplete and inadequate education, teenage drug use, and juvenile delinquency.

Conservatives have sometimes depicted parents as victimized not by social forces, but by the government. In the early decades of this century, the National Association of Manufacturers, mill owners, and other industrialists argued that parents had the absolute right to send their small children into mines, factories, and fields when they needed the children's income. Government prohibition of child labor, they said, was an abridgment of parental rights and unwarranted harassment of families.[27] In the 1920s, conservatives also claimed that the Children's Bureau, income aid to impoverished widows, and "unmarried ladies" who campaigned for improved child-health services all furthered the victimization of American parents by "government intrusion."[28] More recently, the opponents of the Child and Family Services Act of 1975, which would have funded child care and prenatal and child-development services, argued that this legislation was designed to abolish parents' rights to raise their children. "Can the government take away your children?" warned a flyer circulated by the bill's opponents. The flyer goes on to quote the *Congressional Record* in saying that parents in a rapidly changing society might not be "entrusted to prepare their children" for the future. Conservatives generated thousands of letters from angry parents, and the bill was defeated. So strong was the sentiment that this legislation would preempt parental authority that even five years later a conservative columnist, James Kilpatrick, described it as a "hair-raising" concept, "legislation that would convert millions of children into virtual wards of the state, with their every physical, emotional and mental need tended by functionaries at thousands of day care centers."[29] Ironically, this legislation probably would have *expanded* parental control of a broader variety of day-care arrangements (and thus expanded parental choices as well) than in today's ever-increasing, predominantly privately funded day-care "free market." But it was intensely regarded by some groups as a fundamental usurpation of parental rights — another example of government victimization of parents. This sentiment continued to grow in the latter part of the seventies. By 1980, the "pro-family movement," a politically conservative group seeking to cut back or stop government funding of services for children or families, was claiming, in the words of its national chairwoman, "to try to break the stranglehold that the professional human-services types and the bureaucrats have on family life..."[30]

From a different perspective, several recent studies of the family have stressed the victimization of parents by experts and by government. Christopher Lasch, in *Haven in a Heartless World: The Family Besieged* and *Culture of Narcissism,* argues that the rise of children's and family services, helping professionals, and social science have drastically undermined parental self-confidence. "The invasion of the family by industry, the mass media, and the agencies of socialized parenthood," he believes, have destroyed "parents' confidence in their ability to perform the most elementary functions of child rearing."[31] Although far gentler in his depiction, Kenneth Keniston in *All Our Children* sees the parent today as "a coordinator without voice or authority." "If parents are frustrated," he says, "it is no wonder: for although they have the responsibility for their children's lives, they hardly ever have a voice, the authority, or the power to make others listen to them."[32]

CONSEQUENCES OF NEGATIVE PARENT IMAGES

The acceptance of cultural images emphasizing parental weakness, ignorance, passivity, or helplessness has had profound implications for parent-professional relationships, for the evolution of American policies and programs for children, for parent–professional relationships, and for how parents evaluate their own worth and strength.

How Parents Have Viewed Institutions

Many parents do not see institutions — a children's hospital, for example, or the local elementary school, or an adoption agency — as places that either victimize them or compensate for their alleged incompetence. Instead, they see places where a child's life can be saved, where children of blue-collar workers can get the kind of education that enables them to grow up to be teachers in the schools in which their fathers were once janitors, where a homeless child can be assured a loving home. This, after all, is the record of the helping institutions in America, and it made a profound impression on Americans in the first half of the century.

Implicit in the critics' argument that schools, health and welfare services, institutions, and the state are taking over the functions of the family (as if institutions had some sinister capacity to move in and lop off these functions) is a view of parents as passive recipients. My view is different. I believe that many parents worked hard to acquire for their children the circle of protection and the real benefits that the pediatrician's office, the child-health station, the maternity unit, and the school seemed to offer.

Parents did so for sensible reasons: The evidence suggested that these institutions helped children to survive and develop well. Parents in general were not suddenly neglectful or ready to abandon their responsibilities in pursuit of self-fulfillment. In a broad social sense, parents did not transfer child-raising functions to institutions and helping services. Financing them privately or supporting the social policies that provided them from public funds, often at some sacrifice to themselves, parents reached out and brought services for children *into* their families when they decided it mattered to do so.

In previous centuries, children suffered and died while medical experts looked on helplessly. Education, especially secondary education, was reserved for the children of the rich. Childbirth meant intense suffering for the mother and serious risk of death for both mother and baby. But between the end of the nineteenth century and the middle of the twentieth, everything changed. By the mid-1950s, nearly all mothers survived childbirth, and most babies were born without damage. The death rate of white infants fell from 100 per 1000 live births in 1915 to approximately 30 per 1000 live births in 1950. For Black and other nonwhite infants, rates fell from 180 per 1000 to approximately 45 per 1000. Maternal survival was still not always assured for child-bearing women in 1920. Between 75 and 80 white mothers per 10,000 who gave live births were likely to die in childbirth; between 125 and 130 Black and other nonwhite mothers per 10,000 might die. By 1950, however, only 5 white women in 10,000 could be expected to die, as could 25 Black and other nonwhite mothers. Maternal mortality has by now declined to almost zero. Young children also now survive the ravages of childhood diseases. In 1900, approximately 40 out of 10,000 children died between the ages of five and fourteen. By 1950, only 5 children per every 10,000 in that age group died.[33]

Of course, many advances occurred because changes in sanitation practices, flush plumbing, and the pasteurization of milk prevented or controlled the infectious diseases that had been the most frequent cause of children's death. But to many parents the pediatrician's office or the child-health clinic with its dedicated, serious-looking staff must have appeared as the symbol of a new capacity to shepherd children through illnesses which previously threatened their lives. Miracle drugs, miracle doctors, miracle hospitals — or so it must have seemed.

Similarly, many factors contributed to making education more important to Americans. Immigrant children whose parents did not speak English had far fewer chances for success in the new country. There were millions of such children. In 1909, for example, government surveys in American urban schools showed that more than half the children were unable to speak English.[34] Furthermore, as many as one in every three citizens in some states was completely illiterate during the first decades of the century. Today that proportion falls below three in every hundred.[35]

The outward symbol that a factory hand's son or daughter could aspire to a profession, prestige, and a more comfortable and dependable income was public education: the grammar school, the high school, the city university or state land-grant college. In fact, the increasing power of the labor unions, the reduced work week, the minimum wage and unemployment insurance, the end of most child labor, and Social Security contributed to new opportunities for earning a decent income. In addition, during the twentieth century, the American economy developed in ways that made it more reliant on educated workers. By 1970, more than 40 percent of the labor force was engaged in professional, technical, and other such occupations. Less than 5 percent was involved in nonfarm unskilled labor. (In the eighteenth century, by contrast, 80 percent of the work force was unskilled).[36] At the same time, technology created new jobs and enlarged the market for white-collar workers and professionals. Whether or not education was the key to a better life, many parents thought it was and encouraged their children to stay in school.

Over the first half of the twentieth century, as children's services grew, scientists, academicians, and professionals found many new ways to do good things for children. By the middle of the century, even polio, which crippled and killed thousands of children each year, was vanquished. Researchers working on new breakthroughs helpful to children toiled inside the shiny new institutions built for them by an increasing flood of government funds and private donations from a grateful public. To some parents, however, the power of these new "miracle workers" seemed more valuable than their own ability to protect and rear their children. There was a surge of concern about "what the experts say or think should be done." Analysts have described the rush of parents in the late forties and fifties to depend on experts, child-rearing manuals, and popular child-guidance specialists. The expanding market for literature giving advice to parents, with titles such as *Pushbutton Parents and the School, Are Parents Bad for Chil-*

dren? and *What's Right With Us Parents?*, indicated a growing sense of dependence.

Yet, as the previous chapter demonstrates, many parents *never* thought it appropriate to entrust their children completely to institutions and to professionals who could automatically be depended on to act in the child's best interests. As that attitude increased in the 1960s and 1970s, parents had to recognize the prevalence of deficit cultural images of parenthood, assess the impact of those images, and develop a new, more suitable self-image that could serve as a more appropriate metaphor for the relationship between parents and institutions, parents and government.

How Institutions Saw Parents

A convergence of economic, social, and political forces in the nineteenth and early twentieth centuries, as well as scientific breakthroughs in public health and pediatric medicine, meant that child health, welfare, and educational services could and did improve the lives of children and their parents. The imagery of parental incompetence and helplessness so frequently summoned up by scholars, advocates, and public officials in order to win these services, however, had unfortunate results, permeating the structure upon which services were founded. Partly for that reason, schools, hospitals, and child-welfare services evolved into organizations that often excluded parents while helping the child. Especially in urban areas, where the institutions rapidly became large and complex, parents' rights were remarkably abridged — to the point that portfolios filled with professionals' judgments about parents and vital information about children could be opened to almost any school-system employee, but were closed to parents.

The two services that later became nearly universal for children — hospitalized childbirth and elementary education — worked on the assumption that professionals knew far more about children than parents did. Public schools in too many cases educated children "despite their parents" rather than in a combined parent–school effort. Doctors, not mothers, delivered babies, sometimes by using harmful drugs (such as scopolamine) while "protecting" parents from knowledge of the drugs' frightening possibilities. Hospital pediatric wards became places where parents were unwelcome.

It is interesting to speculate on what sort of hospitals and public schools we would have today if assumptions less hostile to parents had shaped their early years. Undoubtedly economic and political needs also contributed to the development of these services, and undoubtedly children and parents benefited from them. But they might have been very different if different assumptions about parents had animated their creation.

One reason institutions shut parents out is a professional need to feel completely competent. The image of the "omnipotent professional," writes the perceptive Mary Howell (mother, pediatrician, and psychologist), is symbiotically dependent on an image of parents as incompetent:

> We [parents] are taught to feel incompetent in every area of expert and professional endeavor. If experts and professionals have a "right" to keep and control their knowledge and skills, we must play the counterrole of incompetence... We are continually led to believe that no one but a professional can solve our problems for us.[37]

This symbiosis also flourishes in the professional perception of parents as victimized to the point of helplessness. Such a perception means that *someone* must help the children, and it reinforces cultural acceptance of professionals as appropriate, effective helpers.

Analyzing causes of friction between parents and teachers, educator Sara Lawrence Lightfoot says, "The cultural images of mother... seem to express the mirror images of the teacher... there is need for strong teachers when mothers are perceived as being less than adequate."[38]

In fact, these mirror images originate historically in the need to establish a professional identity of competence. In the nineteenth and early twentieth centuries, teachers, pediatricians, pediatric nurses, and child-welfare workers needed to prove that they could provide a service that was not only essential to healthy child development but that no one else could provide. Thus, professionals whose lives were bound up in the care and education of children needed to distinguish, in the public mind, their work (and themselves) from parents, whose work, after all, was not (and is not) radically different from the work of many professionals caring for children. Operating factory machinery or computers, repairing automobiles, or designing highways is *fundamentally* different from nurturing and instructing children. Thus factory hands, computer programmers, auto mechanics, and engineers perform recognizably different work from teachers, nurses, psychologists, and social workers. But parents educate their children (teachers) and care for them when they are ill (pediatricians, nurses); they observe and reflect on their children's behavior and construct meanings for or interpretations of these behaviors, which in turn guide their own behavior (psychologists, psychiatrists). They mediate family conflicts (judges, child-welfare workers) and search out needed resources for the family (social workers). In this sense, the actions of child-serving professionals differ from parental actions only in the degree to which professional activity supplies a specialized skill (injection into the proper vein, in the appropriate dose, of the chemical proved by scientific research to be effective in treating a particular sickness), imparts knowledge (algebraic equations, early Babylonian history), or addresses unusual problems (serious mental illness) which are beyond the purview of most parents.

As the helping professions emerged, they followed a common pattern of evolving from the status of an occupation to that of a profession. Part of this "professionalization" calls for proof that practitioners of a skill can lay claim to "certain and exclusive competence."[39] Professional skill, according to one analyst of the process, "is measured by the probability that a layman would fail at the assigned task with varying degrees of practice."[40] Furthermore, professionals are characterized by autonomy, the exclusive ability to define mistakes (nonprofessionals don't know enough to recognize professional failure; only other professionals can do so), and the assertion of the power to define the needs of the client.[41] Thus, in the days when the professions of public schoolteaching, pediatrics, and child welfare were emerging, teachers, nurses, social workers, and counselors had to demonstrate that their skills in caring for children were far beyond those of the lay public — that is, of parents. One way to accomplish this was to describe in harrowing detail the incompetence of parents. Furthermore, these professionals needed to demonstrate that only they could define the needs of the child because parents were either too ignorant or too overwhelmed by stress to perceive and articulate those needs.

Even today, while many of the child-serving professions have gradually earned the status and recognition of professions, others (particularly those in which women or mothers predominate, such as teaching or nursing) are still struggling to establish firmly their claim to that identity. Within the context of large, well-established professions in which service to children is regarded as merely one part (such as the practice of pediatric medicine, considered within the context of the medical profession), those professionals who work with children are typically among the most poorly paid, and often they are less well regarded than their colleagues. Thus, the general pediatrician who spends his or her days diagnosing colds and common ear infections often has less status (and certainly less income) than the eye surgeon. It has been and continues to be an uphill struggle for people who spend their lives working with children to prove firm professional standing.

Consequently, our schools, hospitals, and child-guidance clinics are now often organized around the assumption that professionals have answers and parents have questions. Rare is the practitioner who doesn't believe that he or she is more competent than the average parent; they are taught to believe precisely that in their training. Until quite recently, the very assessment of competence has been seen as something that professionals do to parents, not vice versa.

If the theoreticians are correct, then the widespread use of Incompetent and Victimized Parent imagery may have been an inevitable accompaniment to the establishment of various professions. But, ironically, the very struggle to gain a broad public conviction that activities similar to those of parents have "certain and exclusive competence" is constantly impeded by the depiction of parents as incompetent.

Of all the negative consequences of the deficit images of

parents, however, the most regrettable is their impact on parents' self-images. Damage to self-confidence and feelings of worth is evident in so much contemporary literature written by parents. All the experts may be right, explains experienced mother and author Shirley Radl:

> Anyone, in fact, can be right, because I certainly can't say that I am. Sometimes one thing works and sometimes another thing works. Sometimes I think I'm doing the right thing, and sometimes I know perfectly well I'm doing the wrong thing. And the whole time I'm dealing with [my children], I feel totally inadequate to the task — totally unhelped by any of the experts.[42]

As a growing literature written by mothers attests, this parent's feelings are common. Some of this new candor about self-doubt emerged in the interviews I conducted. It was expressed most easily at the Mothers' Centers, where women are strongly encouraged to be deeply honest about their sense of themselves as mothers. One mother says, "We always seem to wonder what we're doing wrong. It's not the environment, or the child, it's always what *we're* doing...I know I question myself..." Another gently scoffs at her former beliefs that her own professional education (she earned an advanced degree in early childhood education) would protect her from self-doubt. When her daughter was born,

> I thought if anybody was able to handle a young child...I had enough experience and enough background. Well she threw me for a loop; I felt as if I came from Mars and never knew anything. She was extremely difficult and I was unprepared for my feelings of "What am I doing wrong, that this is happening to me?"...I was too educated for that to happen to me, but it happened anyway. And that was an extremely difficult time, wondering, What am I doing wrong?

Self-doubt is painful. Fears about one's ability to fulfill one's chosen occupation are also painful. But self-doubt and fears about one's competence to do a job that, unlike other jobs, is a round-the-clock, twenty-year undertaking that doesn't lend itself well to termination is particularly hard. Lowered parental self-esteem was surely an unintended consequence of the professionalization and institutionalization of children's services, but it was nonetheless a consequence.

The Victimized Parent image generates less self-doubt than the Incompetent Parent image does; at least parents can attribute their failures to overwhelming external forces. Furthermore, some parents really are made to suffer by unhelpful and even inhumane treatment, as the testimony of the parents interviewed for this book also indicates. Racial, sexual, and other kinds of discrimination do victimize millions of American parents. Still, Victimized Parent imagery ultimately reinforces feelings of helplessness. It results in a diminution of self-respect, a loss of self-confidence, and consequently a shrunken sense of one's capacities to protect one's children and rear them well. Even those who use Victimized Parent images to argue against cultural use of Incompetent Parent imagery fail to help parents. Consider language like that employed by author Christopher Lasch, widely hailed as a vigorous opponent of the appropriation of parental competence by institutions and the helping professions:

> Outside experts have taken over many of [the American mother's] practical functions, and she often discharges those that remain in a mechanical manner. In view of the suffocating yet emotionally distant care they receive from narcissistic mothers, it is not surprising that so many young people... describe their mothers as both seductive and aloof, devouring and indifferent...that she appears in the child's fantasies as a devouring bird, a vagina full of teeth.[43]

Such words are hardly apt to bolster either a mother's sense of self-esteem or the energy, hope, and confidence parents need to create "their own agencies of self help" — Lasch's alternative to dependence on professionals and their services.

A NEW IMAGE: THE RESOURCEFUL PARENT

I had trouble in the last few days. I got a note from my son's teacher saying she wanted to see me, and from the time I got the note...I was imagining all kinds of terrible things — what did I do wrong? What am

I going to do? It must be my fault; either I'm giving him too much time or not enough time, or something — and I really thought I was going to go out of my mind. But all I could think of was 'Well, I'll...come here and join a group on mothers and sons or something, because I'm trying to think of everyone I know and nobody's son is like mine; nobody that I know. But I figured if I come here, I join a group, there's got to be somebody else with a son getting in trouble.
— a mother participating in a Mothers' Center

You know the typical thing about parents in the emergency room with children. The typical response is, "But the mother would faint!" But they forget that the child first had something happen to him out in the field and it was very traumatic and the mother probably has two or three other children. She had to put them in the car with her or find a neighbor to take them while she actually drove the car all the way there and didn't have an accident. And she unloaded the child, brought him in to the emergency room, and answered all the questions that are asked. And now they are telling her she won't be able to stand it.
— a parent member of Children in Hospitals

Many women had a lot of strengths, a lot of positive creativity, a lot of good survival skills, a lot of good parenting skills that were more or less going unchallenged and unchanneled...so isolated [were they] in their own individual struggles. So we came together on that kind of premise...unify our energies, our strengths, our creativity, all the good things that we knew existed, and put them into some collective mechanism by which a lot of other people may be able to benefit.
— a leader of the Sisterhood of Black Single Mothers

We don't beg anymore. We don't go "Will you *please* find a program? Thank you." We go in and we say: "My child has a disability. What programs do you offer? I am going to visit them and then we'll decide which one he goes into."
— a parent member of the National Society for Autistic Children

If you become a martyr you are just going to ruin everything for yourself and everybody around you. There is no reason to be a martyr. You can get out with other people that have the same problem and exchange ideas with them and learn how to stand up to the system with them. Learn how to stand up not only to your doctor but learn how to stand up to your

mother or your grandparents or whoever it is that is giving you a hard time. Learn how to look your neighbor straight in the eye and say, "I'm not going to take my child to some stupid medical clinic in Mexico. I believe in my doctors." Look at grandparents and say, "She will not eat that because it is not good for her, regardless of whether she is going to be dead in two months or two years, who knows!" Having the strength to discipline your child instead of giving in to your child because you don't want to live with a monster if your child outlives you — as more and more children are doing, with long-term treatment.
— a parent member of the Candlelighters

Carol: If I'd had the strength to address my alcoholism, five years into the marriage I would have taken the two kids and left Bob — but the bottom line was I had no self-esteem, that's what this thing with Daddy had created — no self-esteem... [Carol is a college professor who as a child was sexually abused by her father and who spent almost two decades in a very unhappy marriage.] Now I have to accept the responsibility for not letting myself be labeled, and that's wonderful. *I* do the choosing.
Patte: You're not a victim anymore.
Carol: No. I'm a victim of nothing except my own choices and it takes a whole different way of thinking to realize that I am not the victim. I'm glad you put it that way. The cycle is broken.
— from an interview conducted by Patte Wheat and published in *Frontiers,* the Parents Anonymous newsletter

The Resourceful Parent image conveys the belief that parents are first and foremost doers and decision makers on behalf of children. Most important for this image is not *what* we are deciding, but *that* we are deciding. The approval or understanding of policy makers or professionals is irrelevant. What matters is that we parents are now thought to be acting on behalf of our children rather than passively waiting for professionals and bureaucrats to do something.

Of course, as we saw earlier, organized groups of parents were active on behalf of their children in the early decades of the twentieth century, and even in the nineteenth century. So it is not surprising that a policy statement published in 1954 by the

National Association for Retarded Children concludes with a statement about parents:

> And his parents [the parents of a retarded child] have the right to determine for themselves, on the basis of competent advice, the course of care, training, and treatment, among those open to them, which they believe best for their family; and to have their decisions respected by others.[44]

In the 1950s, when community-based facilities for retarded children were scarce and institutionalization was regarded as the "right choice" by many, parents were burdened with extraordinarily stressful decisions. But in a sharp break from earlier images of parents of retarded offspring, the Educational Bill of Rights for the Retarded Child emphasizes parental energy and decision making — and respect for parents' choices.

The Resourceful Parent image began to emerge consistently, however, in post-1960s literature, when the trend toward increased reliance on experts was met by a countertrend of dissatisfaction with experts, institutions, and professionals. The grass-roots participation movements of the past two decades, originating in the struggle for civil rights, ran counter to images highlighting passivity and incapacity. Consequently, since the sixties, the literature about children's needs reflects changes in images of parents.

Consider the way in which some contemporary leaders of the children's-rights movement, such as Marian Wright Edelman, founder of the Children's Defense Fund, approach the issue of parents' rights to involvement in children's services. Says Ms. Edelman:

> Parent involvement is... crucial, because when you are dealing with children it seems to me to make sense to try to involve those individuals who have the most influence and responsibility in the child's life... Many professionals don't trust parents. Many parents don't trust themselves. This must be combated.[45]

Like earlier literature, such speeches and articles also emphasize the sufferings of children, the injustices that many children and parents face, or the stress that many families feel. Faded, or fading, however, are the assumptions that parents are either generally incompetent or victimized to the point of being passive and helpless.

This new literature does not assume that because parents are resourceful, government has no obligation to assure fair access to necessary resources. After all, this literature is rooted in the heightened awareness of the 1960s that social forces such as prejudice are inimical to fair opportunities, and in some cases to survival. Consequently, by the 1980s, a new theme is emerging in arguments for government policies and programs: government should meet compelling needs and redress injustice experienced by children and parents, but construct policies from a clear-eyed assessment of the strengths and resources that parents bring to their problems.

In an insightful, cogently argued book, *The Strengths of Black Families,* first published in 1971, Robert Hill sounded this theme. Then the research director of the National Urban League, an organization strongly supportive of effective national policies and programs to aid Black families, Dr. Hill examined volumes of statistical data detailing the characteristics of Black family existence in America, in order to document the personal and cultural resources that Blacks bring to the stresses and injustice they confront. He argued:

> It is our contention that examining the strengths of black families can contribute as much toward understanding and ameliorating some social problems as examining their weaknesses...Systematic examination of the strengths of black families should facilitate the development of national policies and programs which enhance and use these assets to their fullest potential.[46]

This theme reappears throughout the seventies and eighties in books, speeches, and testimony about other populations disadvantaged by illness, handicap, crisis, or stressful life transitions.

In another break from tradition, increasing numbers of books and articles are being written by parents themselves. Here the Resourceful Parent image strongly emerges. Consider the way the Parents' Campaign for Handicapped Children and Youth introduces parents who have just given birth to a handicapped infant to the new assumptions about such parents, in a brochure they distribute:

> Parents are fully capable of bringing up their own children; they have deep resources of courage and dedication needed to face the facts of handicaps, see what's needed and cope with their complex and demanding job.
>
> When problems arise, professionals should be there as *consultants* — to offer information and to suggest choices based on experience. Parents and professionals are natural resources for each other in seeking solutions for problems — and in helping each child grow to the maximum extent possible.

The Resourceful Parent image does not deny problems parents face. Here parents of handicapped infants are acknowledged as individuals under stress, who must "cope with their complex and demanding job." But they are resourceful, and they can work with professionals as equal partners in seeking solutions and solving problems.

While the Resourceful Parent image does flourish in the literature written or published by activist parents, a significant aspect of this literature is recognition that many parents do have impaired self-images and different ranges of resources. It is precisely in the search for better resources needed by their children that parents become more resourceful.

Personal accounts of evolving activists symbolize the possibilities that are available to every parent. One example is "Becoming Involved is Becoming Somebody," written by Gerri Chestor, a parent of an autistic child. Published in "Network," a parents' newsletter from the National Committee for Citizens in Education, the article begins: "I'm 'just a parent' and I'm proud of it." Ms. Chestor describes herself as someone who "was terrified to give a book report in front of my high school class." She matured into adulthood while remaining naive about how the system works and about politics in general; "Nobody could have been less prepared than I was." Her personal odyssey began in the 1960s with a four-and-a-half-year effort to get her autistic son evaluated. Institutionalization or a special school program was then recommended. After talking to "every special education director of every school district and the head of every agency in the state," Ms. Chestor concluded that no special school programs then existed for autistic children in the state of Colorado. Nor did anyone believe that autistic children could be educated.

For Gerri Chestor, placing those telephone calls drew on a special reserve of courage. In the sixties, parents, and especially mothers of autistic children, were thought to have caused their children's condition by some conscious or unconscious coldness. Specialists probably regarded Ms. Chestor's phone calls as impertinent. After all, she had caused her son's problems; why should schools have to live with it? Nevertheless, those calls were just the beginning, as Gerri Chestor evolved into a resourceful and determined parent. At first she simply took her son to school and left him with the first-grade teacher. When that didn't work, she "found out the schools were supported by property taxes" and refused to pay hers for four years. She also withdrew her two daughters from school, violating compulsory attendance laws, as an expression of her objections to her son's exclusion. Along the way, Gerri Chestor learned about legislative politics, first by distributing campaign literature, then by simply walking into big political functions and approaching the "biggest political names there" to introduce herself. This, she explained, helped considerably when she later showed up in the state assembly to testify and lobby. The legislators vaguely recognized her face and felt somehow that they knew her.

Gerri Chestor's activism paid off. In 1970, the governor of Colorado asked to see her and appointed a task force on autism, which recommended the first public school program for autistic children in the history of the state. By 1978, because of "a handful of parents who had nothing going for them but guts and determination," in Ms. Chestor's words, Colorado was serving over 80,000 handicapped children and appropriating $33 million for that education — a far cry from the $3.5 million that such services attracted in 1965.

Gerri Chestor's story is not all that different from those of Mary Akerley, another parent leader in the National Society for Autistic

Children, or Jolly K, the founder of Parents Anonymous, or Bob Le Clair, one of the founders of Massachusetts Fathers United for Equal Justice, or Daphne Busby, leader of the Sisterhood of Black Single Mothers, or Hope Zimmerman, one of the founders of the Mothers' Center on Long Island, or many of the other parent leaders interviewed for this book. Having set out to find or generate the resources they needed, the parents I listened to created not only the new skills but the personal attributes and the new self-images they need to be effective. Collectively, those self-images — of action, competence, power, ability, assertiveness — are merging into a new cultural image: the Resourceful Parent.

Parents engaged in activism not only consciously promote new images of parents, they also combat old ones. The literature about services to children in the 1970s, and even the 1980s, still includes some Incompetent or Victimized Parent images. But more and more often, parent activists are responding to these negative cultural images by asking why images focusing on weakness, incapacity, and incompetence still prevail, why parents are always the ones who need help. The stereotypes they contest include the image of the Candlelighter parent as someone totally "out of it," swept away by the overwhelming stress of having a child suffering with cancer; the image of the abusive parent as a psychotic criminal; the image of divorced fathers as carefree runaways from their responsibilities. Stereotypes like these, say parent activists, are not only inaccurate but constrict the chances that both parents and children have to be accepted by society. Deficit images distort the expectations that others have of both parent and child behavior, and so constrain parents' hopes. Parent activists feel that this is especially unfair because negative images so often result from ignorance.

"At times I hear people mess with us who don't even know us," says Daphne Busby, of the Sisterhood of Black Single Mothers. "All these people coming out with their little matriarchal problems. And if you ask them how many black single mothers do you know, they don't know us." Her own view is different: "A woman having a child and struggling when she could be on her own as a single woman, she's compromised on a lot of things just to raise this child. But that's not given any respect."

Finally, parent activists feel that parents should reject negative stereotypes because in a quiet but powerful way those images make parents feel they should pull back from highly protective and nurturing involvement with their children. Images of "overprotective" and "overanxious" parents, say activists, control parental behavior, an effect that is sometimes intended. A founder of Children in Hospitals articulates the anger that I heard from many parents about stereotypes that obstruct their efforts to protect and nurture.

> Even when we were talking to Dr. R about rooming in, well, he felt that the only time that a parent would be told not to room in is if the pediatrician felt that it was time to cut the cord; if the child was too old or if the parent was pathological. I thought, well, that's just wonderful! How do you decide when would be the appropriate time or if there is a terrible pathological situation? One fellow told me that they watch for incest — a mother who would want to stay with a ten-year-old or a seven-year-old, whatever it was that I had at home at the time, and he said he would watch for abnormal relationships. I said, what are you talking about, and he said, well, you know, incest. I said, you are *kidding*. My seven-year-old would not like to hear that he had to come here alone for anything but I would have to worry then that you are going to assume that we have an incestuous relationship? This becomes so bizarre and yet again this is the attitude — watch those parents — those are suspects.

The reaction of parent activists of being demeaned or excluded is not just verbal, however. It is expressed in action: in their mutual support, in their struggle to achieve basic institutional change in the services their children need, and in advocacy for new laws and a fairer share of the nation's public resources for children.

In sum, both similarities and differences exist between this kind of child advocacy and that of earlier periods in American history. There is still sustained advocacy for a different distribution of public resources to those children who have been excluded from equal opportunity. There continues to be a movement for reform of powerful institutions which hold such sway over the lives of so many children. And as always the advocates of such changes are bound together by a shared vision of what could be and a supporting network of mutual help. Only this time, in many parts of the country, these efforts are undertaken by determined and competent people who have the most to gain or lose by the outcome of their efforts: parents. The policies and programs they work for are shaped around the assumption that parents will be active not just in a one-time creation or restructuring of the services needed by their children, but on a continuing, durable basis. And with that assumption comes a new, more confident, more resilient appreciation of themselves as people committed to one of the nation's most arduous (and most valuable) tasks: rearing children well.

What Parent Groups Provide

4

Lee Lapicki's street seems very silent. Row houses neatly line both sides of the street, edged by clipped, small front yards and swept sidewalks. In this suburb of Baltimore, the well-scrubbed sidewalks do not seem out of place — but the silence does.

I went to Baltimore to interview Lee Lapicki because I had seen her testify in the United States House of Representatives. Representing thousands of parents who struggle with child abuse, she spoke about the work of Parents Anonymous to the congressional committee considering renewal of the Child Abuse Prevention and Treatment Act. She was extremely effective. She was also very honest. During nearly all of her testimony, the representatives listened more attentively than they had listened to any other witness.

I wanted to know more about Parents Anonymous. But as I walked down the street to Lee Lapicki's house, I was thinking about her, another mother raising children. What was it like bringing up children in this quiet community? How difficult would it be, after all the publicity in the local papers describing her as an abusive parent and a leader of Parents Anonymous, to live life normally in a neighborhood like this?

Lee Lapicki is easy to feel comfortable with. She is someone with whom it is possible to raise questions that one wouldn't discuss with other people, at least not in an initial interview. So, as we talked in her kitchen, I asked her about her neighbors' reaction to the publicity when she helped to found the Maryland chapter of Parents Anonymous. What response did she get from the other parents on her block when she started saying on TV that she was an abusive parent who was finding great solace and help in joining together with other abusive parents?

"Absolutely nothing," she said. "There was no reaction. Once in a while, I would see someone on the street and they'd mention that they had seen me on TV. But that was it." My face must have registered disbelief. Lee leaned over and said, "But then, why would they? There never was any reaction to anything I was doing. People here just don't get involved with one another."

The most important thing about mutual support in the parent groups with whom I talked is that it ends that kind of aloneness. Raising a child is never easy, but raising a child among strangers is virtually impossible. Parent self-help and advocacy groups are first and foremost oases — places where conversation, interest in one another, practical tips, friendship, and frequently humor can be shared. In the mutual support encouraged by these groups, parents rearing children under sometimes painful circumstances experience one of the most basic human feelings: connectedness to others.

Contrast the isolation Lee Lapicki felt in her neighborhood with the first meeting of Baltimore parents interested in Parents Anonymous.

> The first meeting was basically getting to know each other — telling your stories about how you were raised, how many children you had, whatever people felt like saying. We kicked everybody out about 10:30 and straightened up and talked, and when we walked outside it was pouring rain and all ten of the women were still there in the pouring rain with their umbrellas, still talking...
> All of these people were sharing and saying, "Please call me," and "Please do this."

Nor is this connectedness special to abusive parents, who very often are almost totally estranged from both family and friends. For example, all kinds of parents often feel very alone when a child has learning problems. The father whose child is failing to master reading may feel quite isolated and ashamed of his child's failure — and, by extension, his own failure as a parent — when he compares his situation with the apparent successes his neighbors or relatives have with their children. The mother whose child becomes the "bad boy," the disruptive child in the class, may pull back from seeking helpful information from other parents, fearful of their increased censure of her child. When the Parents' Union was first formed in Philadelphia, it distributed its phone number and publicized its commitment to parent rights primarily to pull together parents who were weary of prolonged teacher strikes. The group's members soon found themselves handling phone calls from parents experiencing all kinds of problems with their children's education and feeling unsure whether they had *any* rights when they strongly objected to a school's behavior toward their children. "We couldn't turn them away," says Happy Fernandez, one of the founders of the Parents' Union. By the early 1980s, the Union each month handled sixty to seventy cases brought to them by parents, and sponsored a parents' hotline for immediate help.

Mothers of seriously mentally ill children spoke of the isolation they feel in a society that routinely holds mothers accountable for the mental health of their children, and of the eagerness with which they wanted to talk when they met other parents like themselves. One parent activist illustrated this by describing what happened when she and another woman (whose son had been hospitalized with mental illness from age eight) developed a mothers' group that met at the local public library. The library closed at 10 P.M., but the small support group usually refused to stop for the night. They continued their meetings at a local restaurant until it closed, then kept in touch by telephone in between weekly meetings. Over time, the group evolved into the Long Island Regional Council of the Federation of Parents' Organizations for the New York State Mental Institutions. I heard many stories like this.

The relief that parents feel in breaking out of their isolation makes for a powerful cohesive force. Describing the letters received by *Ladies' Home Journal* after it published an article on autism, National Society for Autistic Children activist Mary Akerley says: "The big thing that ran through the letters was, 'We thought we were the only family in the world with a kid like this! And Bernie [Bernard Rimland, a founder of the Society] said we've got to find a way to get these people together and find the other parents; each one of them had thought there was no one else they could talk to. My God, they're coming out of the woodwork."

As parents connect, growth is usually rapid. In 1977, for example, Atlanta parents first began to organize peer groups concerned about drug use. Parents in Naples, Florida, then developed a group modeled on the Atlanta one. Newspaper accounts and government pamphlets described the experiences of these parents. By 1980, there were six hundred such groups and a national organization, the National Federation of Parents for Drug-Free Youth (NFP). The NFP's president, in a "Good Morning America" (ABC) segment, mentioned that a parent-group starter kit was available; the organization received 18,000 requests for the kit.

Children in Hospitals grew from a few parents to hundreds within a year. The Mothers' Center, which began with a group of about fifteen, now reaches out to several thousand women. Black Parents for Quality Education expanded in only a few years from slightly more than a thousand parents to an estimated twelve thousand. Parents Anonymous has experienced incredible growth, from sixty chapters in May 1974 to over five hundred chapters by the fall of 1976, and to twelve hundred chapters worldwide by 1981. The Parents' Union, just a handful of parents a few years ago, has grown to an organization reaching out, through its local school associations, to 24,000 parents.

Parents organize and join mutual-support groups so intensely because such groups end isolation. But they also meet two other important needs. Parents' self-help groups are new communities where effective solutions can be found or developed for problems so new that families, friends, and even professionals don't have all the answers. They are also places where parents, in concert with one another, create a new belief in themselves.

NEW COMMUNITIES

Many analysts of the modern family point out that neighborhoods where families support one another are becoming scarcer in our mobile society. The demise of geographical neighborhoods, however, need not mean that parents are bereft of any support. Transcending the limitations of their immediate environs, they can connect with parents from other neighborhoods to create new supportive communities. In an evolutionary perspective, organized parent groups are an adaptation, made both possible and necessary by the increasing ease with which we move.

Many parents, of course, still rely on their extended families and on informal networks of family and friends to provide the support that they need for rearing children. A fair percentage — parents with handicapped children, single parents, or adoptive parents — are likely to live near their own families and near established friends. Why, then, do so many parents seek mutual support outside these networks?

Change is one reason. Most extended-family and friendship networks rely on child-rearing ideas and coping strategies that emerged from earlier generations and have served well over time. Family and friends are cultural depositories for parents, sources of knowledge about things like colic, skinned knees, the first day of school. They are a storehouse of ideas and suggestions, furnishing help for problems that people raising children have commonly encountered for many years. Nearly all the parents interviewed for this book, however, faced uniquely contemporary problems. Before the advent of highly developed neonatal care, for example, seriously handicapped children would not have survived, or would ordinarily have been institutionalized. Today, there are an estimated 10 million children in the U.S. with handicaps or chronic health impairments.[1] The vast majority of these children live at home. Twenty years ago it would have seemed impossible for large numbers of handicapped children to attend public schools with their friends. Today every handicapped child has the right to public education. Mainstreaming, in which handicapped and nonhandicapped children attend classes together, is often preferred for all but the most severely impaired youngster.

Increases in the divorce rate also mean that many more mothers are bringing up children alone, and many more fathers are coming to grips with child custody decisions and the power of the courts to sever them from their children. The number of children affected by divorce has increased by 700 percent since the beginning of the century.[2] About 10.9 million children grow up in single-parent families today.[3] Remarriage and step-parenting are common; in 1970, about three-fifths of all children with a divorced parent were in families with one step-parent.[4] Between 1970 and 1978, the number of families headed by single men rose by 29 percent.[5] These experiences were much rarer a generation ago.

Adopting a child used to mean receiving a small infant in one's home. Adoptive parents could anticipate rearing a child who had a few concerns about his or her origins or background; more serious problems were unusual. Today adoption is quite different. Many adopted children have been abused or neglected; many have been in foster care for some time. Consider this mother's account, from the newsletter of an adoptive parents' group:

> Twin girls, age two years old, were available. The girls had been separated at six months into different foster homes with separate environments. Both had been plagued with severe illness caused mainly by abusive neglect. Their foster homes tried to bring them back to health but they had a long way to go. Lea Ann had been "branded" developmentally retarded with a possibility of environmental correction and borderline malnutrition. Jenny was a "normal" two year old. We both gulped and took on the challenge.[6]

Change does not have to be extraordinary to be worrisome to parents. Schools now educate children with curricula that today's parents never studied. Where do you turn to be sure that these methods work and are beneficial to children? Then, too, teachers have new rights — a license, it sometimes seems, to analyze the psychological health of a child and write sometimes damaging conclusions into the child's permanent record. Family, neighbors, and friends may be just as bewildered by these changes as any average parent is.

Parents cannot tap older traditions for helpful information about school-related situations like these. They cannot turn to grandparents to discuss safe foods for children taking powerful anticancer drugs, or what to say to the judge making a decision about joint custody, or adopting eight-year-olds who have been in six or seven foster homes. Parents dealing with problems like these need to create new cultural depositories from which they can draw ideas and strategies. They can do so by talking and listening to other people in the same situation.

Other experiences can make it impossible to turn to family and close friends for support. Parents whose children are drifting into regular marijuana use, for example, often shut themselves off in a shamed silence, holding fast to the hope that their adolescents will "grow out of it" and grandparents or family friends will never need to know. Admitting this shame to another parent — often an obviously conscientious and loving parent — who is feeling the same emotion can be a lot easier than telling even a close friend whose children are drug-free. Parents Anonymous participants often remark that telling another, supportive parent that you have battered your children is a very different experience from telling your own mother or sister or friend next door. When Lee Lapicki found out about Parents Anonymous and its toll-free number in California, she called and connected with another understanding parent. "I have been trained pretty well not to show emotions," she said. "One of the emotions I don't show is crying...but I cried to Margo on the phone. I couldn't believe it, but I figured I'd never see her."

To solve new problems and to seek the open communication that some families and friends do not permit, parents develop self-help groups. But as a group evolves, parents support each other in ways that strongly resemble what family members typically do for one another. The first model of mutual support, the family, is so satisfactory when it works that self-help groups either consciously or unconsciously imitate its functions. Many parent activists refer to their organization as a second family. Grace Monaco explains the prolonged commitment of parents to the Candlelighters, even long after the death of their children: "Other members of their second family have given them help and they feel the need to also give that comfort to others." Writing in *Frontiers,* the Parents Anonymous newsletter, a young mother says of her involvement: "Before long I found myself responding, listening, learning, leaning on every available shoulder. I began to feel part of a tight family."

Caplan and Kililea, in the classic text *Support Systems and Mutual Help,* describe eight ways in which extended families support their members. These "support system functions," as they call them, also characterize to a large extent the functions of parent self-help groups. Extended families, the authors say,

1. Collect, store, and share information about the outside world.

2. Provide a receptive group where members can, for the most part, openly report what they have done and how people have reacted to their actions. The other members of the group help the person evaluate his or her own reported behavior and the meaning of other people's reactions.

3. Are a source of belief systems, value systems, and codes of behavior that influence an individual's understanding of the nature and meaning of the universe, or his or her place in it, and of the paths he or she should strive to travel in life. Caplan points out that the strengthening power of these inner "maps" and belief systems are felt more during acute family crisis.

4. Provide here-and-now guidance, especially in crisis or in long-term burdens. The group encourages sharing of the problem, offers advice and guidance, assists members with emotional and cognitive difficulties during role transition, and helps make arrangements with health or welfare agencies, including going with the distressed person to the community institution if needed. The group usually collects and stores the names of dependable professional helpers and has built up a network of relationships with knowledgeable individuals to whom they can turn when a group member is in need.

5. Provide practical service and concrete aid, including gifts, help with shopping and household tasks, and help with individual group members' care of children or the elderly, especially during crisis or transition. The system of regular exchange means that individual group members know they have a right to expect assistance from one another, because they also will be expected to provide assistance to other members of the group when needed. Thus, these services are performed without the recipient's feeling more vulnerable or less competent.

6. Are a "haven for rest and recuperation," a place where it is safe to relax and be oneself, where people are well known and burdens of the outside world can be temporarily set aside. The group also monitors fatigue in a member struggling with crisis, "legitimizing" rest during a period when putting aside responsibilities seems selfish or negligent. Finally, when the group survives over a long period of time, members can observe each other's development over the years and act as a "reservoir

of developmental personality data" about each other.

7. Act as a reference and control group; judge, reward, and punish behavior in an atmosphere of trust and continued acceptance.

8. Validate and reaffirm each individual member's sense of identity and competence. Individuals struggling with long-term burdens, crisis, or role transition tend to forget their continuing strengths, become confused about their identities, doubt their own abilities, and seek reassurance from others. The group reminds each person of past achievements and "validates their pre-crisis self-image of competence and ability to stand firm."[7]

Parents in self-help and mutual-support groups engage in nearly all these functions, with the exception of acting as a reference and control group. Most parent activists with whom I talked explicitly rejected judging one another's behavior and rewarding or punishing group members for violations of the group's code. In their view, parent groups should shield their members from the painful and constrictive effects of being judged as failing to measure up to expectations. This is undoubtedly related to the controlling influence of those deficit images which parent activists refuse to accept, as well as to their perception that excessive professional judgment limits parents' self-confidence and ability to rear children. Then, too, given the variations in child-rearing philosophies in America, it would be impossible to develop a consensus about one appropriate child-rearing code within a parent group. Without this consensus, groups could not control the actions of their members, even if they sought to do so. Finally, most of the parent groups I studied organize in response not to a socially recognizable "failure" of behavior but to parental feelings of chaos and loneliness during transitions or because of stressful biological or social conditions. Negative judgments by the group would just add to the stress.

Parent activists' refusal to create a reference and control group is all the more remarkable because that is the function of so many other self-help organizations. Recovery, Inc., Alcoholics Anonymous, Gamblers Anonymous, and even weight-reducing groups embrace a behavioral or ethical code to which members must adhere in order to remain in good standing. Marie Kililea describes this aspect of self-help as "secular religion." Often, such groups are organized around an "authority-hero" whose personal philosophy and writings are carefully studied and followed. Parents Anonymous does have ten "guidelines for achievement," statements to which members agree. But guidelines are quite different from a code to which members pledge adherence, as is the case with Alcoholics Anonymous.

Parent self-help groups are usually not a substitute for extended families or for informal helping networks among friends. The self-help organization is, in Kililea's words, a "supplementary community," a ring of support around one's first support system, meeting special problems and experiences. For most group members, supportive interactions with family and friends solve many daily problems. Sometimes, as in the Candlelighters and many adoptive parents' groups, extended families enroll in the group's special meetings. But when parents add advocacy for systematic social or institutional change to the emotionally supportive functions of the group, they need the supplementary community even more. Families and friends may initially regard such efforts as foolhardy; professionals and bureaucrats, even when sympathetic, can be antagonistic to a new (and angry) parent group. For parents, confrontations with government or helping institutions can be frightening at first. Fear, a sense of mission, and the conviction that eventually, if the group stays together, conditions will improve for their children drive parents into closer interdependence within the group. At this point, the supplementary community strongly resembles the "beloved community" of the early civil-rights movement, which supported activists during jailings, beatings, and bombings, as well as the strong sense of sisterhood which has characterized much of the women's movement.

By listening to and supporting one another, parents choose to define themselves as competent, independent of how professionals behave toward them or their children. Within the group, individuals develop the skills and the courage to call on professionals when their "certain and exclusive competence" is needed, mediate the uses to which that competence is put, and prohibit future professional involvement with the child when it appears unnecessary or undesirable.

NEW CONFIDENCE, NEW SELF-IMAGE

Parents involved in mutual support in self-help groups believe that their organizations increase their confidence and enable them to develop new, more positive self-images. Philip Roos, a psychologist and parent leader in the National Association for Retarded Citizens, describes the common reactions when parents are told that their children are handicapped: loss of self-esteem, shame, ambivalence, depression or chronic sorrow, self-sacrifice or adoption of a "martyr" approach to life, and defensiveness and acute sensitivity to perceived criticism of the child. Roos also describes "existential conflicts" that such parents struggle with: feelings of disillusionment, aloneness, vulnerability, the basic unfairness of life, the insignificance and meaninglessness of human existence, apprehension about the future, and the sense of their own finiteness and mortality.[8] Parents facing extreme stress, as in a child's hospitalization for serious surgery, chronic conditions, or the death of a child, or the milder but still painful stresses associated with prolonged conflict in a school situation, feel they must contend with these burdens and existential conflicts as well. Some of the parents I interviewed also felt their self-confidence threatened because of abrupt life transitions — in childbirth or divorce, for example. The new mother or the father who has gained custody of his children and begins taking responsibility for their daily care may experience feelings of uncertainty and incompetence as well as loss of self-esteem.

Newsletters of parent groups often include articles describing feelings like these. Ultimately, these responses to children's suffering or to sudden life changes, together with the continued impact of deficit images of incompetence and victimization, dislocate positive parental self-images and impair self-confidence. In mutual support, activist parents help each other take apart destructive self-images and build and sustain constructive ones. Three functions are central to this effort: (1) "releasing consciousness," (2) offering practical assistance, and (3) renewing parents' spirit, determination, and enthusiasm.

Releasing Consciousness

In mutual support, parents talk and listen to one another in what the organizers of the Mothers' Center call "new and deeper ways, in a nonjudgmental, empathetic atmosphere." In the words of these women, they "release consciousness," or transform their awareness, of each self as a parent, of all that one is and can be as a parent, and of the barriers to being that parent. In hearing and understanding the ways in which others cope with child-rearing problems, parents develop a greater consciousness of their own strengths but also a sense that imperfections are acceptable.

Modern parents are subjected to enormous pressure to be perfect. "Mothers in particular," says Angela Barron McBride, writing in *Growth and Development of Mothers,* "have come to represent man's projection of the ideal. The very word 'mother' has all sorts of meanings that bear little resemblance to a real person; it has become a *metaphor.* 'Mother' represents a set of behaviors and hopes that no flesh and blood woman could ever meet."[9]

Choosing depression over anger is not unusual for people caught in a web of conflicting stereotypes and expectations; passivity frequently results as emotional energy is diverted into trying to reconcile the demands of external images and expectations with the realities of personal, daily experience. Mutual support brings parents out of this lonely struggle. By focusing on their own needs, mutual support encourages parents to express what they really feel instead of what they think they are supposed to feel. Parents learn an interesting lesson, in the midst of so many encounters that involve seeking help for the child; they learn that they can be listened to for their own sake, and not only because it might help the child.

The late Jolly K's testimony before then senator Mondale, when the Child Abuse Prevention and Treatment Act was first introduced, presents an example of the effect of mutual support on parents. She described a mother jailed for child abuse and neglect who benefited from the parent group established in jail:

> While working with this mother, we saw her as a very, very passive person who did very little to assert what she wanted, what her feelings were, or her personality. The more and more

we worked with Betty, the more of a person she became. She started viewing herself as first of all a human being, worthy of saying, "I feel this way," or "I don't agree with that." She learned how to be able to stand up and say, "I am a human being. I have feelings. I have the right to say I have feelings."[10]

The Mothers' Center provides another example. After childbirth, a woman's concern and interest focus on the helpless infant. Hundreds of articles each year advise her of the importance for the child's future development of doing the right things in those early weeks and months. A mother's needs and feelings are often ignored. According to a Mothers' Center publication,

> pregnancy and the demands of child care bring about a chaos and disorganization of the individual and the family. Programs at the Center help a woman/mother reestablish her adulthood, integrate the new status of being a mother and cope with the process of becoming a functioning adult. The feelings of isolation and depression diminish because of the experience in groups at the Mothers' Center.[11]

All parent mutual-help groups respect the parent's need to feel competent at what she or he is doing. All design their discussions, meetings, and practical supports to promote self-esteem. In sharing their knowledge, parents discover that they too can acquire the power that professionals have — the power of highly technical knowledge. Writing in the magazine *Children Today,* for example, founders of the Mothers' Center describe how the Center pools its meager resources in order to send at least one mother to professional meetings. The authors explain: "We have been generally welcome at professional meetings and although we have frequently been told that the presentations would be too complex for laymen to understand, that has not been our experience."[12] Hope Zimmerman, one of the Mothers' Center founders, described the experience of attending a conference where the findings of two prominent researchers on parent-child attachment were presented; these scientists had demonstrated what "we had discovered in the course of talking to one another" — that parents' experience of attachment in the perinatal period is powerful, has long-lasting impact, and is very sensitive to institutional interference.

Parents also discover similar feelings of power and self-confidence when they find they are mastering the "inner secrets" of the educational process, despite the obscure technical jargon used to communicate that information to the public. Organizations like the Philadelphia Parents' Union and the United Parents' Association of New York City spend many hours patiently decoding *stanines* (a score in educational testing that reports a child's position relative to other children of his or her age), *percentiles, rank ordering* — terms that so often cloak test results behind screens of language foreign to the typical parent. The pleasure of attending conferences when workshops on testing no longer sound like so much jabberwocky, or of accompanying a frightened parent to a session with the local principal and watching her demonstrate her newly mastered knowledge of testing and its implications, is indeed "consciousness-releasing."

Discovering that we can develop the same explanations for significant events and problems and that we can communicate in the same language as scientists and professionals makes parents conscious of our own power. Beyond that, we can learn to read the professional literature and acquire enough familiarity with concepts and language to be able to understand and synthesize those findings for many other parents. The Parents' Union, for example, in the early 1980s was publishing a fact sheet for parents entitled "The Key to What You Need to Know In Parent-Teacher Conferences," in which they carefully charted and explained the complicated system of "levels" that were used to explain a child's progress through the Philadelphia public schools. In that city in 1981, expected achievement levels did not have the same numerical value as the child's grade; children in grade 2 were not expected to finish level 2 in math and reading. Rather, children in grade 2 were supposed to have completed levels 4 and 5 in math, levels 5 and 6 in reading ("pupil competencies"), and levels 5 to 8 in "new reading." Children in grade 5 were supposed to have finished levels 11 to 13, 10, and 10 to 13, respectively. Pity the parent of three or four children, trying to keep the dizzy array of numbers straight! While it's exceptionally unfortunate that a child's progress in the basics has to be expressed in such a complicated format, the fact that the Parents' Union is willing to track down and chart this information into a usable, intelligible framework makes a vast difference, not only to the parents benefiting from the fact sheet but to the parents doing the analysis. Never again will they feel as vulnerable as they undoubtedly did when the "facts" about their children's achievement levels were first given to them.

A similar consciousness is encouraged by the parents in the National Federation of Parents for Drug-Free Youth. "Have confidence in your ability to make a difference," urges one of their early brochures, which begins by providing parents with a scientist's assessment that "there are over 7000 scientific publications on marijuana. Not one gives marijuana a clean bill of health." Parents are referred to materials that help them understand and use terms such as *cannabinoids* (a derivative of the scientific term *cannabis,* a genus of plants which includes hashish and marijuana).

Some parents even move beyond fact sheets and pamphlets to establish their own journals and create their own literature. All these experiences, which liberate consciousness, inevitably transform and strengthen their commitment to mutual support.

In listening and talking to one another, parents also hear how others have challenged the power of institutions. The realization that it is possible to assert oneself successfully emerges. At the same time, parents become aware that the power of professionals is not magical. They hear accounts of encounters with experts that have diminished parents, made them feel less competent. Feelings of anger and hostility naturally result. In expressing their anger within the supportive group, parents rid themselves of negative self-images and start to build a new understanding of themselves as confident, knowledgeable activists.

Practical Assistance

In mutual support, practical action flows from the talk and sharing. All groups collect and provide information that parents might otherwise futilely search for. Some of this information is needed for day-to-day coping with children who have special needs. For example, the information generated by research breakthroughs about mental retardation or learning disabilities is often not very accessible. Parent groups gather and report the most recent knowledge.

Frequently, information helps parents understand and beat the system. For instance, parents provide each other with both formal and informal evaluations of different programs and their staff. The Parents' Union distributed throughout Philadelphia a wallet-sized "Parents' Rights Card," which lists for parents all the rights assured them under local, state, and federal policies. No longer can parents be told, for instance, that they cannot request that their children be excused from science or health courses on religious or moral grounds. They only need to check their card to see that they are entitled to the request and that it is the Pennsylvania state government that established this right.

Other, less formal kinds of help from parent groups might range from finding the best treatment center for specific types of cancer to locating a pediatrician willing to buck the hospital that doesn't allow parents to stay overnight, to identifying who in the vast educational bureaucracy has the responsibility for classroom placement and/or transportation of handicapped children. Beyond these referrals is the advice that only parents who have experienced the system can give: a thorough description of the kinds of questions that parents seeking to adopt will be asked during an evaluation by an adoption agency; likely attitudes of agency workers; a personal account of the demands that are likely to be placed on fathers seeking custody of their children. "We do get calls," says Grace Monaco, "from parents who say, 'My child has just been diagnosed; what do you suggest?' And I'll have to find out what's the profile of treatment in the community. Have you talked to your doctor about this? Has he consulted with anyone? Has he called NCI [the National Cancer Institute] for a second opinion, for assistance on where to go or what to do, on what kinds of programs are available?"

The National Federation of Parents for Drug-Free Youth encourages groups to develop practical assistance uniquely suited to the needs of parents of adolescents: peer groups that work out a set of standards about teenage social activities and drug or alcohol use which all the members of the group stand by. These endorsed standards then become a helpful bulwark against the adolescent plea of "Everybody else's parents are letting their kids do it!" In Georgia, parents who in one evening meeting had learned that even their twelve-year-olds were using drugs and drinking came back for a second meeting, at which they decided that all of their youngsters using drugs would be immediately grounded for two weeks, with all parents cooperating in upholding this penalty. The group then drew up a list of rules about both social activities and drug, alcohol, and tobacco use, which the entire group endorsed. Finally, parents cooperated to discover the best scientific information available on drug use and adolescence to identify drug-free activities for teenagers in the community, and to take turns driving their children to and from these activities. It took months before the struggle to wean their adolescents from drug and alcohol use, to help each other enforce the group rules, and to involve these young teens in alternative activities produced results. Parents gave each other needed emotional encouragement during the worrisome time between shocking discovery and hopeful signs of healthy recovery. But the practical assistance of both a parent-developed, communal set of standards and mutual research, carpooling, and chaperoning made the essential difference. Writes one parent: "The parents' united front gradually reversed the peer pressures among the kids."[13] These twelve- to fifteen-year-olds began to develop other shared peer values, to agree that "it was much more fun to dance, to play ball, to white-water canoe, to act in plays, to work at part-time jobs, than it was to 'just sit around getting stoned.'"[14]

Frequent, honest talk helped the parents in this Georgia support group buoy up each other's spirits and determination. In nearly all parent groups, both group and individual parent-to-parent counseling is an important source of support. In the late 1970s, for example, Fathers United for Equal Justice in Massachusetts sponsored a group every other week to provide information and emotional support to fathers in various stages of divorce. The New York City Council on Adoptable Children holds regular discussion groups. One COAC newsletter lists an interracial family group, a black adoptive parent group, and a single adoptive parent group, each discussing concerns shared by parents and children in that particular type of adoption.

Also in New York City, parents of public schoolchildren are trained by United Parents' Associations to lead informal discussion groups aimed at "helping each other over rough spots by sharing experiences." Other groups try to provide supportive information on an ad hoc basis as well as in regular group meetings. Says Daphne Busby from the Sisterhood of Black Single Mothers, "We call a meeting as we see a meeting is required..."

Telephone counseling is another major activity. The New York City COAC estimated in the late 1970s that they received between seventy-five and one hundred calls a week from parents seeking information as well as help. The Long Island Regional Council of the Federation of Parents' Organizations for the New York State Mental Institutions took calls from those worried about the effects of medication (and overmedication) on their children or other relatives. These parents received concrete information about what to watch for regarding tranquilizers or other drugs. Telephone counseling can be very demanding, particularly for those dealing with their own stress or who are new to counseling. Lee Lapicki describes some of her feelings when she started: "The first couple of calls were panicky. One of the phone calls I had gotten was from a woman who had her two children removed for beating them with a chain. And that was my first — I'd had no training for crisis calls; what I did was just listen... but it was still awkward and awfully difficult for me not to judge."

Accessibility is a major concern of parents offering supportive counseling, since the inaccessibility of the traditional services is one of the reasons parents turn to self-help. One way of being available, used by Fathers United for Equal Justice, is an answering machine, which records messages twenty-four hours a day. Each evening the fathers take turns returning the day's calls. Other groups urge people to call on several other parents, not just one. Explains Lee Lapicki: "So we say [when you feel that you are losing control]...you have ten or twelve phone numbers of people in our group whom you can call rather than dump on the kid." Spreading telephone support over the members of a group is possible, particularly in smaller groups where parents have gotten to know each other. But even when the self-help organization has a central office and telephone number, the kind of counseling it offers is distinct from the professional type. Says Daphne Busby about their telephone counseling:

> Not only crisis, it doesn't have to be a crisis...Sometimes we like to hear about the good things too. But very often it can be crisis averting. Very often you are home by yourself and you have a problem that is eating on your mind and you may not have the kind of relationship with your family that you would like, or maybe they live far away...and you are kind of tired and...you may just need somebody to encourage you to hang in there, somebody who can go over to visit and just get your mind off things or somebody who will even take your child overnight...

While this sort of personal involvement tends to be more characteristic of local groups, some national groups engage in mutually supportive telephone counseling over a wide geographic area. The Candlelighters, for example, feel that not every parent wants to talk regularly with other parents, but they may still seek the support only another parent can give. That kind of parent may require a hotline in which "you can call up as an anonymous parent and talk." In her paper "Family Support Groups," Grace Monaco says:

> The Connecticut Candlelighters have a telephone lifeline which has become a daily vehicle for the emotional support of families in their area. It is a credit card number funded by a local foundation. The line has been used heavily for information concerning immunization against flu, nutritional information, questions on insurance and medical bills, measles, chickenpox outbreaks, information on blood programs and zoster immune plasma availability. Most commonly it is used to let out pent-up emotions, and to share good news when a child has successfully completed surgery or chemotherapy.[15]

The National Committee for Citizens in Education maintains a national toll-free number (800-NETWORK) to answer parents' questions about public education. They published a book, entitled *You Can Improve Your Child's School,* based on the questions parents responded to through their toll-free number.[16]

Another concrete support that some parent groups offer is case advocacy, in which parents help each other represent themselves in negotiating the services needed from an institution. Here again, personal experience helps ensure success. Explains Daphne Busby:

> Members who know the rights of welfare mothers, because of their own personal experiences, have gone down to the welfare office with other members. A lot of times people have no preparation for knowing just what to expect, what kinds of things you are going to be asked. That can be a traumatic kind of experience, when you do not know what to expect.

The Parents' Union flatly tells parents upset by the disciplinary suspension of their children and planning to appeal, "Never go alone to a suspension hearing...Contact Parents' Union for a parent advocate."

Finally, some groups sponsor alternative services — schools, adoption services, halfway houses — as a practical support to parents. In organizing alternative services, parents often feel ambivalent. Often the group would prefer to see the established services do a better job. Running their own program for their children, they fear, is another drain on time and energy. But when no other service is available, a parent-organized and -administered alternative is a valued support.

Renewing the Spirit

In the camaraderie of the group and in their commitment to preserving openness and humanness among themselves, parents renew and energize each other. When I visited the Federation for Children with Special Needs, in Boston, I intended to interview several of the people who had formed this unique coalition from organizations representing parents of handicapped children across the state. The Federation offers a parent-run referral and advocacy service, funded in part by federal money. A mother of a retarded child having trouble with a local school district, for example, can pick up the phone and call the Federation. Another parent, personally experienced with the problem and well versed in the law, will answer, listen, and help.

On the day I went to Boston to interview Federation parents, they had just been visited by a team assessing how well the federal funds for the project were being spent. The parents working at the office were shocked and angered by what seemed to them to be the brusqueness and impersonality of the federal evaluation team. Some deplored the apparent indifference to the complex network of mutual support relationships within the staff. "That's what makes this whole thing work," said one. "If they've missed that, how can they possibly understand what we are doing here?"

Feelings ran so high that I scrapped plans for extensive interviewing. Instead, I witnessed a dozen women renew their sense of commitment to each other and face their feelings of fear of the power that the evaluators might wield. Over lunch together, they joked and laughed, planned a weekend retreat, and encouraged each other to be persistent in difficult cases they had taken on.

There are other ways in which mutual-support groups focus on renewal of spirit. One is the emphasis on equality within the group. Frequently groups are composed of parents from different socioeconomic classes and backgrounds. But the members typically structure the organization to preserve a sense of equality. "All programming is open and nonexclusive," says the Mothers' Center brochure. "People are encouraged to think in new ways. Our job descriptions exemplify nonlinear thinking. Titles of coordinator, facilitator, and consultant are nonhierarchical." The mutual-support group offers a striking contrast to stratification in the surrounding society. If everyone has the right to both give and receive, if all the groups' members are treated with respect, the individual's confidence is renewed.

Parents aid each other through sharing good news and laughter as well as sorrow and pain. "We would like to start a Good News Column," the fall 1977 issue of the Candlelighters' newsletter states. "Please send us some news items that are happening in the treatment of children with cancer. Good things in therapy, in living, in caring. Good news of children coming off drugs, of good neighbors and friends, of celebrations, of your own personal triumphs. We want to share them.'' Other newsletters describe hospitalizations of children carried out in supportive ways, or handicapped children who have finished their education and are functioning in the world. In group meetings as well, communication is not always problem-oriented. Members of Parents Anonymous are encouraged to share their pride in overcoming potential crises. Parents in the Candlelighters are encouraged to meet socially and to talk about family events other than the child's cancer. Says Grace Monaco, speaking from the personal experience of her daughter's death:

> We have come out of the experience of my daughter Kathleen succumbing to cancer a much stronger family unit than before, with a perspective on how important it is to live every day as well as you possibly can, get as much happiness out of it...
> Our sense of humor has improved considerably because we like to find things to be happy about...I think that is the big lesson to be taken out of parents' groups. It's a very disruptive lesson to some of the parents themselves who first come into a group...they walk into a room and here are silly giggly people who are having a marvelous time with each other and socializing and talking and that is what they should be striving toward.

Laughter renewed the spirit among the Georgia parent group confronting drug problems. Writes Marsh Manatt:

> Many of the parents were depressed and confused by the ease with which their children admitted lying, breaking the law, stealing money from home, and turning on other children...As the parents gazed with foreboding at the long road ahead, their main consolation was the continuing contact with the other parents, the sharing of information, insight, grief, and, surprisingly, laughter.[17]

Many of the parent groups sponsor social events such as picnics, potluck suppers, and holiday parties where the whole family can come together. The Sisterhood of Black Single Mothers pools its resources so that members can have a ''mother's day out'' to see a play or share a meal. Adoptive parents plan family celebrations so that both parents and children can meet others like themselves, feel less "different," and celebrate the fact that the hard times which characterized the lives of many of the older children before adoption can be consigned to the past.

Finally, parents renew each other with their conviction that the organization to which they have committed their efforts will survive, overcome obstacles, and eventually improve the lives of other parents and children. Mutual-support groups, of course, do not always continue. But even when a group is transient, just coming together in mutual support for a brief period can profoundly alter the lives of parents and the ways they view themselves. In the early part of the 1970s, a group of single mothers established MOMMA, a national mutual support organization. MOMMA no longer exists as a national network. But I found Lynn Hartwell, one of its founders, in California, working on a project related to the status of women. When I interviewed her, she said, "One of the most interesting parts about MOMMA is the growth and development of the women who were involved in it from the beginning five years ago. Half of them were either on welfare or in a very bad place. But the women who came to MOMMA for two or three years of friendships and relationships saw things change greatly. We are all working now. Our lives are much more upbeat. We influenced each other to believe that we *were* capable."

Of the parents I interviewed, some interrupted careers after involving themselves in mutual support and began entirely new occupations. Some went to law school. Some found the confidence to leave safe, secure positions and work part-time at jobs they really enjoyed, so as to have more time and energy for family or for building the self-help organization. One mother active in changing hospitals won a seat on the local school board, and brings to that arena her conviction about parents and child-serving institutions.

As the individual lives and the images parents have of themselves change, ripple effects are felt in cultural images of parents. The successful survival of the group or of individual members is in itself an affirmation of the competence and the power of parents. Daphne Busby explains:

> Some of the talent and creativity and energies and intelligence that comes out of welfare mothers in our organization is incredible. Okay, it would be incredible to somebody who believes that everybody on welfare is lazy. We know that is not true because we see it is not true. We are the proof that it is not true.

Other parents bring a new confidence to their relationships with professionals. Parents Anonymous now puts out literature that professionals can use in learning how to identify abusive parents — but their literature has a section in it called "Look for Strengths," which lists the many different strengths that abusive parents show and that they can draw upon to move themselves away from their abusive impulses. The National Society for Autistic Children also produces literature for professionals describing parents of autistic children in ways entirely different from the kinds of images that were so common a decade ago.

Perhaps the most telling sign of the new self-confidence that parents in groups feel is a statement from a mother involved with Children in Hospitals. Brandishing an agenda for a soon-to-be-held professional conference on early intervention with handicapped children, she said: "Here they are talking about what it means to be parents and they haven't got a parent on the panel. So I think here is a good example of professionals who have not even stopped to look at where they could invite a parent in to give their insights. It's just shocking to me."

A decade ago, parents wouldn't have talked like that about a conference sponsored by doctors and psychologists. And if self-help and mutual support among parents continue to expand as they are currently, ten years from now parents will be regularly sought out for leadership roles in professional training seminars and conferences.

Shaking Up Institutions

5

The temperature stood at 9°F on a bitterly cold morning in January 1972 when a group of parents assembled on Victory Boulevard in Staten Island. Just beyond the wide boulevard loomed the quiet buildings of Willowbrook. When the group had gathered, the parents sat down, blocking traffic in the streets. Then they entered the institution's grounds, linked arms, and began the long walk up the drive to the main building of Willowbrook state hospital, home for thousands of retarded children. The doors were locked. The parents broke into the institution, fought with the institutional police, and confronted the director of the hospital with their knowledge of the terrible abuses committed against retarded children and other patients at Willowbrook. "Then," says Max Schneier, who led the march, "we went into Building Six, which we knew was the worst one. Some of us were so appalled that we had to run out of the building and vomit in the yard."

That night millions of Americans saw what these parents had seen and heard, as TV sets transmitted the horrors of Willowbrook into kitchens, living rooms, and bedrooms. The public responded; the governor was besieged by angry calls. He immediately earmarked about $5 million for Willowbrook.

But Max Schneier and the other parents who marched on Willowbrook were not convinced that this would make much difference. For years, says Schneier, visiting parents had not even been allowed to enter the locked wards where their children were living. The doors to those wards were always locked. Why should any real change occur? The public furor would fade, and Willowbrook would quietly return to its former status as a peaceful-looking, little-known institution whose walls contained thousands of retarded children, heavily dosed with powerful tranquilizers, poorly fed, unbathed, often unclothed, neglected in their own excrement.

To prevent this, the newly formed Federation of Parents' Organizations for the New York State Mental Institutions kept up a persistent demand for change. Seeking long-term improvements in Willowbrook and other state hospitals, they broadened their activities beyond dramatic confrontation. Over time, they and others exposed not just the abuses on the wards but the nature of the system that had allowed Willowbrook's horrors to occur. Eventually, they helped open up to the public eye one of our most closed systems: publicly funded mental institutions.

PERSONAL PAIN AND INSTITUTIONAL REFORM

The vigor and passion that parents bring to advocacy for large-scale change spring from acute, painful experiences. For some parents it's the death or maiming of their children. For others it's the terror of small children in hospitals where parents are prohibited from staying close to their youngsters. For still others it's watching their children endure humiliations because they are handicapped or ethnically "different." Activist parents may be responding to the anxiety of sending children to schools that are unsafe, schools where some children are assaulted and abused by others. In less extreme situations, parents whose children are failing to master the educational basics experience a protracted sense of pain and anger.

Most of us in this country want to believe that the services we have put in place for children work well. We want to think that our institutions are fair, humane, and helpful. Facts sometimes show otherwise, however. As we saw earlier, public education seems to be failing quite a few American children. Some 13 percent of all seventeen-year-olds are functionally illiterate: they cannot read, write, or do simple sums, let alone fill out job applications.[1] For every one hundred students who graduate from high school, twenty-nine drop out. For every two Black or Hispanic high-school graduates, one drops out.[2] *Small Futures,* a study for the Carnegie Council on Children, estimated that "between 10 and 15 percent of American children are getting either no schooling or schooling that prepares them for nothing."[3]

Consider Philadelphia, home of the Parents' Union. With more than 230,000 students in 1979-1980, it was the fourth largest school district in the United States.[4] It has more than 20,000 employees in the public schools; in fact, the system is the city's second largest employer.[5] That means there is one employee of the public schools for about every twelve or thirteen children. The Parents' Union estimated in the early 1980s that its own annual budget of $275,000 was "equivalent to what the school district spends in less than four hours." Yet almost half of the students who entered high school then dropped out before graduation. The causes of such school failure are, of course, ambiguous; there is not enough consensus yet among either American parents or American educators that certain school practices help and others harm.

But lack of consensus is not the case in child-serving institutions such as foster-care agencies. Within our system of social services, children without parents (or separated from their parents) are particularly vulnerable to "getting lost." There are about half a million children in foster care, costing $2 billion annually.[6] The cases of these children should be reviewed at least once a year and preferably every six months, to determine whether they should be returned home or adopted into a permanent home. Such decisions affect the security of the childhoods and future functioning of foster care children. In some instances, when the decision is made to return them to homes where they were previously injured or abused, the children's safety is at stake. A mid-1970s analysis of state-required reviews in a California county, however, showed that approximately two-thirds of the hearings took two minutes or less. About 6 percent took ten minutes or more, and the longest review took twenty minutes.[7]

Testifying before the Senate Finance Committee in 1976, then New York City Comptroller Harrison Golden described this situation, which still held in the early 1980s:

> Despite massive federal outlays for foster care services, no one presently knows exactly how many children are in foster care, let alone how long they have been there or whether they should

be there at all. What we do know from a number of local studies, as well as from a recent GAO audit, is that foster care around the country is generally a poorly managed enterprise.[8]

The conclusion is inescapable: In some of our most essential public services to children — schools and foster-care and mental institutions — children are at risk of being harmed.

Nor is risk to children's well-being confined primarily to public institutions. Hospitals serving children in the U.S. are largely private institutions. While in the past decade there have been great improvements in permitting parental presence, particularly "rooming in," during a child's hospital stay, a 1982 survey found that one-fourth of all hospitals still restrict visiting hours for parents.[9] The choices are narrowed: either sleep here or visit only when it fits hospital routines. Thus, children of parents who must spend the night at home with their other children or who hold down jobs with irregular schedules are subjected to the terrors that result from restrictions on parental visiting hours.

Finally, policies and practices in judicial systems are often harmful to children. Judicial tolerance for drunk driving is a primary concern. Less than 1 percent of all drunken drivers are arrested, and if someone *is* arrested, the chance that he or she will receive a serious penalty is "mathematically insignificant."[10] Cindy Lightner of California organized Mothers Against Drunk Drivers when she discovered the history of the man who killed her child: After three arrests for drunken driving and a scattering of mild fines and probations, this man was arrested a fourth time for intoxicated driving and hit and run, and then released on bail. Two days later, he hit and killed thirteen-year-old Cari Lightner.

Facts, studies, and personal experiences like these reflect many individual experiences of suffering by children and parents. These painful experiences propel parents into seeking others like themselves who will listen and talk about their own frustrations, their own rage. In a group, individual experiences coalesce. The result — fueled by hundreds, sometimes thousands of individual parents' encounters — can fundamentally alter an institution's policies.

Eventually parents move beyond an awareness of personal harm to a consciousness of systemwide harm or widespread violation of the rights of children and their parents. The awareness that one's own retarded child may be lying in his or her own excrement in one institution evolves into the knowledge that most retarded children within a given system of institutional care are vulnerable to such abuses, and why. At times, parents who aren't even aware that they or their children have rights guaranteed by law and policy, develop a broader consciousness when they discover that a hospital or school system has officially endorsed parents' rights statements. Consequently, this discovery leads to a deeper analysis.

In that analysis, parents typically move beyond individual blame-fixing. As they gain experience in reform, they realize that institutional harm of children and parents is usually not intentional but is inextricably linked to basic failures in the institution itself. Their analysis thus leads them to the conviction that the institution must be fundamentally changed if the rights of children and parents are going to be respected. To do that, parents must do more than physically gain entry; they must penetrate the complex policies and procedures of an institution's operation. And they must exercise some influence over the resources on which the institution depends.

As parents develop the analytical and political skills of advocates committed to fundamental change, they gain a broader and more subtle understanding of the word *institution*. For most of us, *institution* conjures up images of large, dull edifices. But in the vocabulary of advocates, the little neighborhood school and the system of public schools to which it belongs are institutions. So is the community hospital, and the local adoption agency — and the systems of laws, regulations, and policies, both formal and informal, that prescribe how they are to be run. Says Al Kahn, a Columbia University professor and author of several books on helping services in America and abroad, "The institutions that are advocacy's targets are not always the entire system: e.g., schools, clinics, or courts. Sometimes the institutions are the processes: e.g., planning, coordination, administration, budgeting, and the like, or casework, group work, or psychotherapy.

Sometimes they are the professional cadres: e.g., doctors, social workers, police, judges, and agency staff."[11]

Systems, processes, professions — acquiring mastery of all this has been the province of experts, not parents. But in the last two decades, the power of experts, once so glamorized and welcome, has come under challenge. Writes Don Davies in a book edited by him, *Schools Where Parents Make a Difference:*

> Many Americans are fed up with the "best and brightest" making the decisions for them about wars, taxes, zoning, hospitals and schools...They are suspicious of politicians and professionals and experts. Some are retreating into apathy; but others are organizing with like-minded people to build healthier communities and institutions and...to make government and institutions more responsive, more accountable.[12]

Willowbrook symbolizes the features of child-serving institutions that parent activists describe as most harmful or potentially harmful. First, institutions with hidden, tolerated incompetence unfairly win parents' trust by claiming to be competent. Second, the policies of the institution act to close out parents who seek to know what actually happens; thus incompetence is protected and preserved. In the case of Willowbrook, the doors were literally locked. But parents feel that other institutions, such as public schools, are also closed. Says one parent activist: "You can walk in the door, but you're not very welcome."

By forcing the closed institution to open, even temporarily, and by exposing its internal workings to the public eye, the parents at Willowbrook demonstrated that even a small number of parents can challenge the power of experts. But more significant for parent activism, the parents' march and its aftermath demonstrated that what parents can uncover and what they can do about these problems are worth the risks and the extraordinary persistence needed to shake up institutions fundamentally.

WHAT GETS PARENTS STARTED

According to parent activists' accounts, many parents do not choose involvement in institutional reform as much as it seems to choose them. A few moments of anger and insight into a particularly damaging situation propel some into a commitment which they maintain for many years. For others, it is a much slower process.

Why do some parents and not others commit themselves to challenging and changing powerful institutions? First, parents who choose institutional reform are assertive — perhaps some more visibly than others, but even the quiet activists have a steady forcefulness. Second, parents who choose institutional reform discover that establishing what they see as basic rights necessitates long, repeated confrontations. In the course of interviews, I heard many examples of such confrontations. One parent, a member of a group concerned with childhood hospitalization, described her attempts to find a hospital where she could stay overnight with her four-year-old. Her pediatrician informed her that she could not, and furthermore should not, stay with her son. "It's not going to hurt," the doctor said. "He will only be scared." This mother persisted, and consulted with a specialist. "He was very brusque," she reports, "and said that there was no reason for me to be there, and there weren't any hospitals he had ever heard of that allowed that." When she named some hospitals that permitted parents to stay with their children, the specialist told her he was not on the staff of those hospitals, so she would have to accept that she could not stay with her child. The mother then walked out, saying she would find another doctor. But, she says:

> I would not have had the nerve to do that, if I had not had a sister who was a pediatric nursing instructor and...I knew there were a lot of medical reasons, psychological stuff that was already written up that would back me up. So I had reassurance and back-up that a lot of mothers would not have had. By the time I walked out on my pediatrician I was shaking and crying because I had just said, "Doctor, you are wrong." And that is very difficult for somebody nonmedical to say. I was not questioning professional judgment about what needed to be done, but only what my child needed psychologically.

Confrontations like these are exceptionally painful, reflecting particular fears that many parents experience if they anger a physician.

Other parents, even when they feel less vulnerable, may find confrontations just as painful. A mother of an autistic child describes her battle with the local public school. A school official called her, explaining that they were about to offer a special program that they felt would benefit her son, who was in a private school. She explains: "I said I don't want to change him and they said, well, you can't turn it down until you look at it. So I went and looked and I liked it and I took Eddie and my husband and the three of us said, yes, this really looks nice. So I called up and said fine, you have my approval, you can enroll him." This process complete, the mother spent the summer looking forward to public school for her son. Her child was particularly eager to go to what he described as "a real school." But: "They called up in August, a week before school was going to start — no, two weeks, because we were on our way to the beach for a week — to say we couldn't get the funding, no program. I had to tell Eddie. He cried and cried: 'I want to go to a real school. They said, you said...'" So, she says, "I got back on the phone and I just raised hell. I said you *will* provide an appropriate public program for this child. Now you stirred him up and he is ready." She gave the school three options that would meet with her approval and said she would call in a week, after coming back from the long-planned family vacation.

With the opening of the school year just a few days away and with no arrangements, it was not enough to assume that the school would find a good educational setting for her son. This parent actively investigated possibilities. "A school near us had a learning disability program with vacancies on every level," she explained, "and I got the principal of the school to go to bat and help me too." She arranged for the required evaluation of her son. School officials then hesitated to place her child because he wouldn't get psychotherapy, which used to be thought of as a crucial aspect of treatment for autism. The mother objected: "I said he doesn't want it. He said he doesn't want it. He wanted to be normal. He didn't want any of those trimmings that nobody else in the family had... Well, they fussed and fussed and he had to start back in his private school but with the understanding that they would phase him in." Again the parent objected, pointing out,

"You don't phase in kids with autism. They are confused enough by their environment. You don't send them to this school for part of the day and that school for part of the day."

As every parent activist does, this mother began to feel she would be seen as unreasonable. She began to get intimations from school officials that "being reasonable" was necessary when placing autistic children. "I said I am not being unreasonable. A normal child has problems dealing with this kind of nonsense." She explained again that autistic children find it extremely difficult to master environmental changes. The school suggested that at least for the first week, the child would ride to the public school on the school bus, be picked up at 10 o'clock by his mother, be driven to the private school, and then be taken home by his mother at the end of the day. Finally this parent quieted her uneasiness about bringing her autistic child into a radically new environment under such confusing circumstances: "I thought, well, you've won the war, you've lost a battle, what's the difference. You have to compromise at some point or they write you off as totally unreasonable."

This example illustrates the kinds of confrontation with the system that parent activists engage in, as well as the anxiety and fatigue that repeated confrontations engender. Observers agree that when parents can take other, less time-consuming, less threatening routes to obtain the right kinds of services for their children, they will try them first. But for many parents the choices are few and mostly unpalatable: either change their demands, abandon their fight (which feels like an abandonment of the child), or rely on continued, bitter, risky arguments to secure children's rights.

The only other choice is to bring about change in the institution on which they must depend. As Grace Monaco says:

> It comes right down to the fact that unless you have an impact on the professional that is treating your child, things are really not going to be that much better. You can provide emotional support to help you get through things, but you can't make things better for all parents unless the system itself changes.

The parents' march on Willowbrook was a moment of high drama. It marked a turning point in the history of residential services to the retarded and the mentally ill. The novice activist, captured by such drama, would find it easy to believe that courageous confrontations such as these are the stuff of institutional reform. The reality, as the experienced well know, is quite different.

Systematic change is a laborious process. "There are times we get the feeling we ought to just dissolve and forget this whole thing," says one parent activist. "But to be an organization that's constant, always there, always firm or has a good foundation, eventually the change comes through."

Exposure of the shocking abuses at Willowbrook helped mobilize public support, but it still took a court case, long hours of tedious participation by all kinds of advocates on commissions, and prolonged political activity to maintain that public pressure for improvements in state mental hospitals. Even after all this, the unusual step of a successful disaccreditation of a very large state hospital by the Joint Commission on Accreditation of Hospitals was necessary to bring about significant change. Ten years later, mental institutions are more open but the struggle isn't over.

Public-school reform is another area demanding extraordinary persistence. Sometimes this occurs because cultural cycles repeat themselves. In the first three decades of this century, the public schools in New York City struggled to educate millions of children newly arrived from Europe. In the most recent three decades, those same schools have struggled once again with the challenges of educating children migrating into New York — this time principally from the rural South and the islands of the Caribbean.

Furthermore, large systems are inert; after periods of intense advocacy for change, when the watchfulness of the advocates inevitably relaxes, they have a tendency to slide back toward the more comfortable ways of the past. Says the United Parents Associations' author of "Sixty Years of Parent Involvement":

> Issues have a way of coming full circle. Every decade has seen campaigns for adequate budgets, equitable financing, quality educational programs that meet children's needs. Every decade

has tried to secure and protect the rights of children and parents — to confidentiality, to consultation, to creating a sound home-school-community relationship.[13]

In situations where institutions seem intractable, parent-to-parent mutual support is likely to prove absolutely essential to sustaining parental tenacity.

WHAT WORKS

The basic choices open to parents seeking fundamental change in harmful or unhelpful institutions are three: change the institution's actors (or their behavior); change the institution's rules; change (or in some way influence) the flow of dollars that fund the institution. As I listened to parent advocates, it became clear that the best of those choices is the last. When an organized group of citizens can influence the way in which both private and public institutions are funded, then the actors, their behavior, and their rules can be changed.

Sifting through parent analyses of the strategies involved in institutional reform, I could discern some common strategies that have been used to gain influence over an institution's resources. Fact-gathering and public exposure of hitherto accepted practices are the first steps. Then, with private institutions financed by individual consumer dollars, effective advocates inform consumers about the choices they can make with those dollars, and encourage choices supportive of children and parents. With publicly funded institutions, effective advocates learn to use different branches or different levels of government to assure that public dollars are spent only when institutional conditions helpful to children and parents are met. Conversely, parent advocates working for change in public institutions learn how to obtain withdrawal of public funding when the conditions in these institutions are demonstrably harmful.

These strategies are described more fully in the remaining pages of this chapter. When parents are successful in bringing about fundamental change, it is primarily because they use these approaches with steady, tenacious persistence.

Getting the Facts

The most immediate task of parent groups who have committed themselves to institutional reform is to get the facts: which issues are linked to delivery of a particular service, which current policies and procedures does the institution rely on, and who or what controls those policies.

Getting the facts is one thing; finding out how a public school, a mental institution, or a court system really works is a different matter. Most parent activists form friendships with someone on the inside of the system who provides them with basic facts, copies of organizational charts, operating policies, and staff memos. Obtaining such materials is typically time-consuming, even in a public agency where they are supposed to be public information. In a private institution, insiders may be the only source of information. Says a parent activist concerned with hospitals, "I think it's awfully nice if you have an inside pipeline. If you can get on the pediatric ward and find a nurse who is sympathetic to your needs...she feeds you the information of what's coming down from the top."

The more closed the system is, the more important it is to have inside friends and the harder it is to find them. Reprisals against insiders who provide information to advocates may be severe, especially when that information forms the basis for exposure. The two physicians and the social worker who tipped off Federation parents about the terrible abuses in Willowbrook were summarily fired. Federation parents fought to have them reinstated.

Sometimes an inside friend includes someone in the media who has reported on a particular system and knows a lot about it. A group of adoptive parents in Pennsylvania, struggling to expose a local judge's racist attitudes toward transracial adoptions, found an invaluable ally in a local reporter. She showed the parents how to file a complaint with the state's court administrator and judicial board, and at times not only identified high-ranking officials in the state government but quietly made arrangements for parents to meet with them.

When inside friends cannot provide necessary data, parent activists learn how to ask the system itself. Recommending that parents approach the school system for information related to school policies, budgets, reading scores, and goals, Happy Fernandez gives some concrete suggestions:

> Make requests in writing whenever possible and keep a carbon copy of all requests — even those that are handwritten... Don't be put off by educational jargon. If you don't understand such phrases as "standardized tests," "line-item allocations," "learning disabilities," do not let embarrassment keep you from asking what they mean. Sometimes educational jargon is used to cloud the issue or to create "insiders" and "outsiders"... Be persistent. Keep asking. In one school district it took parents eighteen months to get the reading scores for each school published in readable form.[14]

Parents find it easier to acquire the facts from the system if they have already learned who makes decisions in that institution, and who or what influences and controls them. Many of the parents I listened to had acquired their understanding of decision making through case advocacy.

Case advocacy involves representing your own interests or the interests of others in trying to get the right decisions made — or the wrong ones reversed — for an individual child. By engaging in case advocacy, parent activists identify an institution's decision makers the hard way — by going from one to another and learning who has the authority to make which decisions. Some parents urge starting right at the top, with the person who can exercise the most control, and working your way down. Others feel strongly that parents should begin with the decision maker closest to the child. Says Mary Akerley:

> You always start at the lowest level and go up. Talk to your kid's teacher. Find out if he or she is the problem or if he or she is a victim of a decision made at a higher level. When you've identified that, you will move. You never move up without telling the person you have been dealing with that you are going to move up. If you make enemies on your way up, they are going to kick you on your way down... Then you go to the principal and if it's not really his fault you go the area superintendent and on up as high as you have to go. But you don't write to your congressman your first day out.

Don Davies, director of the Institute for Responsive Education, agrees and adds, "Going through those steps will give you a good grasp of what the nature of the problem is or what people say it is and how they respond to it. Then you go to the school committee." Acknowledging parents' discouragement in making their way through so many steps, Davies says, "That doesn't mean it has to take months and months — that can all be done within a few days."

Davies is used to advising parents about this sort of thing; his organization publishes material describing how parent groups go about analyzing school systems. Other groups publish similar guides for parents. The National Committee for Citizens in Education, for example, puts out "Who Controls the Schools?" and the North American Council on Adoptable Children distributes the parent-authored "Citizen Action Manual," which explains typical agency decision-making processes regarding adoptable children.

No analysis of an institution is complete without a careful look at who benefits from the present operation. Father advocates in Fathers United for Equal Justice advise that the current system for divorce and custody adjudication produces millions of dollars in legal fees, and that any attempt at divorce reform must take that into consideration. The New York City Council on Adoptable Children has uncovered and publicized the enormous financial incentives for keeping children in foster care instead of allowing them to be adopted. In New York City, explained Sherry Bunin, an adoptive parent active with COAC, much of the foster-care revenue comes from the federal government. The agency that moves the child out of the system loses the foster-care maintenance funds. In addition, the state and the city each pay half of the required fee for placing the child in an adoptive home.

In the education system, parent groups have encountered another group organizing to achieve more power over decision making: the school system's employees. Some of the parents I listened to believed that union leaders who represent teachers in the collective-bargaining process often oppose any further opening up of the school system to parents. Closure, which brings relative tranquillity, tends to benefit teacher unions, especially in collective bargaining. As one parent put it, teacher unions think that parents should "make cookies but not policy."

Public Exposure

Helen Moore, president of Black Parents for Quality Education, describes the importance of alerting other parents:

> Many of the parents really did not recognize that the schools were inferior because their children were getting As and Bs on their report cards. The standards meant that their As and Bs would perhaps not compare with the standards of the people in the suburbs or in private schools. So we woke the community up in those areas.

In complex institutions (like large urban school systems) or those used by only a small percentage of the population (like pediatric wards in hospitals), practices that may be harmful to children are not visible to the general public. Parents whose experiences have made them acutely aware of such practices must first help the public understand that some institutional practices are harmful, and why.

One way of heightening public awareness is to evaluate systematically an institution's performance, and publicly distribute the results. This tactic has been used with great effectiveness by two groups of parents focusing on childhood hospitalizations. In the early stages of their organization, both Children in Hospitals and Parents Concerned for Hospitalized Children meticulously surveyed all the hospitals in their metropolitan areas, asking each hospital to describe its policies on overnight stays by parents and parents' presence during treatment procedures. The results were tabulated in chart form, printed, and made available to the press and the general public. Hospitals wondering how they measured up and parents seeking information about comparative hospital policies requested the survey results, which were also picked up by the local media and discussed in the papers.

Changes were dramatic. Children in Hospitals reports that the percentage of metropolitan Boston hospitals allowing parents twenty-four-hour visiting rights on pediatric units increased steadily from 16 percent in 1973 to 77 percent in 1980. The percentage of hospitals providing rooming in for parents increased from 42.5 percent in 1973 to 93 percent in 1980.

Other types of systematic public evaluations are being used to change the courts. Judges have a great deal of discretion, particularly in deciding appropriate sentences for people found guilty of crimes. When a typical pattern of judicial decisions seems to be harmful, some parent groups engage in court watching — actually attending trials, documenting the decisions made by judges, and profiling for public distribution the types of decisions. A 1982 newsletter of the National Federation of Parents for Drug-Free Youth describes the court-watching activity of a Virginia parent group concerned that drug-related crimes against children were being treated lightly by some judges:

> A group of about 25 citizens take turns attending court cases and making their presence known. They are supplied with dockets listing significant drug cases to be tried in Circuit Court. They attend all of these trials. They also attend other trials to determine if drug cases are handled differently.[15]

This group felt that decisions were considered more carefully by judges simply because parents were listening and taking notes. Court watching similarly helps parent advocates concerned with drunk driving to assess whether newly enacted laws (for example, legislation specifying different measurements of intoxication) are known and enforced by local courts.

Individual local courtrooms are usually open to the public. But exposure of performance in large public institutions is quite difficult, as Willowbrook exemplified. The more complex the bureaucracy is, the harder it is even to obtain information about the institution's practices. Some parent groups find it more effective to persuade others to conduct an evaluation of the institution, particularly when the others have a legal relationship to the disbursement of funds. The request by New York COAC (and other advocates) for an audit of the city's use of foster-care funds is an example. Comptrollers, in charge of disbursing funds, can investigate how those funds are spent more easily than a parent group can. The New York City comptroller's audit of foster care documented that many children were shifted through a series of institutions and foster homes for most of their childhoods. As an official report, the comptroller's audit received wide publicity.

Parent advocates frequently go to the media with documented accounts of harm being done to children within institutions. But such action risks distortion; the message in the newspaper or the item on the six o'clock news is not always what parent activists want to communicate about themselves. Some activists recommend that parents choose which newspaper or magazine they want to write about their group, analyzing the articles of a particular periodical over a period of time and reading back issues if necessary. In that way they can identify those reporters or columnists who will be sympathetic and knowledgeable and avoid those likely to focus on the sensational aspects of the story.

Finally, in the effort to marshal public support, parent advocacy groups use materials they have developed: newsletters, pamphlets and handouts, films and videotapes. Many groups sponsor a publication service, selling books or other information by mail. Publication services make the newest information far more available to parents; they also make the parent group much more widely known, since libraries, other organizations, and the media pick up and publicize materials bearing the group's name and statement of purpose.

Consumer Pressure

Parent advocates soon learn that control over funding is the most effective lever in achieving institutional reform. A striking dichotomy emerges from parents' descriptions of their strategies. Those who were working to change private institutions — hospitals or agencies financed by consumer dollars or by private insurance payments — needed approaches different from those necessary for changing public institutions such as schools, agencies, and other government services. Many parents voiced the conviction that private institutions were more responsive to change. On the other hand, a systematic and successful redirection of the flow of government funding, as in the case of federal aid for educating handicapped children, has an impact on many private institutions seeking federal funds. Says a parent active in changing hospital policies toward parents:

> In terms of local community hospitals, I think the biggest impact we can have comes through, you know, I'm a consumer, I'm going to use your facilities, now what is it you're doing that you ought not to be doing and vice versa. And you can put the pressure on your doctor, so to speak. I will go someplace else if I can't get what I need here. That, of course, is in a metropolitan area where you have a choice. In a small town you don't have a whole lot of choice.

Choice helps bring about institutional reform. This is especially evident in the work of parents advocating change in hospital practices. Children in Hospitals successfully encourages parents to choose institutions with more provisions for parent involvement. Dramatic improvements in Massachusetts hospitals came about in part because hospitals with prohibitive policies toward parents feared the loss of patients. A similar strategy has been used over the past fifteen years by the organizations advocating prepared childbirth and father participation in labor and delivery.

Today, with the declining birthrate, parents advocating change in hospitals find that consumer choice is increasingly powerful. Fewer children, fewer pediatric hospitalizations, a growing number of hospital beds to fill — these provide economic incentives toward change. The Mothers' Center on Long Island found that local hospitals in competition for maternity patients were willing to listen to a group of mothers who brought them a survey of the obstetrical policies favored by hundreds of mothers in the area.

The emergence of more radical, alternative practices to hospitalization — the home-birth movement, for example — is also a stimulus to change. A parent recounts the impact of the home-birth movement in Dupage County, Illinois:

> Many of the doctors now, where they used to say, oh well, we have to keep the mothers in for three or four days, they are so elated to hear about these schemes where the mother comes in for four hours and gives birth and goes home. Because, my God, we got her in the hospital for four hours, that's four more hours than those home-birth people. Where ten years ago the idea of having a mother in for four hours and letting her go, they would have torn the building down before they would have considered that.

While our current economic climate works to the advantage of parent advocates, it also means that threatened institutions may react angrily. The survey of area hospitals provided to parents by Children in Hospitals represented an implied boycott to institutions already fearful for their economic survival. Because they recognize that their influence derives from the economic implications of their power of referral, members of Children in Hospitals strive to maintain independence and avoid being "captured" by medical institutions hungry for better public relations. This group does not directly recommend a hospital; instead it offers its survey to parents who request it, and volunteers to put them in touch with other parents who have used various hospitals.

The consumer pressure that works well in a community-based hospital often does not apply to the larger, more academic and research-oriented hospital. Boston Children's Hospital Medical Center, for example, may have less awareness of community pressures than a local hospital because Children's draws its patients from all over the world, and many parents come long distances with seriously ill children in the belief that this hospital offers the best hope for the treatment of rare disease. Parents Concerned for Hospitalized Children encountered a problematic situation with several of the large specialist hospitals in Chicago:

> I think your leverage at the specialist hospitals has to do with, you're a big institution, you're supposed to be a leader and we see that you're not doing what you're supposed to...so the prestige is their vulnerable place vis-à-vis other big hospitals. It's economics that eventually is the lever you have at the local hospital.

Teaching hospitals are less pressed for patients but they are dependent on research and training funds. The prospect of looking foolish in a local survey, of being identified as less progressive than a small local hospital, is unattractive to a hospital trying to convince a government official or private foundation that it is forward-thinking.

Both hospital parent groups found it effective to approach the public-relations departments in all of the hospitals and tell them their concerns. In the specialized hospitals they also went to the heads of departments, particularly mental-health departments. Frequently they found very sympathetic professionals who formed strong if quiet alliances and joined them in bringing pressure for change.

The Public Dollar: A Harder Struggle

Mobilizing economic incentives toward reform when institutions are dependent on public money can be arduous. The legislative branch (Congress, state legislatures, county commissions) authorizes the expenditure of public dollars; the executive branch (federal agencies, state agencies, the mayor's office) distributes those funds within the guidelines set down by law. And governments are not moved to action by individuals; it takes organized groups working together over a long period of time.

Parents who have taken up the challenge of reforming public institutions usually develop a strategy finely tuned to the realities of modern American government. They get one part of the government, either a particular level or one of the three branches, to influence the decision making of another part. The American system of checks and balances makes possible this type of citizen activity. In some cases, this means going to the courts to mandate executive-branch action. In others, it means persuading an executive to help lobby the legislative branch, or the legislative branch to pass a bill requiring change in the courts.

Parent activists also use different levels of government to influence each other. The power of the federal government can be brought to bear in changing state- or city-administered institutions, and state governments can be persuaded to influence federal decisions. These particular strategies, of course, are most effective when change is needed in a service supported by funds flowing through different levels of government.

Advocates trying to find economic incentives to change publicly funded institutions must ask several questions. What are the sources of funds to these services? From what level of government do they originate? By what power are they spent? What is the statutory base of the funds? What regulations govern their use? How does the institution qualify for them? This analysis is often more involved than it looks at first. Many people begin with the impression that local services are financed by local government funds. Digging deeper, parents find that what seemed to be county or city funds are in fact federal funds disbursed through the state government. As this kind of tracing proceeds, some parents may become discouraged by the complexity of the system and drop out. Most of the parents I listened to, however, are determined to master the complicated patterns of public funding and to direct funds in ways that better protect their children.

Parent activists use three primary methods for achieving greater control over public funds. First, they persuade legislative or agency officials to attach conditions to funds that their children receive or are supposed to receive. Second, if the funds already have conditions, parents exhort and encourage compliance with those requirements and expose services in violation of them. Finally, parent activists turn to the courts for help in establishing and enforcing their rights and the rights of their children.

Of all the approaches used to effect institutional reform, none is more challenging than the attempt to attach conditions to the flow of public funds, especially when those funds are not likely to be increased. In some states, adoptive parent groups have used this strategy with success. Citing the horrible impact of multiple foster homes on children, adoptive parents have successfully lobbied some state legislatures for laws requiring that funds used to maintain children in foster care be dispensed only when each child's case is periodically reviewed and adoption opportunities are explored.

Attaching conditions is most frequently used within school districts where education funds are raised through local taxes. Local school boards, with semiautonomous power over funding for the community's public schools, often respond to a well-organized parent group, particularly around budget issues. The school board, after all, must be voted into office by parents who pay the local property taxes.

The newsletter "Citizen Action in Education" describes a classically effective parent strategy. A group of mothers in a typical suburban school district became concerned about inadequacies in their children's school. The school board, unresponsive to their carefully researched claims, did react when matters turned to electoral politics. The article concludes: "Parents won the changes they sought, not because of the ways they presented the 'legitimacy of the issue' but because of the threat of votes against the budget. This is what 'local control' in the suburbs is all about."[16]

When local funding is controlled by state legislatures, parent activists have a harder task. If the political officials from the city or county government lobby the state legislature against "encroachment" on "their" funds by parents interested in attaching conditions to the use of those funds, even sympathetic state legislators can withdraw their support. Frequently, experiences like this have prompted parent advocates to seek increased spending on children's services — new funds which carry with them different and more stringent requirements on how they are to be spent. But this usually requires the passage of new laws, a subject for the next chapter.

In situations where existing law does specify that public funds can be given only to institutions meeting certain standards in their policies and practices, however, parent groups can control the flow of funds. Institutions receiving Medicare or Medicaid funds, for instance, must be accredited; that is, they must be shown to care for patients skillfully and humanely, according to professionally established criteria. The Federation of Parents' Organizations for New York State Mental Institutions brought about changes in New York's Pilgrim state hospital because of one political action. They stopped the flow of Medicaid and Medicare funds to the hospital by seeing to it that Pilgrim lost its accreditation from the Joint Commission on Accreditation for Hospitals. "We got disaccreditation," says Max Schneier, who then headed the Parents' Federation, "because we could prove that Pilgrim State didn't meet the standards in the Joint Commission's own manuals." When the New York state government did not demand change at the disaccredited hospital, the Parents' Federation filed a brief seeking to stop the flow of federal Medicare and Medicaid funds into the state on the grounds that Pilgrim violated federal regulations by not being accredited.

The Department of Health, Education and Welfare ruled that the millions of dollars given to the hospital by the federal government should be stopped. As Schneier explained, "All hell broke loose then." The state government was immediately responsive. Schneier's group negotiated for improvements at Pilgrim, then helped the institution win back its accreditation and its federal funding.

Parent activists also use lawsuits. These serve two objectives: They interfere with the flow of funds to institutions that violate the law, and they establish entitlement to rights, or enforce rights that have been abused.

In 1975, the Philadelphia Parents' Union filed a suit charging that the board of education had illegally entered into a contract with the teachers' union because it had permitted items of educational policy, in which parents had a significant stake, to be defined as "working conditions." In 1977, the courts refused to void the contract. But the Pennsylvania State Supreme Court ruled that parents can challenge in state court the collective-bargaining agreements between the teachers' union and the board of education. In this one case, the Parents' Union set a precedent helpful to parent groups all over the country who want more say about school-board-and-teacher contracts.

Successful lawsuits to defend the right of informed consent or the right to due process also have been brought by parents. Some lawsuits, especially those supporting education to the handicapped, were brought to effect fairer distribution of public goods and services.

The Willowbrook suit, *New York State Association for Retarded Children, Inc.* vs. *Carey,* demonstrates the powerful inducements toward change produced by a successful class-action suit. The trial lasted several months.

> During that time, more than fifty witnesses appeared on the stand and nearly 3,000 pages of court testimony were recorded. Noted physicians, researchers, professors and parents appeared as witnesses and reported bruised and beaten children, maggot-infested wounds, assembly line bathing, inadequate medical care, cruel and inappropriate use of restraints and insufficient provision of clothing.[17]

The result was a historic decree that mentally retarded persons have not just a statutory but a constitutional right to protection from harm. In addition, the decree set as a goal for Willowbrook the preparation of each resident for eventual life in the community at large. This proved to be invaluable in bringing about institutional reform for the treatment of the retarded throughout the country.

A single lawsuit, many parents remarked, does not produce change in isolation from community attitudes. Litigation is influenced by a community's awareness, sometimes based on the shock of exposure of abuses. The Willowbrook decision was won in part because, in the words of the judicial memorandum, "During the three-year course of this litigation, the fate of the mentally impaired members of our society has passed from an arcane concern to a major issue, both of constitutional rights and social policy."[18]

Parent advocates sometimes reject lawsuits as too time-consuming, costly, and risky. After absorbing great amounts of work and attention, lawsuits can end in failure. The New York City Council on Adoptable Children, for example, helped to bring a class action suit, *Child* vs. *Beame,* on behalf of five Black children who had been in foster care most of their lives. Lawyers argued that the children were being denied their constitutional rights because no efforts were made to find them permanent adoptive homes. Anticipating an agency's response that the children's age, race, and long stays in foster care made them "unadoptable," the adoptive parent group set about documenting that it was possible to find permanent families for such children. Going through their files of about four hundred families, they recruited prospective parents for these five children. One hundred and fifty families showed strong interest in adopting them. During the three weeks that the judge was making the final decision, COAC tallied some sixty calls from Black families who wanted to adopt children.

The judge's dismissal of the lawsuit in 1977 was a great disappointment. COAC's commitment to the case had been strengthened by the process of assembling the evidence. Even the experienced eyes of these adoption advocates were astonished by the sheer bulk of the records that had been kept on these children for years and years. One child had been seen by over three hundred professionals in the course of his lengthy foster care stay. "No one," said one adoptive parent angered by the virtual truckload of records, "wanted to shake the system."

Even when lawsuits are successful, parent advocates find that it is often not enough to seek protection from existing laws. Instead, they must often obtain new laws which either authorize or mandate change in institutions, and which fund those institutions so that changes helpful to parents and children can be carried out. Paul Friedman, one of the nation's leading legal experts on the rights of the handicapped and a brilliant analyst of the Willowbrook lawsuit, touches on a strong current of consciousness among many of the parent activists I listened to: "The ultimate solution for improving the care and habilitation of the mentally ill will not come from the courts. It must come from the legislatures and from a reordering of basic fiscal priorities."[19]

Working for Laws That Work for Children

6

Wednesday, October 1, 1980: Outside the high black wrought-iron fence surrounding the White House, a small group gathers, carrying placards.

Not unusual for the broad sidewalk in front of the North Portico entrance to the Executive Mansion. Tourists gather here in clumps, of course — a good spot for photographs of loved ones, happy parents and children on holiday, pleased to be preserved for posterity together in snapshots with the tall white columns of the President's House as a background.

Demonstrators for many sorts of causes gather here as well. Sit-ins, pickets, rallies — people with passionate beliefs and deep anger come to this spot. On this Friday, there are few children, but the adults who are carrying placards are clearly parents.

These are parents whose children have been killed or crippled by drunk drivers. One father carries a hand-lettered sign: MY SON WAS KILLED. WHY? He explains: his little boy was eight years old. A moment's violent impact from several tons of steel, and an eight-year-old is dead.

In the group are Dot and Tom Sexton, so freshly bereaved that opening their grief to inquisitive journalists is exceptionally hard. Barely two months have gone by since they buried their fifteen-year-old son, killed by a drunk driver. The Sextons explain why they have come to the President: When brought to justice, this drunk driver had received two years' probation and a $200 fine. Dot Sexton is quoted in the newspaper accounts that week, saying, "You can't sit on your hands when your child has been dealt this injustice."

Two years later, when passage of national legislation addressing drunk driving seemed imminent, I interviewed Dot Sexton over the telephone. She has a gentle, even voice. She has other children, who were getting ready to go back to school. We exchanged good-humored comments on the improvisations mothers engage in when they work at home.

In the two years since she picketed the White House, she has definitely not been sitting on her hands. For in two years, the state of Maryland, with prodding from Mothers Against Drunk Drivers (headed in this state by the Sextons), has made scores of legislative and administrative changes aimed at reducing drunk-driving-related deaths. From the perspective of one who has watched the years of struggle it often takes to get changes in state adoption, foster-care, and special-education laws, I say, "In just two years — amazing."

Dot Sexton explains that enforcement is what matters now and talks of breathalizer tests and blood-level percentages and legislative changes MADD will try for in the upcoming session. She describes her disappointment that some of the new laws they had supported were not enacted.

Then, in response to one of my questions, she talks of her son. The gentle voice breaks. "He was sitting in the back seat, returning from a fishing trip with another family. Tommy lived for about an hour after the crash. You know, he had celebrated his fifteenth birthday on Monday — and then on Saturday he was dead...Last week, seeing all his friends come back from vacation, I found myself watching them, wondering what Tommy would have looked like now."

In a few minutes, her voice steadies again and we return to analyzing mandatory jail sentences, legal definitions of felonies and drunk driving, statistics on accident and fatality rates. Dot Sexton's voice alters only once more during this interview. We are speaking of a new Maryland law that changes the drinking age from eighteen to twenty-one, and of various lobbies that had opposed MADD in the fight to get this law enacted. She explains: "The death rate for teens is very heavy on the weekends. As parents, we had lost children; we felt that no one else should have to lose a child that way." When Dot Sexton says that, her voice gets very clear, firm, and strong.

George Will, the conservative columnist, expressed it succinctly in a 1982 *Washington Post* column about drunk driving: "MADD is evidence," he wrote, "that there is no political force comparable to the fury generated by injuries done to children."[1]

On September 29, 1982, the House of Representatives unanimously approved the Howard-Barnes bill, a $125 million federal program to counteract drunk driving. Within days, the Senate followed suit. It was almost two years to the day since a small group of politically inexperienced, aggrieved parents had picketed the White House, asking that national power be used to protect the nation's children better.

MADD was a very new organization when it took its case directly to Congress and the President. For other groups, years of frustrating work at the state level precede a concentrated effort in Washington. But nearly all parent groups striving to change public institutions seek the help of an ultimate American power: the power of the national government's law, the law of the land.

Thus, in early October 1980, Mothers Against Drunk Driving were joining a tradition. Now, like parents of handicapped children, children with cancer, or children with educational disadvantages, like adoptive parents and parents angry about too-easy access to illegal drugs, they can be found climbing that rather small hill that supports one of our three most powerful national institutions: the United States Congress. Laws are enacted by Congress, not by the President, so it is here that parent advocates focus most of their work. On occasion, however, many of these groups have brought their case to the smaller but nonetheless imposing white building 1.2 miles away from Capitol Hill. Here, sometimes inside the President's working quarters, sometimes outside the high fence that surrounds the President's park, parents call for the involvement of the chief executive in securing help and improved protections for themselves and their children.

In a democracy, this is as it should be. When our government funds public schools, child-welfare agencies, law enforcement and judicial systems, then parents, whose taxes finance those government funds, should expect government to set and enforce fair and effective standards of education, help, or protection in these public institutions.

The preceding chapter discussed how parents are shaking up publicly funded institutions to get fairer, more helpful — in some cases, less harmful — institution-wide policies developed and followed. This chapter describes the successful strategies parent advocates have used to get a sluggish, unresponsive bureaucracy — the federal government — to respond to *them,* and in so doing to bring the resources of the national government to promote institutional change.

I have particularly focused here on the strategies used by the Candlelighters, the North American Council on Adoptable Children, the National Coalition of Title I Parents, Mothers Against Drunk Drivers, and the many groups representing handicapped children. This chapter also discusses the role of parent advocates not just in getting laws passed (enactment) but in getting them to work (implementation). To illustrate this effort at implementation, I have used some features of the Education for All Handicapped Children Act to show how parents of handicapped children have won for themselves a unique role in making sure that the laws they have secured work well.

GETTING LEGISLATION PASSED

A new law can mandate institutional change — for example, declare that public schools must serve children. A new law can help institutions change by offering new funds to help states achieve specific purposes. Thus, adoption subsidies, newly authorized and funded by federal law, help child-welfare agencies recruit parents willing to adopt children in need of extensive, special care. Or a new law can offer a blend of both help and authority: Legislation passed by the Congress in 1982 to deter drunk driving provides $125 million in incentive grants to states, but only to those states that meet standards to improve protection against injury or death from drunk driving. Child-welfare legislation in 1980 also made extra funding available if agencies used it to prevent family break-up or to reunite families.

Typically, parent advocates, weary of the slow daily struggle to shake up institutions, turn first to local or state laws. Most groups discussed in this book have sought and continue to seek state laws that spark institutional change previously resisted by counties, cities, towns. Just as typically, state laws are often inadequate. The poorer states have too few public revenues to fund the newly authorized or mandated change. Less progressive states have entrenched traditions which treat some threats to child health and safety as more tolerable than others, some children as less "equal" than others. Finally, some states are so intensely populated with children who need help or who have health and educational problems needing resolution that even well-financed state coffers or good intentions are not enough to stimulate fundamental change in schools, courts, law enforcement, and child-welfare agencies.

So ordinary parents learn to do what high-priced Washington lobbyists like to think only they can do: put together a legislative proposal, get it introduced in Congress, and get it passed.

Timing, coalition, a groundswell of demand, precedent-setting lawsuits, and some friendly (and powerful) insiders — these are the elements in getting legislation passed, whether in state capitols or in Washington. Lots of legislative lobbies can get laws passed. Whether those laws will help the people for whom help is intended is sometimes another matter. Parent groups bring to the legislative process several assets important to enactment *and* to implementation. One is a geographical base of interested people. Defects in legislative proposals can be spotted and removed as they are circulated through a large national or statewide network. Another is familiarity — with the needs of children, of course, but also with the local system that will implement the law. Parent advocates know the local system and local problems in ways that few political figures ever will.

In the late 1970s, for example, the Candlelighters formulated a legislative proposal that would distribute five regional pediatric cancer centers across the country to serve both as a backup to physicians treating children with cancer and as a nucleus of knowledge about pioneering research and treatment in pediatric cancer. This proposal originated through a grass-roots process. Explains Grace Monaco:

> We developed this approach through a vast correspondence. Parents wrote in saying that in my locality there is only a

30 percent five-year survival rate for acute lymphoblastic leukemia at our local facility, vis-à-vis what I've heard is sixty percent or upward in the major centers. What can we do about this? So we formulated a proposal... We then circulated that to all the groups. The groups gave back comments pro and con, talking about how they wanted to maintain as much local treatment as possible, but they knew that there was a benefit to referrals in the region and that we have to have a balancing and what we really needed was a tumor board. So parents really developed the project. We have had about six months of correspondence going on.

The Education for All Handicapped Act (PL 94-142) was refined through a similar process until the best features of state laws mandating public education for the handicapped had been adopted.

Evidence that a national legislative proposal has been developed through a widespread grass-roots network is quite reassuring to a legislator willing to introduce a bill, for in the refinement, parent advocates make sure that the new law is likely to work well for children — and that an involved constituency of parents around the country will be attached enough to this legislative approach to work tenaciously for its enactment.

Not that a member of the House or Senate can be expected to listen only to the parental perspective. The Candlelighters eventually proposed the creation and funding of a network of "centers of excellence" in pediatric cancer research and treatment — centers that would provide expert medical and scientific backup to local hospitals. (Families often need to have their children treated close to home, but the local hospital may be unfamiliar with all the most recent life-saving breakthroughs in cancer treatment.) The proposal met resistance from some cancer specialists; it will need refinement through those networks, too, before a bill capable of winning broad-based support (and minimal opposition) can be introduced.

The 1982 laws on drunk driving were initially introduced in a more stringent form by Representative Michael Barnes and Senator Claiborne Pell in 1981. This bill was not enacted. Transportation safety experts, state government representatives, law-enforcement officials, and Mothers Against Drunk Drivers worked with interested members of Congress to shape a legislative proposal that could be voted into law. Parent advocates learn over time to anticipate lawmakers' need for a legislative proposal that will work well from a parental perspective and at least reasonably well from the perspective of other influential groups concerned with the issue.

Network: Grass-roots Lobbying

The network is a major asset in organizing political support for the legislative proposals parents favor. In congressional districts around the country, parent advocates stimulate the flow of letters and phone calls urging support for a proposal from the representative from that district. "Letters are very important to House members," says the legislative handbook drafted by the Candlelighters for their national network, "because they are the principal means of contact with the people who vote every two years." The handbook then lists a dozen suggestions for making letters effective. Most parent advocates stress the importance of writing at critical moments in the budget cycle (the annual pattern of executive-branch and congressional decision making that results in appropriation of funds). Others emphasize personal visits to Congress as a way to underscore what the letters have been saying. Then Representative Shirley Chisholm, speaking at the October 1977 conference of the National Coalition of Title I Parents, advised:

> Get together with other PAC [Parent Advisory Council] members in your area and set up a meeting with your representative in his or her district office. At the meeting, make it clear that the Title I parents intend to closely monitor their support of Title I, and that you expect to see them work on behalf of strong legislation for Title I. Then again in January, when the budget process begins, write to remind them that increased funding for Title I must be a top priority.[2]

Congress is not the only focus of grass-roots lobbying. Ms. Chisholm went on to urge parents to write to the President, who would be proposing his own plans for Title I. The Candlelighters' handbook gives detailed analyses of the executive-branch budget processes leading up to the President's decisions about funding requests for the cancer program, and urges parent advocates to become involved in the budget process of the National Cancer Institute.

Other parents mobilizing grass-roots lobbying reach out to local community leaders and political figures for support with legislators. Adoptive parent Gerald Adcock, who campaigned for the passage of the Opportunities for Adoption Act in 1978, gives a case in point. "It's important to reach the politician where it counts, where he feels it," he says. He recommends enlisting the help of local religious leaders, newspaper editors, and mayors in order to bring an issue strongly to the attention of a local group's congressional representative.

Finally, grass-roots lobbying includes a focus on the congressional or state legislative committee that has the specific authority to consider and report out legislation in the area of interest to a particular group. Explaining in the late 1970s that Congress would soon hold hearings on renewal of the Cancer Act, Grace Monaco said:

> So we will have our parents locally, here in Washington, talking to each member of the authorization committees, Kennedy's committee and Rogers's committee, presenting our position paper, our statement on what is needed. At the same time we will be having the parents' groups across the country contact their congressmen and senators at a local level, urging them to support this particular approach.

The importance of the legislative committee to a bill's passage into law is gradually learned by most parent groups. In Congress, most of the work needed to enact a bill is done in the committee with jurisdiction to begin the authorization of new law in that area. The first, unsuccessful drunk-driving bill was introduced in the House by Representative Michael Barnes, who clearly has a strong personal commitment to this issue. The second and successful bill, however, was introduced by Mr. Barnes and Mr. Howard of New Jersey. In 1982, Mr. Howard chaired the Public Works and Transportation Committee, which had jurisdiction over this issue in the House of Representatives. Support from a committee chairman means far greater chances of success.

Grass-roots lobbying depends on keeping the network alert and knowledgeable about the issues, the political process, and the alternative pieces of legislation introduced. Newsletters of parent groups abound with summaries and advocates' analyses of bills. These analyses really matter, say parents, because many people new to advocacy are initially intimidated by legislative language. A clear description gets them past that barrier. Analyses are also useful when congressional representatives ask advocates for opinions on alternative legislative proposals. Newsletter articles not only prescribe the "how-to's" of getting legislation passed, but also describe and analyze success stories. These testimonials are evidence that the time and effort spent in getting a law passed are worth it. Other stories in national newsletters highlight how parents in one state have been able to encourage parents from other states. National conferences often focus on political education: seminars on legislative process, workshops to share effective advocacy techniques.

As parents undertake political self-education, a common awareness transforms the group. From a collection of individual parents scattered throughout many communities, they evolve into advocates with a grasp of the technicalities of getting on the House calendar or of legislative formulas for allocating funds. As they become part of an advocacy community, members of a national parent network say they learn to time their efforts so that the Oregon parent group reinforces the efforts of the Massachusetts group and together they alert the California group to give them needed support with a key member of the congressional committee. In each of the national networks, a central person (or persons), acting as a switchboard operator, transfers information rapidly throughout the network. By virtue of his or her pivotal position, that person possesses a range of valuable information about activities in many regions.

The Association for Children with Learning Disabilities is noted for its well-organized national parent network. Chapters are organized in cities, counties, and towns; these merge into state chapters linked by a national board. Parents make use of this organization to move information about a legislative proposal rapidly throughout the state. Potentially all individual members (numbering 80,000 in 1982) can be mobilized to contact their congressional representatives. Robert Russell, one of ACLD's founding parents, says that it was his responsibility during one of their first lobbying attempts to alert the ACLD board vice-president who had the task of mobilizing the state affiliates. When Russell got the signal from Washington, he called the vice-president and found she had all the telegrams ready to go. "I made that call on Tuesday," says Russell. "By Thursday night I got a call on an unlisted phone from a New Jersey parent I didn't even know, urging me to contact my representative." Russell reports that within a week, legislative aides were calling to pledge that their members would vote for the bill and to plead with ACLD leadership to halt the torrent of letters, since their offices were swamped with mail.

The Insider: Personal Lobbying

When I asked Grace Monaco to describe what worked for the Candlelighters in getting legislation passed, she succinctly replied: "What works is knowing whom to talk to and how to talk to them." Only an insider close to a state capital or to Capitol Hill really knows that. All the parent groups that have focused on getting laws passed have at least one or sometimes several lobbyists who visit the offices of legislators and get to know the aides responsible for their areas of interest. Those insiders know that legislative aides can become effective advocates for the group's objectives. Most important, the lobbyists develop a relationship with the staff directors (or counsels) to the committee(s) that review legislative proposals that interest the group. Robert Russell described the surprise of the ACLD leadership when, in their early legislative work, they discovered that even though a powerful senator had agreed to introduce legislation that would help learning-disabled children, they still had to convince the committee counsel, a "mere" unelected staff person, of the merits of their approach.

Sometimes the organization's chapter in the state capital or in Washington is given the responsibility for monitoring developments and keeping in touch with the member or committee whose job is to mobilize the network. Sometimes the organization establishes an office, especially in Washington, and either hires a "government affairs specialist" or persuades a parent advocate with lobbying talents to volunteer for the job. Parents interviewed for this book recognized that while all group members active in legislative advocacy learn that access to legislatures is not difficult to obtain and that a wide range of people can be effective lobbyists, some seem to be born with an instinct for it. Describing one of NSAC's leaders, Mary Akerley says: "If she dies and goes to hell, she will lobby to get into heaven and will probably make it."

As they develop their advocacy capabilities, most parent groups struggle with the concept of lobbying and its political connotations. Concerns about losing tax-exempt status or endangering the source of funds are common. Most groups resolve this by learning the details of lobbying laws and regulations. Some establish two separately funded arms of the organization, so that only one concentrates on lobbying. Others keep careful records of the amount of time actually spent in lobbying versus other activities.

In the early stages of legislative work, advocacy groups usually discover that getting a law that authorizes a certain amount of money for children is only half the battle. A legislature still has to decide how much of the amount they have authorized will actually be appropriated. In Congress, special appropriation committees make these decisions within the framework of budget targets set by the legislature. Over time, as the leaders of parent groups realize that their newly enacted law will be meaningless if funds are not appropriated to support its implementation, they encourage parents to lobby both authorizing and appropriation committees.

Getting "Regs"

Another early lesson, say parent advocates, is that even with a law and an appropriation, there are several more innings to the ball game. At the federal level, the agency within the executive branch that will have responsibility for administering the program writes and publishes regulations that govern the conditions under which funding can be distributed to the states or agencies applying for it. Parent advocates have to make their perspectives known to the agency writing the "regs." Usually drafts of the regulations are published in the *Federal Register,* and public comment is solicited. Mary Akerley describes the extraordinary process by which regulations were developed for the Education for All Handicapped Children Act — a process that reflects the grass-roots parent involvement that helped bring the law into existence:

> After the bill passed, there was an extraordinary process for the regulations. You know, usually the administering agency curls up with some of its staff and they write regs and publish them in the *Federal Register.* People scream about them and then sometimes they change them and sometimes they don't. What happened on this one was that before they drafted them they got together about 150 people from all over the country; I am, of course, one of them. They locked us up in Reston for three days and said, "Draft regs." They broke up into teams, each working on a separate section or subject in the bill, and they made sure that each team was balanced. It had a consumer on it, someone from BEH [Bureau for the Educationally Handicapped, at that time a bureau within HEW which was responsible for special education], someone from the state education agency, and I think someone from a private school; all the different perspectives were represented. Then our draft went to BEH and it was refined and refined and refined and every time they re-refined it we all got copies to look over and comment on. This is before it ever appeared in the *Federal Register.* They also had a series of public hearings across the country for citizens to come and say what they thought those regs should be. As a result they are probably the best set of federal regulations ever drafted. They were very responsive to this kind of public input before they were drafted. Which is the way to do it. You don't have to make so many changes.

Using the Media

Parent advocates also rely on newspapers and TV to aid them in getting laws passed. Some favor using the parent network to generate editorials and newspaper articles in a variety of cities. Gerald Adcock recalls advice about going to the media obtained from Capitol Hill friends when NACAC was working to get the Opportunities for Adoption Act moved through Congress. "Then," he says, "we went to the papers and we began to get the support of the prominent columnists, people who could write, who were read and who didn't mind sticking a knife in where it ought to be stuck..."

Getting favorable editorials in the Washington papers, particularly a day or two before a vote is scheduled, is another strategy. Grace Monaco describes another approach, used by the Candlelighters:

> We also have a practice of saying thank you. If a congressman and a senator have been particularly good to us or responsive to what we need, we write letters to the editors of the papers, all the papers in their district, in which we say thank you very much for having a congressman or senator that really is interested in and willing to take a stand on X, Y and Z. You are really lucky to have him...We don't tell Congress or send letters to the editors of the papers saying that you have a lousy congressman because he is not doing a damn thing for us. That doesn't achieve anything...

Piggybacking and Coalition

Whenever possible, parent activists propose joint support on issues of mutual interest to large, powerful groups. The Elementary and Secondary Education Act is typically supported by a variety of professional, labor, and civil-rights groups. So the National Coalition of Title I Parents "lobbies the other lobbies" as well as seeking particular support for the issues that matter to the parent constituency. NSAC might try to persuade the National Association for Mental Health to back its proposals. The Candlelighters might approach the American Cancer Society. MADD works alongside the National Safety Council and national associations of law-enforcement officials. If the other lobby offers its support, parent advocates are quick to spread the word around the appropriate congressional offices that "both so and so and we support these provisions."

Coalitions seem to have a critical role in getting legislation passed. The Education for Handicapped Children Act, parents consistently pointed out, was passed by a coalition of advocacy groups. So was Chapter 766, the Massachusetts special-education law, the Adoption Assistance and Child Welfare Act of 1980, and the 1982 drunk-driving legislation.

The Uncontroversial Issue

Widespread public acceptance of an issue contributes to legislative success. Who would oppose the right to education? ask parents, in analyzing the passage of the Education for All Handicapped Children Act. Mary Akerley explains: "We didn't do anything unusual or spectacular. Everybody was united on it. There was no controversy."

Controversy is minimized, of course, when a problem is perceived as an "act of God"[3] — a handicap, injury, or health impairment which could strike anyone's child. We all feel the need for improved protection against those problems; we generally agree, however vaguely, that "something should be done." Public emotional agreement supports a bill's chances for enactment, unless the parents become too emotional themselves. Then they can be written off as "hysterical," dismissed gently but firmly as insufficiently rational to propose and analyze legislation.

So powerful is public sympathy for childhood cancer victims, for example, that the Candlelighters deliberately restrain themselves from making emotional appeals. Says Grace Monaco:

> We approach lobbying from the point of view of a very close analysis of the need, very close relationship of our statement to the legislation that is being proposed... It is sufficiently emotional to them just knowing that you are a parent with a child with cancer or who has lost a child to cancer or who has a child who has survived cancer, sitting there in front of them testifying. That's all the emotional reminder they need.

Obtaining broad support for what the public perceives as an "act of will" — problems occurring from apparent negligence or weakness on the part of the people needing help — is often harder. Here the question of whether the parents involved "deserve" the assistance of a national law and of national funding may be controversial, and is certainly an obstacle to enactment of laws. Case in point: adoption assistance. Most of us will not experience an act of God that requires us to need adoption subsidies. Some Americans in the past have questioned whether such need reflected a deficiency of will or some withheld commitment or ulterior motive. Much work had to be done during the 1970s to educate lawmakers about the sometimes staggering expenses involved in adopting health-impaired or multiply-handicapped children. Many explanations had to show that lack of subsidies closed adoption opportunities to all but affluent parents, typically white affluent parents — a fact particularly regrettable to Black and Hispanic families of modest income, since large numbers of children waiting to be adopted were Black or Hispanic. However, an uncontroversial, demonstrable cost-effectiveness rationale finally won enough consensus for enactment of the Adoption Assistance and Child Welfare Act: the state was already paying large subsidies to maintain children in foster homes or institutions; with lesser subsidies, these same children could be adopted by their foster parents or others. One way or another the state would spend funds on adoptable children (many of whom had been abandoned or battered by biological parents). With adoption assistance, the state, the children, and parents wanting to adopt all benefited.

Gerald Adcock of the North American Council on Adoptable Children illustrates how the investment theme helped Congress understand adoption subsidies as uncontroversial:

> Where is the controversy? What's the loss to the nation? There is none. It costs a few dollars maybe, but in adoption or foster care or child welfare, dollars spent are going to be returned with a handsome investment. A congressman votes for energy saving, he's going to make somebody mad. He votes for defense, he's going to make somebody mad. He votes against it, he's going to make somebody mad... What's adoption? It's a winner. From the time it goes down the runway to the time it's airborne, it's a winner.

IMPLEMENTATION: MAKING THE LAW WORK

When a new law is passed, it is a very exciting and hopeful moment. But many things have to happen before actual practice really changes at state and local levels. Agencies must be notified of the new legal provisions and requirements that they are now expected to uphold. Decisions have to be made about who gets funded and for what purposes, and about how to assure that the money is spent in ways consistent with congressional intent. Practitioners, the people who deliver the services, must learn new practices. Sometimes a new group of practitioners must be specially trained. A monitoring process to observe the nature and extent of changes in actual practice must be established, together with the means for reporting to the public and to the funding authorities on how well the provisions of the new law are being carried out. Seeing a law through this series of events, called implementation, requires persistence.

In the implementation of all laws authorizing services to children, both power and responsibility for overseeing actual change is assigned to some individuals. Typically, these are agency representatives or, at times, groups of professionals. In the 1970s, however, a fundamental break from that tradition was made in one significant law: the Education for All Handicapped Children Act (EHA). In this case, parents are by statute given the right to share in the power and in the responsibility for making the law work well.

EHA "is a fairly unique law in that consumers have been given the responsibility for implementing it and monitoring it," says Dorothy Dean, former executive director of the Parents' Campaign for Handicapped Children and Youth. In the late seventies, the Parents' Campaign, which then housed a federally funded project called Closer Look, was answering a thousand letters a week from parents seeking information about special education for their handicapped children. With a parent board of directors and a mostly disabled staff, the Parents' Campaign organizes its knowledge about implementation of EHA into publications that can be distributed to very large numbers of parents and professionals throughout the states.

The individual role of parents in getting the right kind of services for their handicapped children and in holding school systems accountable for the education of their children is a unique feature of EHA. Parents have carefully spelled-out rights, notably the right to contribute to an Individual Education Program (IEP) drawn up specifically for their child. The IEP must describe the placement plan for the child and the specific educational objectives which will be accomplished through it. Parents have the right to withhold consent to the IEP. If they disagree with it, they have the right to a hearing by an impartial hearing officer (not an employee of the school district or anyone involved in educating the child). During the hearing, they have the right to counsel, to cross-examination, and to call witnesses. If they disagree with results of the hearing, they can appeal, bringing a lawsuit into state or federal courts if necessary.

For all of the individual power that parents possess under this act, implementation is slowed by the lack of a formal process at the state or district level in which local groups of parents can influence school-system decisions. One parent explained: "So there are individual concerns and there are group concerns, and right now I think the individual parents' part is almost working better than the group concerns." She goes on to say that the state councils required by the 1975 law to review special education in each site may include only one parent representative. Further: "Parents don't have any training for participating in those kinds of forums. They're overwhelmed, all those professionals and one parent." And, unlike Title I parents, who during the 1970s were eligible for federally funded training about the Title I law, the parents of children eligible for EHA funds have no right to organize to enable them to understand the law, its regulations, and its implementation. On the other hand, Title I parents do not have individual parent rights that compare with the rights assured parents of handicapped children. There is no IEP which parents can approve or disapprove for children receiving Title I services. Sometimes parents don't even know that their children are in Title I classes.

As I listened to parent activists, I heard several common prescriptions for achieving meaningful parent roles when laws are implemented. These included building parental awareness of the new legal rights provided by the law or its regulations, reeducation of professionals, parent-to-parent help with case advocacy (making the law work in individual cases), and tenacity.

As the staff of the Parent's Campaign for Children and Youth often explain, what makes services for handicapped children change is parents' actually *feeling* that they have the right to affect the institution and then acting on that feeling. This consciousness is strengthened by the successful passage of a new law, but can be weakened by the lengthy struggle for implementation. The years of effort it took to win strong legislative recognition of parental rights in the Title I law is a good case in point and may have contributed to the ease with which the Reagan Administration in 1981 obtained removal of those provisions.

With new legal rights come new responsibilities for parents. They are no longer outsiders; they are part of making the new law work. During the phase of beginning implementation, tangible successes are rare and public impatience with continuing problems can arise. This can be particularly discouraging for the leaders of activist groups. Implementing a new law, especially a precedent-setting one, means taking risks and making decisions that are not easy, comfortable ones. When I asked Bill Anderson, a longtime member of the National Coalition of Title I Parents, what makes a difference in accomplishing implementation, he said: "Several things — the attitude of the people you're dealing with and your own attitude. There has to be a willingness of both parties to buy into the process. If there's going to be success, we'll take some glory. If there's going to be failure, we'll take some of the lumps."

But even as new insiders, advocates don't feel they should simply expect that the institution they've long struggled to change will inform all parents well about the new legal rights they have to mandated change. Parent-to-parent training and information sharing, say parent advocates, is the best way to build both awareness that new legal rights exist and skill in exercising those rights.

"Implementation of this law [EHA]," says one parent activist for handicapped children, "will depend on independent groups providing information to other parents and informing each other. So I would say that's the first step, informing people about their rights and then training them. Because the system is very rough and it's all weighted in favor of the system."

A parent of a handicapped child in Massachusetts working for implementation of special-education laws echoes this emphasis: "Our law (Chapter 766) and federal law give parents a great deal of power, but they have to know what it is they are entitled to do and what their child is entitled to have. And the only way to do that is to educate the parent through materials and training." The Massachusetts Federation for Children with Special Needs is funded to provide this information and training. But it is one of only a few parent-run centers in the nation supported with government funds to inform and train parents, despite the many new state laws in special education and landmark federal legislation.

Parent advocates implementing special-education laws object to governmental uneasiness about funding the training they need to promote school-system change. While most recognize that legislators are bound to worry about funding parent activities that may cause them political problems, one wondered, "If they didn't want it implemented, and to support what it takes to get it implemented, why did they pass it in the first place?" Another urged that "congressmen understand that advocacy does not mean anything except getting what is due an individual — the services that they are entitled to by law and taking care of the things that have fallen through the cracks. But they get so defensive... It's not militant," she explained. "It's simply trying to make the system work."

Legislation that adoptive parents helped to enact — the Child Abuse Prevention, Treatment, and Adoption Reform Act of 1978 — did provide funds for training and technical assistance. While the law did not specifically direct that parent groups were to be strongly considered when these funds were awarded, the final House-Senate conference report (the official Congressional report summarizing the legislation and its history, and clarifying the purpose of the law) did. In light of the intense parental involvement in enactment of the first federal law concerned with adoption reform, the language of the report is significant:

> Adoptive parents are included as being eligible to receive Federal funds in the carrying out of this provision to provide technical assistance... in order that they may be an integral part of carrying out this adoption proposal [the new law]."[4]

Language like this breaks ground; it recognizes that parent advocates motivated deeply to work hard for a law's enactment are important allies in getting the law to work well.

Education for Professionals

Parent advocates working to improve the law come up against some of the same barriers that parents face in institutional reform: the recalcitrant attitude of some professionals, or just plain professional ignorance of the law. However, in special education, say parent advocates like Al Katzman, then head of the ACLD Advocacy Committee, "The attitudes have turned around dramatically from what they were twelve or fourteen years ago." The staff of the Parents' Campaign for Handicapped Children and Youth reported that in the late 1970s, inquiries about special education from professionals doubled. They interpret this as a sign that professionals are not only listening more to parents but also seeking parents out to obtain accurate, updated information on the new developments in special education.

Innovative training of parents and professionals together reflects a new emphasis on equality. Elayne Brodie describes a course in which parents and teachers learn the technical aspects of Title I: "The teachers and parents are trained together and graduate out of these classes together. Every teacher doesn't understand what the federal jargon is about. Every parent doesn't, so we're going through it together."

Case Advocacy

Another aspect of implementation is case advocacy. Parents at the Federation for Children with Special Needs are especially committed to responding to the parents who call on them for help in getting what their children now have a right to. Some calls coming into their parents' center may require hours of telephone negotiations with the parent, school officials, and a variety of state officials or lawyers. These cases, say the staff of the Federation's referral service, activate their own memories of painful efforts to get their children taken care of, and elicit a strong sense of commitment.

Sometimes trained parent advocates are sent out to accompany a parent to the IEP meetings. Advises Closer Look:

> Bring along a helper to the IEP meeting, if you will feel more comfortable or secure. More and more people are getting

special training to act as advocates for parents in these new and unfamiliar circumstances. Your helper can rehearse with you ahead of time, explain what will go on and how decisions about the IEP will be reached. Ask members of your local parent organization if they are aware of this kind of help. If you can't find someone trained as an advocate, try to get assistance from another parent who has been through it. Experience is a great teacher, and you can benefit from it.[5]

Involvement in case advocacy leads some to an analysis of the systematic elements that block a new distribution of public services. Says one: "Doing this case by case is going to be meaningless unless you get the people at the top, the policy makers, to understand and agree."

Parent advocates who have won laws providing a better distribution of public resources for their children come up against the fact that if the new distribution is to be implemented through the existing system, that system still has to change. This can be discouraging to people who believed that passage of a new law would in itself change things. But many of the parent activists with whom I talked are making long-range plans to implement the laws they worked so hard to pass. When I asked a parent affiliated with the Federation for Children with Special Needs what her organization planned to accomplish over the next ten years, she replied: "I think monitoring is a major goal... It's not really enough to just get something set up; systems fall into patterns, ways of doing things that are easy for them, and families of children need to know when something is happening with their system that is not in the best interests of the child."

THE BATTLE TO KEEP WHAT WE'VE WON

While effective implementation of the legislation will be an important challenge to parent activists, just the battle to keep what has been won may also absorb their energies over the coming decade. This is particularly so as elections bring into power men and women whose positions on legislation may differ greatly from those of previous administrations. Parent groups as well as organizations generally concerned with child welfare and education experienced this intensely in early 1981. The new

Reagan administration proposed consolidation of both the Title I educational program and the Education for All Handicapped Children program into one block grant with virtually no federal requirements. States were to have far greater freedom, a proposal distrusted by parent advocates who had spent decades, often unsuccessfully, trying to persuade state governments to recognize the rights of their children to equal educational opportunity. The Reagan White House also proposed placing the new Adoption Assistance and Child Welfare Act, which had been designed to require state governments to rely less on long-term "temporary" foster-care arrangements, into a block grant for social services whereby the new federal requirements would be repealed.

Reacting strongly to the loss of these targeted programs, parent groups and other advocates opposed the block grants. By June 1981, broad coalitions had won key votes supporting their position on EHA and the child-welfare law in both the Senate and House. By October 1982, parents had convinced the secretary of education to withdraw proposed changes in the regulations for education of handicapped children — changes that parent advocates strongly opposed as a dilution of both parental and child protections. During the same period, however, parents active in education for low-income children eventually lost the rights guaranteed to parents in Title I of the Elementary and Secondary Education Act.

Thus parents learned the fragility of victories won in the seventies. After all, the federal laws that meant so much to them could be almost entirely repealed if a strong and persuasive White House wanted it so. But they also learned to rely on the same diligence they had used to secure passage of the laws in the first place. Proposed repeals could be opposed and at least some important victories scored, even in the face of formidable opposition. The power of the President of the United States — whose help Mothers Against Drunk Drivers sought that autumn day in 1980 — is formidable. But as the parents of handicapped children learned in 1981-82, when a President sought legislative and regulatory changes parents assessed as harmful to their children, even presidential power can be feebler than sustained, skilled, broad-based action by ordinary citizens.

Parent Groups:

Common Problems, Common Practices

7

As I listened to activists describe their organizations, many parents asked me if others were struggling with similar problems. Had other groups found especially effective solutions to problems? Did other organizations begin in the same ways and follow similar lines of development?

Many similarities do exist. There are common ways in which parents find or organize self-help and advocacy groups, and there are common problems. In almost all of the organizations, the leadership struggled with the use of private homes as a base for operations, ambivalence about funding and expansion, relationships with professionals and professional services, decisions about coalition politics, case versus class advocacy, and alternative services versus advocacy. Finally, many of the parent groups were pioneering new concepts for human services and new ways of bringing parents and professionals together.

GETTING ORGANIZED

Parent self-help and advocacy groups usually organize either rapidly, in response to a dramatic event, or over time as parents with similar perspectives meet informally.

Among the mothers who founded the Mothers' Center, for example, bonds of trust grew up over the course of a six-week group discussion about pregnancy and childbirth. The New York City Council on Adoptable Children also came together gradually as parents who had adopted "hard-to-place" children met and slowly analyzed their experiences.

The National Society for Autistic Children had a different

beginning. NSAC organized because of the unprecedented response to an article written by a mother of an autistic child in Chicago and published in the *Ladies Home Journal*. Bernard Rimland, who lived in California with an autistic son, started corresponding with the article's author, Rosalyn Oppenheim. Together they tried to answer the many letters from other parents. Out of that flood of correspondence grew a network of parents around the country whose experience of mutual support transcended distances and sparked the founding of a national group.

The parents who founded the Candlelighters came together because a legislative crisis threatened to disrupt the chemotherapy their children needed to survive. Explains Grace Monaco, "When we had gotten together for the first four or five months and had achieved our first legislative objective, it occurred to me very strongly that what we were really doing was providing a self-help support system, and I said what we are really doing here is we have found we have to talk to somebody, we found each other, we are really enjoying talking to each other, we are learning a lot, we are growing, we are finding it easier to cope with the problems we are having with our kids, and that is what we should be encouraging, as well as the legislative approach to the issues."

Recruiting Parents

When leaders seek to enlarge the group, they most often turn to the media, particularly newspapers and television. One woman's experience in joining Children in Hospitals illustrates the power of television shows to recruit parents and to offer significant relief to a stressed parent:

> As the mother of a boy with asthma severe enough to cause him six hospitalizations in a ten-month period prior to his second birthday, I have many times been thankful that I accidentally happened upon your broadcast on Channel 44.[1]

Members of Parents Anonymous are often encouraged through television to join the organization. Lee Lapicki, for example, watched a noontime TV talk show on which a member of Parents

Anonymous described her experiences. One phone call later, she was connected to the national mutual-support network and committed to beginning her own mutual-support group in Baltimore.

For Mary Akerley and her husband, an advice column in the evening newspaper provided the needed clues.

> A long time ago the *Washington Post* had a columnist whose name was Mary Hayward. Mary took every letter very seriously. And about the time this happened I knew, and my husband did, that there was something wrong with Eddie, but we didn't know what it was. We had never heard of autism. We knew very little about retardation, but he didn't seem to act like what a retarded child would act like. Anyhow, one day I happened to read Mary Hayward...it was a letter from a woman in Virginia who I now know very well, saying that she had seen so and so's letter and she wanted to offer some help. She represented the Virginia Chapter of the National Society for Autistic Children and they had a free reading list on autism. And I guess at that point we had heard of autism and it seemed to sort of fit.

Some groups place ads or arrange for feature stories. In Maryland, Mothers Against Drunk Drivers recruited members by sending letters on drunk driving to the editors of every newspaper in the state. Ninety percent of the papers printed these letters; the response from other bereaved parents and concerned citizens was immediate and strong.

Sometimes parents hear about mutual-help groups in other, larger organizations, such as La Leche League, the Childbirth Education Association, or the local Parent-Teacher Association. Some parents are referred by human service agencies. Abusive or potentially abusive parents are frequently asked to attend Parents Anonymous meetings by the courts or the child protective services system. Parents of adopted children sometimes find out about a local Council on Adoptable Children from adoption agencies. And sometimes sympathetic professionals on hospital wards or in schools will help parents connect with a group. One Virginia mother sought help from her physician for her powerful, painful grief when her child was killed by a drunk driver. Her doctor listened, then reached for his prescription pad. Under the Rx he wrote "MADD."[2]

Groups often encounter barriers to recruiting other parents. Parents of children in institutions fear that their child may become a target for institutional anger, without their knowledge and beyond their control. Such incidents may not be common, but they occur. The June 1976 issue of the newsletter published by the Federation of Parents' Organizations for the New York State Mental Institutions reports: "Thanks to the efforts of the Federation, the group president's son was transferred to a new facility and is showing signs of quick recovery from the beatings and medication poisoning that he had been subjected to."

Black parents for Quality Education respond to this fear by maintaining secrecy about their members. Parents of hospitalized children are aware that those who refuse to join them before or during a child's hospitalization may come around afterward. "When your child is there," says a parent active in changing hospitals, "you're going to do everything to not rock the boat, because you know it involves your flesh and blood."

The fear of reprisal is not always for the child. Sometimes parents worry about the loss of their jobs or those of their relatives. Another parent of Parents Concerned for Hospitalized Children remembers that early in the organizing, "We even had someone whose mother was about to lose her job because of what she was doing with this group, and her mother was, I believe, an aide in a hospital. She just finally came to us and said, 'I've got to stay out'..."

Not all of the parent activists I interviewed had such experiences, but from time to time the subject did come up. Max Schneier points out that once parents are organized, the institution's managers and staff are more likely to fear losing their jobs than parents are. And Happy Fernandez, organizer of the Philadelphia Parents' Union, notes that parent fears about reprisal may not materialize. "Some parents," she writes, found that "persistence, knowing the facts, or acting with a group of parents turned the official's attitudes into one of respect."[3]

PROJECTING A SERIOUS IMAGE

One of the parent groups' early concerns is the kind of image they project. All agree they want a serious image, but this means different things to different groups. For some it means not seeming radical or threatening. "You know there are philosophies about these groups which say the more noise you can make the more you can get done," remarks a member of Parents Concerned for Hospitalized Children. "We didn't see it that way." Successful advocacy, say some parents, depends on appealing rationally to decision makers. Says a leader of the Candlelighters:

> We do not come in and say you are killing our children because you are not giving us enough resources. That doesn't do anything. The reason we have been so successful is we have been able to say to Congress, this is the problem and this is the way to meet it, and this is why it will work. And we do this in a very unemotional framework.

Other groups find, to the contrary, that being "radical" helps them to be taken seriously. Says Helen Moore, describing the early efforts of Black Parents for Quality Education:

> We were making a lot of noise, holding up meetings, keeping people from speaking, including Mary Ellen Reardon [head of the Detroit Federation of Teachers], and all that; they just couldn't do anything with us. We broke up more meetings, we kept things from happening, we were just very boisterous. But we made our point and we did what needed to be done.

The Parents' Union seems to have pursued both ways of declaring itself to be serious. Members meet monthly with the superintendent of schools. When a class-action lawsuit ended arbitrary student disciplinary transfers (those conducted with inadequate regard for due process), the Parents' Union wanted to be able to say that every school knew this ruling had taken place, so they sent each one of the three hundred Philadelphia principals a copy of the judge's findings, by certified mail. This impressed many principals, and gratified some, who explained they wouldn't have known about the ruling for months because it took so long for information to trickle down through the school system. But the Parents' Union also holds rallies outside City Hall. In the fall of 1980, when a teacher strike threatened to disrupt education for weeks, the Parents' Union disrupted traffic. They chose a Friday afternoon, hoping their action would stimulate the speed of the negotiations scheduled to continue over the weekend. "I had never blocked traffic before," says Happy Fernandez, a slim, soft-spoken mother of three. "But a group of us just went and sat down in the street. We couldn't see if it was doing any good — we were soon all cordoned off, you know. I thought, oh dear, this is going to be useless. But friends from all over the city called us later and said there *had* been traffic jams for blocks. People were mad and they were demanding action." By early the following week, the strike was settled.

Projecting a serious image depends also on taking the lead and pointing out the kinds of changes you want rather than primarily objecting to what you don't want. Being politically realistic and knowing when to compromise is part of this, say some activists. Getting influential supporters to back the group's demands is also important. Judy Grove of Parents Concerned for Hospitalized Children (PCHC) explains:

> It is always helpful to say, as you're talking with these people, well, Doctor such-and-such told us, and last week when we met with Mrs. such-and-such from the psychology department; we keep dropping these names, that makes a difference. They listen to professionals.

This is not always as easy as it sounds. Despite all of PCHC's early emphasis on a moderate image, Judy Grove says, "It took us about four months, four or five months, before we could get an honest-to-God M.D. who would say, 'You're on the right track,' even though the American Academy of Pediatrics had been saying this since 1961. None of the doctors out there wanted to be associated with some kind of subversive consumer group who was going around saying the hospitals were not doing the right thing."

In the end, most parent groups gain respect and a reputation for seriousness by, as they put it, "doing your homework" and learning to quote authorities, philosophical approaches, program guidelines, and standards that are familiar to professionals. In mastering this knowledge, parents lay claim to greater equality. They also use the very tools that professionals use to acquire and maintain power to challenge that power.

Having parents who are also professionals is another way of garnering support. The parent professional can "cross over" when it is helpful, gathering information, disseminating the group's perspective, and in general representing the organization. The Candlelighters, the National Society for Autistic Children, and the Association for Children with Learning Disabilities have professional psychologists, lawyers, researchers, and educators among their parent leadership. Several of the people I interviewed thought that this had contributed to these groups' successes.

THE HOME BASE

One of the most interesting features in many groups is that parents, and particularly mothers, fit functions of mutual support and advocacy into their lives and their families. The kitchen table, the home telephone, and the living room become a center for a circle of parent activists. Even national organizations are run out of the homes of individuals. An editor's note in the summer 1978 issue of *Adoptalk* provides a glimpse of this:

> NACAC is staffed entirely by volunteers. There's no "place of business" — central office is a chaotic corner of the Dunn household; *Adoptalk* is produced at a makeshift desk in my bedroom and pasted up next to the washing machine. Phones and letters are answered, book orders filled, and information sent out by volunteers, by NACAC board members and regional reps across the country and Canada committed to the permanent placement needs of children.[4]

By 1980, NACAC had moved at least part of its operations into a Washington, D.C., office. But still parents continued to work for adoption reform from living rooms and kitchens all across the country. Working from a home base may in itself be supportive for some parents, particularly for mothers in the early stages of becoming committed to parent-group activities. Working at home, mothers overcome some of the everyday barriers to involvement in advocacy, such as the difficulty of finding child care.

But the home base has its own stresses. As the group expands and parents become more involved in mutual-support activities, leaders are troubled by the intrusion of the group into their lives. "I'm a twenty-four-hour crisis line," says Lee Lapicki. "I worked from my home with three little kids during the time I had all my problems... but I got the crisis line out of my house a few days ago. I cannot handle that — my kids resented it. It was to the point where they didn't even pay attention because I was on the phone so much." Often at this point group leaders require a central office. Some groups have invented new approaches to staffing. In 1979 the original Mothers' Center was coordinated by not one but three parents who combined the time they wanted to spend with their own children with mutual-support activities. The availability of regular child care at the Mothers' Center office is another way in which the mothers in this group have integrated parenting with the other aspects of their lives.

FUNDING

One constraint on relocating to an office is the lack of funding. As the volume of phone calls and correspondence grows, the organization, previously dependent on volunteer time and the personal financial contributions of parents, outstrips these informal resources. This is particularly true when the group has decided to establish a national presence. Parents Anonymous, the Association for Children with Learning Disabilities, and the National Society for Autistic Children all reached the point when the kitchen table was no longer enough.

In order to be able to respond to thousands of parents across the country, a national organization must hire clerical help. The telephone, including expensive long-distance calls, has to be paid for; funds for people to move around the country and help start satellite groups are needed. But raising these funds is hard. Groups that have decided to focus their efforts within a community can sometimes obtain support from small local foundations or churches. Usually this amounts to just enough to help out with typing, or with a token rent payment.

The grass-roots nature of a parents' group works against successful application for foundation support. Many groups in the first few years are not incorporated or tax-exempt, as they must be for such funding. Many parents have not had experience in writing grant proposals. Beyond that, foundations have traditionally been unenthusiastic about funding the lobbying and legislative advocacy that wins a fairer share of public resources. Those few sources that will do so prefer to support efforts that will have a clear and discernible product — a successful lawsuit or a blue-ribbon commission report — rather than basic institutional change. So parent groups engaged in long-term reform of institutions may find themselves rejected by private funding sources. In addition, the government will usually not fund advocacy. Stung by the sixties, politicians fear that advocates stir up political trouble. They frown on even the kind of advocacy mandated by law — parent involvement needed to implement the wider educational opportunity called for in a new piece of legislation, for example.

Not all parent groups desire either private foundation or government funding. Some groups fear being dependent on someone else's money, especially if that money appears to have strings. They believe that their work would become bureaucratic and impersonal, just like the more traditional human services. Among some groups the resolve not to depend on foundation or government money is linked to a sense of pride and self-affirmation in surviving without large amounts of dollars. Often the solution is to connive at gaining resources: to rescue equipment from places ready to throw it out, to persuade friends to donate their services, or to convince a larger friendly organization to help out with space or clerical needs. Grace Monaco says:

> We are no bureaucracy. We never will be a bureaucracy. I doubt if we will ever be an organization that has paid directors or paid executives and all that kind of thing. What we are is a vast communications network that helps us help each other. I have managed to connive myself a full-time secretary from another organization concerned about cancer. I'm going to try to connive myself one more because I really need it.

Other groups support themselves by pooling their resources and developing a dues system. Still others have resolved their conflicts by deciding on the essential functions for which funding is needed — an office coordinator, clerical help, a long-distance telephone. They concentrate on seeking funding for only those actions, while other tasks are performed by volunteer labor. Black Parents for Quality Education use their network of friends and contacts with entertainment or other celebrities to produce large and effective fund-raisers. Many groups have discovered that conferences can be a very effective source of funds, particularly when product advertisers are allowed to display their products — for a substantial fee.

EXPANSION TO A STATEWIDE OR NATIONAL ORGANIZATION

Ambivalence about seeking sources of funding is often linked to conflicts about expanding the group. The attraction of informal, open, and supportive relationships as well as the strong pull of parents' own occupations and family lives often constrain the group's expansion. On the other hand, parents want to reach out to people in other communities so that they too can experience mutual support. Successful legislative advocacy also requires expansion. In some cases, particularly in the Candlelighters, the Association for Children with Learning Disabilities, and Parents Anonymous, the founding group has deliberately built a national network of support groups.

Most parent activists are aware that a group will be comprised of a core of active leaders and "maintainers," surrounded by a larger number of members who support the goals of the group. Parents from the large outer circle move in and out of the core as other demands on their time and energy fluctuate, and as crises flare up and resolve.

Parents working for institutional change often ask, "How big should we be?" Nearly all of the parent advocates interviewed would agree with Crystal Kuykendall, who says, in the booklet "Developing Leadership for Parent/Citizen Groups":

> The first thing to understand is that you don't need all of your parents to bring about the changes you want to see. Too many parent groups wait around for 50% of the school community or at least 25% of the group membership to show up at meetings before taking any kind of action or lament when only

eight out of forty members show up at a council meeting. You do not need 100% involvement to be effective.[5]

Kuykendall believes that only 5 to 10 percent of the organization's members need to be active leaders, or as she puts it, "workers."

When the core group is also involved in telephone counseling or in serving on government and other official committees that influence institutions, a much larger group is necessary. "We just need more involvement of parent members so desperately," says Helen Moore of Black Parents for Quality Education. "The group cannot continue as it has, as active as we have been infiltrating all the different committees of the board of education."

But other groups expressed concerns about growing too big. "Part of our problem," says one leader of Children in Hospitals, "is that if we had greater visibility in the community or even in the state, we'd have a lot of difficulty handling the kinds of calls that we would be getting. We have difficulty handling the calls we get now. So it's a difficult kind of commitment to know how much we should expand." In the late 1970s, the Sisterhood of Black Single Mothers echoed this concern. "We can't really handle fifty women a day who would call and say, 'I need help,'" says Daphne Busby. "We are not equipped to handle that kind of situation. So we have not been doing that kind of outreach."

In some highly successful grass-roots groups, developed in a particular part of a state or region, the group leaders are not enthusiastic about expansion. Several of them explained that while the spontaneous nature of their group works very well, it will not necessarily work for others, who have to develop something uniquely suited to their own communities. Other groups fear that as they expand, the name and identity of the core group will be used to promote a different agenda. Judy Grove speaks of the choice not to expand Parents Concerned into a larger organization:

> We made that choice very deliberately. We did have people calling and saying, Would you come out and set us up, will you give us the charter from your organization, give us some official standing in relationship to you. We finally came to the

conclusion that we simply couldn't do that, that we had other responsibilities and to use our name as a branch would mean that we would have some responsibility for what they said. And we didn't want to go that way.

Parents Anonymous shared this concern. Its "Chapter Development Manual" urges people to clear publicity sent to newspapers and other media sources with the national office first so that a "unified image" can be maintained. In fact, said the late Jolly K, a cofounder of Parents Anonymous, their fears were never realized. "Each chapter takes on its own personality, but surprisingly, they all adhere to the overall Parents Anonymous philosophy," she explained.

Jolly K also described the early days in the group's evolution as a national organization, when parents in the core group worried about what expansion might mean for them and their lives. Parents Anonymous was swamped with letters from parents seeking help in all different parts of the country. But the core group of leaders preferred the activities of mutual support to administering a central office. "As Parents Anonymous got big," explained Jolly K, "we resolved the situation by hiring an administrator. There wasn't anything written that I had to be the administrator. My big fear had been that I would have to get involved in day-to-day paperwork. But eight and a half years later, I'm still doing the creative work." Then she went on to point out that I had reached her not at the central office but at home, where she still worked most of the time. She counseled other parent activists to "select the niche that you want and that provides the least strains on the other aspects of your life, and then figure out the other niches, and then recruit or hire other people to do those."

Fear of growth may originate from the core group's feeling of closeness, friendship, and trust. In many of the parent groups, underneath the flurry of press releases, public meetings, correspondence, and telephone calls is a steady flow of mutual support. Organizational tasks are shifted and responsibilities are shared in response to changing stresses in members' lives. Sometimes this pattern moves into the family lives of the parents. When I arrived to interview a founder of the Mothers' Center, she greeted me somewhat distractedly because her two older children had been sent home from school sick. But that posed very little problem as other mothers arrived. One woman cleaned up the kitchen, a second fed the baby, and a third sat at the table talking to me.

Even in a national group, the feeling of mutual support can still be very strong among the core. Parents I interviewed spoke warmly of other activists, sometimes thousands of miles away, and recounted incidents when they had helped each other out. The sense that they could count on each other to come through was strong.

In part, concerns about expansion also reflect parent advocates' fears about diverting too much energy from other responsibilities, especially child-rearing. Mothers particularly feel this conflict, like mothers everywhere in our society. But when groups achieve successes in changing institutional policies and practices or in getting legislatures to pass new laws, the self-images of the mothers involved begin to change. They begin viewing themselves as people with skills highly valued in modern society — political savvy, administrative ability, or good organizational sense. Often these changes occur slowly. Several of the people described their accomplishments and expressed almost a feeling of surprise that "a group of mothers, just a handful of mothers," had been able to accomplish so much. But many fear that the organizational demands that may follow success will inevitably take them away from their families. Said a parent in Children in Hospitals: "Well, you know, there are other groups like ours in other areas, and the thing is that none of us, because we have children, are ready to become professionals who do this full time, at the expense of our own families."

The underlying question for mothers in advocacy groups is whether they see themselves as people with identities distinct from their role as mothers, or whether they maintain the mother identity as the overriding one. This is a highly personal question posing distinctly individual choices, which each mother resolves in her own way.

Some groups are consciously structured to support parents as they work out these choices. Some are organized so that work can be done in modular projects which can be picked up by other parents if a member must withdraw temporarily to be with a sick child. Explains Grace Monaco:

> We have less predictability in who is going to be able to be consistently involved because of the nature of the children's illness. We've had somebody who might be involved like crazy for a couple of years and all of a sudden say, if somebody has a child who has gone into a relapse, you have to forget about me for six months because I don't know what I am doing. What we try to do is to carve things up at the outset so that parents can work at something that they have interest in. They can have a project which takes a definite time limit.

The Mothers' Center, too, makes it possible for members to move in and out of projects. In the early 1980s, groups of mothers just becoming involved in mutual support met for seven weeks, after which they could choose to move on to smaller, less structured conversation groups or to train to become peer counselors for other mothers. Thus the women at the Mothers' Center were free to share intensively the mutual support of the group in one part of the cycle and less intensively in another part, and then return to deeper involvement. The leaders described this process as specifically geared to the needs of mothers, whose children make multiple and varying demands on their resources.

Unlike many American organizations, parent self-help and advocacy groups support the integration of work and family. Joan McNamara, the former editor of *Adoptalk,* describes in the newsletter her response to the arrival of another child. "With a brand new baby son added to five other small McNamaras, one of whom just arrived this winter, it is clear that a maternity leave is due, a 'family break' to tune into husband and kids again, where it all started." Joan McNamara's family break, however, was not going to be a complete break from the NACAC; she planned simply to take a more supportive background role within the organization for a while.

The donation of time is also a stabilizing force within the group, permitting long-term survival in the event of financial difficulties or loss of funds. The Parents' Union for Public Schools deliberately regarded its 1980 staff of twenty-five as people whose primary job lay in supporting the volunteer work of parents — building on and increasing the parental commitment of time to the goal of improving Philadelphia's public schools.

Although individual parents make different choices about their own identities, most parent self-help and advocacy organizations establish an identity quite separate from that of professional services, even those that share their objectives. Partly they try to avoid affiliation with an institution or agency which may try to direct the group toward its own purposes. For example, Children in Hospitals' first encounter with Boston Children's Hospital demonstrated that the hospital's objectives were different from the parents'. Often groups find it useful to avoid even the appearance of such an affiliation, because of parents' negative feelings about the institution or agency. The "Chapter Development Manual" for Parents Anonymous says:

> A state, county, or private agency or facility may not start a P.A. chapter. They may endorse and legitimize the need for P.A., they may refer members, they may support and encourage...but they may not start or be directly involved with the operations of a chapter. This firm rule is necessary in order to negate the anti-agency feelings that so many troubled parents have. Because P.A. is a private organization, and not an extension of any other endeavor, private or public, we have no wish to be seen as a direct part of any existing agency or private concern. We, of course, will be cooperative with these agencies, but will remain autonomous.[6]

The manual also urges Parents Anonymous chapters not to meet in a setting associated in any way with the removal of children to foster care, which would make parents uneasy.

The Candlelighters encourage hospitals and treatment facilities to sponsor group meetings for parents, but urge that their own gatherings should not be held in institutions where members' children are being treated. They want to give parents a break from the stresses they associate with their child's treatment; they also hope that in another setting, parents will feel freer to express their feelings about the treatment, including anger and hostility.

Anger at Professionals

In the earliest, most intense phases, parent groups usually exclude all but a few professionals. At least in these beginning stages, parents often passionately despise managers of institutions that they feel are failing their children. "If a bureaucrat gives you what you are entitled to, he is your friend. If he doesn't, he is your enemy," says the influential pamphlet "How to Organize an Effective Parent Group and Move Bureaucracies."[7] "Parents who succumb to friendly relationships with bureaucrats, with its give and take," the pamphlet's author warns, "will find that they wind up doing all the giving and the bureaucrats all the taking."[8] Parent activists also reject academicians who write textbooks that describe parents as incompetent or victimized. "You take a look at some of the textbooks used in graduate schools," says one member of the National Society for Autistic Children. "If autism is mentioned at all, see how they describe the parental, particularly the maternal, dynamics, and you'll throw up."

Parents involved in self-help groups *are* angry at professionals and feel deceived and mistreated by them. When professionals don't listen or dismiss their views, their anger increases. Further, professionals are often wrong. They insisted for years that children with Down's syndrome should be institutionalized at birth, that separation of hospitalized children from their parents was not harmful, that routine general anesthesia in childbirth was the treatment of choice. In light of this record, parent activists ask, what do professionals expect when a child's health, safety, and future development may be at stake? Parental acquiescence might mean risk to the child's well-being; over time it would diminish parents' protective energy.

Besides these factors, two others are at work. One is the image of omnipotence cultivated during the process of professionalization. The other is adult bonding to the child, especially the young child. Caring for or educating a young child is frequently tedious and demanding; when adults are not emotionally attached to the children in their care, boredom or fatigue may dampen their desire to do well. Fortunately, infants and young children seem to begin life with the capacity to charm, persuade, or otherwise entice adults into deep, long-lasting attachments to them. Cultural values strengthen adults' propensity to feel this. Once they have formed intense attachments, however, adults tend to compete overtly or unconsciously with other adults who are attached to the same child.[9] That rivalry frequently expresses itself in debates over who knows what is best for the child or who can make better decisions. Western literature is replete with sketches of this kind of competition between mothers and grandmothers. I believe the same dynamic enters into the relationship between parents and other people caring for children. One classic case in point: nurses in the newborn nursery often express competitiveness toward new mothers, and vice versa. As in any intimate, one-on-one relationship, hostility is present between two competitors for the same loved one. In individual parent-professional relationships, some competitiveness, and consequently some anger, is unavoidable, since attachment of adults to children for whom they are responsible is desirable and benefits the child.

With regard to professionals' attitudes toward organized parent advocacy, some initially react with hostility — and stay hostile. But others are very supportive. Their reception is often warm indeed. Explaining the relationship of the professional sponsor to the Parents Anonymous group, Lee Lapicki says, "The sponsor is the support system of the group leader, and the group leader is the support system to the group. That's basically how it works. With myself, my sponsor is my best friend. I absolutely love her." Other parent activists expressed their appreciation of professionals who supported them even when it was professionally unwise to do so. The leaders of Children in Hospitals recalled a stormy meeting between angry parents wanting serious change and angry professionals and administrators rejecting the parents' demands. Still, the parents noted, "They chose the speaker, but Gordon Harper, who was one of their psychiatrists, backed us from one end to another." These activists also acknowledged the work of Dr. T. Berry Brazelton and other child-development specialists in persistent advocacy for hospital policy change. They felt their own activism supported professionals' ability to work on the inside for change. "It gives them the incentive and backup to be able to say, 'We've got to make these changes because the people are demanding it and if we can work from the outside and the inside both, that's more effective than only from one side.' " Parents active in public-school reform and parents of handicapped children deeply respect some professionals who, they feel, stood by them when it was unpopular to do so.

Eventually, almost all parent groups, strengthened by mutual support into a deeper confidence in themselves, develop a non-blaming attitude toward professionals and institutions — even while actively demanding change in professional behavior or institutional practices. As the president of the National Federation of Parents for Drug-Free Youth wrote in the winter 1982 NFP newsletter, in describing the growth of the parent movement against drug use: "Parents quickly realized that trying to find someone (schools, police, drug professionals, lawmakers) to blame was not going to solve the problem, but rather was counter-productive." This realization, I believe, is linked to the realization that parents' blaming themselves is counterproductive, for it saps the energy needed for solving the problem.

What often emerges between parent groups and professionals is distinct and separate but mutually respectful relationships. Al Katz, author of *The Strength in Us,* a book about self-help, sees this as a primary characteristic of self-help in general.

> Self-help groups...tend to minimize the role of the professional, as compared with more conventionally structured social agencies. Some self-help groups have deliberately and systematically excluded professionals from leadership roles — Synanon, for example. The professional may be accepted in such a group as an observer, but unless he shares the common problem, he is not considered to be a member, nor does he generally participate in decision-making processes. Other groups may include the professional as a member, but his role tends to be more that of a rank-and-file participant than that of a leader, decision-maker, or teacher. If he functions as a professional at all, rather than as member-participant, his functions are those of a consultant, resource advisor, evaluator, or expediter.[10]

This relationship is far different from the one that Christopher Lasch and other contemporary analysts of the helping services ascribe to parents and professionals. Describing in *Haven in a Heartless World* what he sees as the "proletarian" role of parents, Lasch attributes it to the powerlessness of parents in their relationships with professionals. If parents organized and hired their own experts, he argues, things might be different.[11] Of course, in both a literal and a figurative sense, most parent self-help and advocacy groups have done just that. When they feel that an expert would be useful to the group, they hire one. In addition, they *become* their own experts.

Parents groups frequently work with professionals whom they have selected and/or approved, whether formally hired or not. "Certainly in our group there is a peer relationship between the parents and professionals," says Mary Akerley. "We hand-pick the professionals we will work with." Equality exists even in Parents Anonymous, despite conventional wisdom which suggests that parents under the kind of stress that impels them to injure their children could not sustain a peer relationship with professionals. While each group in Parents Anonymous is supposed to have a professional sponsor, he or she is supposed to take a nondirective role in the group. And in Maryland, at least, Lee Lapicki screens those people who ask to become sponsors.

Finally, many parents personally express compassion and concern for dedicated professionals with extraordinarily difficult jobs. Grace Monaco, in reflecting on the stresses that professionals undergo in working with cancer patients, says:

> The strain on one family, of course, is a tremendous strain, but when you think of professionals who deal with hundreds of children a year, a good number of whom are going to die, with whom they have developed a close relationship, you can understand that the pressures on them in maintaining an intact family of their own can be devastating.

Members of Parents Anonymous concern themselves with professional burnout — the erosion of the ability to sustain sensitivity and commitment as a result of overlong exposure to human demands. A leader of Children in Hospitals talks about the anger parents feel at lab technicians who repeatedly prick the fingers of young hospitalized children, then goes on to say:

Then again, how can we deal with lab technicians to make them feel less guilty? It must be very difficult to be a lab technician in a pediatric hospital. You either have to say that 'I am not a vampire going around pricking a lot of children' or else you get in touch with 'Yes, this is really difficult.'

Many parents talk about professionals as human beings who struggle with their own feelings related to serving human needs. So although parents in self-help groups strongly assert that they are, in their role as parents, as competent as professionals, they often go beyond their initial anger to note that all human beings, whether professionals or parents, have difficulties meeting the needs of others. In fact, activists aware of the strain on professionals often suggest the formation of mutual-support groups among people staffing children's services.

COALITION POLITICS

The commitment to retaining a separate and distinct identity does not prohibit a parent group from forming coalitions with professionals or seeking to share its knowledge with sympathetic (or not so sympathetic) professionals. But not all parent groups favor coalitions. Some, particularly as they begin to get organized, distrust the motives and tactics of other groups and will not recruit potential allies. Others fear that the time and energy spent in developing or maintaining a coalition will be wasted. Still others worry that membership in a coalition may inhibit the group's more aggressive advocacy stances. In a large coalition with many perspectives, it is likely that the militancy of any one group will have to soften.

Most parent advocates prefer to develop coalitions that can easily be put together and dissolved. Black Parents for Quality Education, for example, keeps the best features of a small organization, capable of quick decision making and rapid response, and a large coalition which can exert political muscle, by mobilizing and supporting only issue-focused coalitions. Black Parents achieves part of its objective through a small network of parents (who in turn can mobilize a much larger community if necessary), and push for specific changes as part of short-lived, broad-based coalitions.

Other groups coalesce with professional organizations concerned about similar problems when that seems helpful. Mothers Against Drunk Drivers has worked closely with state and local police, lawyers' organizations, and automobile-insurance associations to win new laws against drunk driving. Parents of handicapped children are often willing to seek out professional organizations in education and to take on certain issues together. Once relationships are established, the coalition can assemble and dissolve as circumstances dictate.

CASE VS. CLASS ADVOCACY

It is apparent from my interviews that many groups struggle with the nature and depth of their involvement in case advocacy (focused on individual rights), in contrast to class advocacy (focused on the general rights and needs of children or parents). Black Parents for Quality Education, Children in Hospitals, Parents Concerned for Hospitalized Children, the North American Council on Adoptable Children, and the Federation of Parents' Organizations for the New York State Mental Institutions all struggle with this conflict in deciding how to allocate their time and energy. At some point in their organizational development, groups resolve this conflict, usually choosing class advocacy. This is particularly difficult because many groups evolve slowly. Coming together first for mutual support, helping each other as individuals, they secure some protection from an institution's practices. Then they may become involved in helping other individual parents, and slowly grow into case advocacy. As members of the group become more deeply aware that the problems are systemic, and more discouraged about the possibility of effecting change through case advocacy, the group becomes more involved with trying to change the policies and procedures of the system itself, not just the behaviors of certain individuals. Class advocacy, with the promise of long-lasting benefits to all children, becomes the focus.

As a group evolves toward class advocacy, parents experience an ethical dilemma. Parent advocates usually know a lot about the impact of everyday institutional decisions on the lives of children. In addition, they are very close to the pain to which many children and parents are exposed. Parents I interviewed were asking themselves whether it is right to turn their backs (as they see it) on the individual struggles of group members or of other parents, which they understand so well. A group leader's decision to focus energies and time on getting the school board to appoint parent representatives to some decision-making committees puts basic change before individual crisis. If at the same time the children of group members are suspended unjustly or beaten in school, the group will have difficulty sticking with a long-term strategy without immediate intervention.

With increasing clout, an organization can allocate less time to achieve the same results: "When there is a problem, when a parent calls us from a different school, we go in there and say this is what has to be done. Sometimes we don't have to do anything but show our faces and then the problem is solved," says a leader of Black Parents.

The Federation of Parents' Organizations for the New York State Mental Institutions has also brought its strength into individual parents' struggles to achieve better conditions for their children. Agnes McLean, from the Long Island Regional Council of the Federation, described how the cooperation of one group of parents at one state hospital with another group at a different state hospital effected the transfer of patients from one institution to another, even when the hospital administrations had concluded that transfers couldn't be made. At other times, the leaders of the Federation have called the appropriate decision makers for parents anxious about excessive medication. Frequently the leaders of Children in Hospitals know the decision makers in each hospital from their policy-oriented encounters; a few telephone calls will help a parent who has been told that it is "against the rules" to stay overnight with a child or to be there while the child is anesthesized.

Many parent advocates find that even when reforms are implemented, case advocacy is necessary. Some of an institution's staff will continue to resist changes in basic policies or procedures. Parents need the support of the group to insure that their children benefit from the basic changes that the group has brought about.

ALTERNATIVE SERVICES VS. ADVOCACY

Another difficult conflict for parent advocates is whether to develop alternative services or to invest time in advocacy for basic changes, which might remove the need for alternative services. Some of the parents I listened to have strong convictions that advocacy groups should not use their energies to develop services their children need. Says Mary Akerley, "We say don't let your board of ed off the hook. If you start a program then they won't have to. What we do recommend is a compromise position. If the parents want to, start it, but then you get them to take it over and you get out. You're in the advocacy business, not the service business."

Other groups see it differently. The development of alternative services is, of course, an expression of mutual support among parents whose dependence on institutional services has been painful. Sometimes parents faced with unresponsiveness in institutions take matters into their own hands. In New York City, when agencies were labeling children "unadoptable" because adoptive parents "couldn't be found," the Council on Adoptable Children maintained an aggressive recruiting service to provide permanent homes for older, handicapped, minority children in foster care. The New York City COAC, like many other groups of adoptive parents nationwide, contacted newspapers and radio stations, maintained files on telephone and written inquiries from parents, and called child-care agencies to inform them of prospective parents.

Adoptive-parent advocates feel that their services do not let publicly funded agencies off the hook. Rather, the message is that what can be done by parents operating on a shoestring and on volunteer time certainly can be done by the system. Publicizing the success of their alternative service leads to advocacy for institutional change.

The National Federation of Parents for Drug-Free Youth developed a nationwide network of alternative parent education and support services because professionals and institutions were not reaching families in ways that worked well enough. Now local groups of parents working against teenage drug use have realized that their own steadfastness and effectiveness in opposing easy access to drugs have made it impossible for public or private agencies engaged in half-hearted drug-prevention work to claim that "it just can't be done."

The Mothers' Center strives to resolve the conflict between alternative services and advocacy by providing alternative counseling services for mothers but using the data generated in those sessions for advocacy efforts carried on in other committees. In this way members take advantage of their mutual-support services to bring about (as they phrase it) "repair of traumas," but also basic institutional change.

SUSTAINING A GROUP

Since parent advocacy groups extract a good deal of personal sacrifice and time, they often find that they must continually show measurable success. Organizations that showed a pattern of decline in advocacy efforts (sometimes followed by a cycle of renewal, sometimes not) were those working to change large, bureaucratic, publicly funded institutions, particularly big school systems and mental hospitals. Over the past decades, advocates for systematic large-scale improvement in these institutions have sometimes turned their energies, after years of frustration, to the creation of alternatives — the community-based group home for mental patients, or the alternative independent school. Middle-class parents, who may be able to pay privately for responsive and effective care or education for their children because of second jobs or two incomes, are understandably more inclined to divert their time and energy away from the advocacy group and into acquiring that additional income if tangible improvements don't occur as a result of sustained advocacy. Even parents who have no choices, either because their incomes are low or because the services needed are so expensive (as is the case with serious illness or handicapping condition), may turn away from a "losing" organization if at least some victories are not snatched from highly resistant bureaucracies.

Some organizations work to prevent this loss of hope by carefully outlining small but measurable and attainable objectives. The Parents' Union's "Two-Year Plan," printed on a 1980 fact sheet available to all parents, is broken down according to System-

Wide Action, Local School Action, and Individual Assistance to Students and Parents. Under each category are listed a half-dozen objectives, such as:

- Negotiate...for specific changes in four critical areas — Reading, Discipline, Special Education and Student Involvement (System-Wide Action);
- Research suspension patterns and take action to reduce suspensions by 10% in 20 schools (Local School Action);
- Assist at least 250 students and parents who need help with suspension, transfers, abuse and other problems (Individual Assistance to Students and Parents).

These goals seem a lot more possible to achieve, and thus more worth working for, than a more abstract "increased responsiveness in the public schools."

Other groups sustain the commitment of their members by publishing accounts of what they've already achieved — victories that some of the parents can remember being involved in. When Children in Hospitals reports on its latest survey of family-centered improvements in Boston-area hospitals, it frequently lists the results obtained by earlier surveys, displaying in statistical format the improvements over the years.

THE NEW PIONEERS

Parent self-help groups have pioneered new approaches to professional training and to human services generally. Nearly all parent groups involve themselves in efforts to educate professionals, believing that changing professionals' attitudes is fundamental to achieving basic institutional change. All of the groups, for example, have sponsored conferences to which they invite professionals.

Recently some groups have become involved in local community and four-year colleges, and even graduate and professional schools, to explain their perspectives and feelings as parents. Such seminars lead students to a much richer understanding of parents, advocacy, and the problems children and families face. Other groups accept invitations to appear at professional conventions and describe the work and convictions of parent activists.

Effective parent-run peer counseling, halfway houses, and hotlines offer new options in the delivery of human services. Parent advocates clearly feel that their services are the equal of those offered by private family service or publicly supported mental-health or child-welfare agencies. Most also feel that while the sort of support that they receive from and offer to one another is of a very high quality, parents can and should be involved with other professional services. Parents Anonymous, says Lee Lapicki, "will make mistakes just like any other agency, but I think it is an excellent support system. It works well with any other kind of service. Parents in Maryland, and probably in a lot of other states, will use other services." Self-help groups occupy an increasingly respected place in the range of human services.

News of another interesting development in human services fills the recent issues of group newsletters. These accounts describe how parents have become partners on teams — consultants in childhood cancer units, members of court-appointed teams evaluating foster-care records, part of citizen-review teams looking at institutionalization. Parents are also required on the evaluation team planning a child's placement, by the Education for Handicapped Children Act.

Parents are helping to invent new concepts in human services which would seem very strange indeed to some of the nineteenth-century advocates who helped develop services like public schools, hospitals, and mental institutions. Then the objective was to separate children from the insidious influence that parents were thought to exert. Now parents are increasingly seen as partners with a rightful role in the development of services for their children. The concept of the professional's role is also changing. As Lee Marcus writes in *The American Journal of Orthopsychiatry,* professionals are beginning to see themselves differently. "The clinician should have practical solutions to real problems, be willing to work directly with the child, work for community involvement such as appropriate school placement, and in general take the side of the family with a lifelong disorder."[12] Marcus's comment refers to the relationship professionals should develop with parents of handicapped children, but it points to a new understanding of the general professional-parent relationship. All parents may not be experiencing a "lifelong disorder" but they do face the very real demands of a lifelong commitment.

A Look Toward the Future

8

Out beyond Montgomery and Selma, through Lowndes County and across the Black Belt of Alabama, small, fragile-looking buildings cling to the line where back road and field meet. For two cold February days, Sophia Harris, whom I had come to visit, drove with me down more than a hundred miles of country roads, pulling over now and then to stop at one of these small buildings. Inside, young children — three, four, and five years old — played, rested, and ate under the care of women who combined the gentle manners of the South with a wary vigilance. Some small children and a few adult women, together in low-roofed buildings across Alabama's poorest counties, may not seem a matter of much significance. But what I saw during those two days of visiting and listening embodies the whole point of parent self-help and advocacy, and symbolizes the implications of this national phenomenon for the 1980s and beyond.

The small rural centers in Alabama symbolize the deeply felt aspirations held in common by the many different parent groups described in this book. In fact, they are a prototype of what parent advocates in so many parts of the country are struggling to achieve — an active community of self-help and mutual support, a fairer distribution, sustained by tenacious advocacy, of services needed by their children, and a children's service that is extraordinarily open to parents.

I was in Alabama to visit Sophia Harris, the executive director of the Federation of Community Controlled Child Care Centers of Alabama (FOCAL). FOCAL is a network of day-care centers founded in the sixties and early seventies by parents and civil-rights workers. Some of the programs I saw were housed in the frame schoolhouses that had been public schools for Black children before integration. Others were sheltered in small buildings at the edges of fields where butter beans or soybeans were sown, picked, and sold to supply income for the program. Kept alive by communities who have raised livestock and crops, quilted, stitched, argued, protested, and sung at choir recitals to support their children's day-care program, these centers are very important to Sophia Harris and to FOCAL. But to the communities they serve, they are a lifeline.

In the almost eighty centers which make up the Federation of Community Controlled Child Care Centers of Alabama, parents and program staff together make the policies and run the programs. Traditional lines of distinction between parents and teachers are blurred. Some of the teachers have children in the center; some decided to work in the program because of their own experiences as parents. Each center is viewed as a place where parents and their perspectives are welcome, where staff expect to give *and* receive support from parents and other members of the community. And when FOCAL convenes statewide meetings or training sessions, parents and teachers travel over the back roads from all parts of the state to participate.

Sophia Harris describes why FOCAL was founded:

> Basically, the purpose of FOCAL was first of all to promote the whole concept of community and parent control... People were very concerned that with the licensing standards coming out, this was just the beginning of something to take away their program and to force them out and say, 'You're not educated enough'... People who served on the board represented these people and they still do, because they are the people from the community, they are the low-income folk, some of them are parents, some of them have been parents in the sense that their children have been involved in the program. I think you'll find, with most of the centers, there's not a great deal of separation between parents and providers.

Staff members' sense of partnership and mutual support moves them to share the stresses and the triumphs that parents experience in their daily struggle to assure that their families survive. One center director from FOCAL describes the power of the county welfare officer in rural Alabama:

A Look Toward the Future 179

> In the county office, each case worker is assigned to so many families and they control whether that family gets food stamps, day-care services, welfare payments, whatever. And basically they are very powerful folk in the lives of a family. Our basic problem has been that a great many of the case workers are older folks who have been there for umpteen years who are not about to change in their belief that welfare folk are basically no good.

She helps parents face that power.

> Sometimes I will see a person in need and I will talk to the person and send him down to the food-stamp office and I will call them and tell them that I know this person needs help and they need some food...it always takes somebody in our county, somebody has got to vouch for them...I really try to help people with jobs, with food, with places to live, with any kind of problem. They don't mind calling me out of my bed at 12 o'clock at night. If they got a problem, they call me.

In FOCAL centers, self-help and advocacy translate into support for survival. Parents help the centers survive — which is not easy in a state where Black community-controlled centers have been viewed with hostility and too often excluded from public funding. The center director and the teachers in turn help the parents survive by providing good parent-controlled child care for those who would otherwise be cut off from jobs and training, and practical knowledge of food stamps, health care, and job opportunities. Most important is the warm, brave companionship that FOCAL center directors and teachers give parents who have to seek assistance from a powerful and sometimes inimical system.

Thousands of miles away is the flat, open expanse of Salt Lake City, Utah. Utah is a hub of traditional American values. Its residents have a reputation for hard work, thrift, devotion to family, and deep respect for education. During the 1970s a higher proportion of the Utah population aged three to thirty-four years was enrolled in school than in any other state in the Union.[1] Utah also spent the highest rate of per capita income on education of all the states in the nation[2] — and had the highest level of completed schooling, too.[3] Yet despite this large overall investment, Utah's schools also have a comparatively low *per pupil* expenditure — $1,676 per pupil in 1978–1979.[4] Perhaps the state's history of high productivity — its citizens are reported to have the highest per-hour productivity rate in the nation — flows through the public schools as well. The public in this state seems to enjoy effective and continuing education at comparatively low costs.

The Salt Lake City school, I was told repeatedly by leaders of parent participation in public education, are a model of what schools could be if they would just take seriously the legitimate desires of parents to influence what happens to their school-aged children. Governed by parents, teachers, and principals, the schools are open and accessible. Intrigued by the apparent embrace of such a modern concept in a city known for its conservative, old-fashioned values I went to Salt Lake City myself in 1981.

Any passenger on a flight into Salt Lake City would be struck by the gradual descent into an ample, expansive valley. The city itself reinforces this feeling of space and access, with very broad streets and lots of sunshine, lots of air.

Openness is also a remarkable characteristic of the Salt Lake City school system. A parent or group of parents who is dissatisfied with what is being taught or how the schools are teaching it is not required just to swallow anger. They can take their objections to the School Community Council right at the child's school, state their case, and get some accommodations made. The council, composed of eight parents, seven teachers, and the principal, is designed to "provide a cooperative means of improving educational programs and conditions within the school."[5] By working toward consensus, the council should devise a way of meeting parents' objections. Parents who aren't satisfied with its solutions, however, can take their case directly to the superintendent of schools, initiating a "request for review of services" by filling out a form available to "any individual who wishes the District to review the services provided by an employee or by a program of the District." From there an open process is followed. The principal of the school meets with the people involved and tries to resolve the situation; if unresolved, the request for review is sent to the superintendent, who sends an impartial "learning specialist" to the school. This specialist meets with all the parties involved, prepares a report to the superintendent, discusses the findings with the employee who is being reviewed, and then sends copies to the superintendent, the individual(s) asking for the review, the principal, and the person reviewed. If the solutions proposed at this point are still unacceptable, parents can take the matter to the school board. Superintendent of schools Dr. Donald Thomas estimated in 1981 that of the forty to fifty reviews conducted each year, only ten have to be resolved at the superintendent's level. In the eight years that he had been superintendent, only two reviews had ever had to be resolved by the school board.

No issue is too small or too large to bring before the School Community Council. Past issues include the proper way to teach reading, parent concerns about where children are taken on field trips (one high-school class had gone to the local Planned Parenthood Association), how much free time the schedule permits adolescents during the school day, the timing of parent conferences, and the content of textbooks. In resolving the issues, says Superintendent Thomas, the council looks for the "preponderance of feeling" among parents and school employees. Sometimes it conducts surveys of parent opinion. It is empowered to set up ad hoc committees to investigate matters of special concern, but is urged to avoid taking a simple vote to arrive at the best solution. Rather than setting up winners and losers, the process is aimed at developing a consensus about what should be done.

The School Community Councils cannot make decisions that violate current board policy or state and federal law. Of course, in concert they can influence or argue for changes in board policy. As a district-wide endeavor, they are also a good source of successful campaigns for school-board membership (two former parent members of School Community Councils were serving on the seven-member school board in 1981).

However, each school is free to decide such matters as what hours it will be open; how often, when, and where parents will meet with teachers; how adequate supplies and textbooks are. Some schools have decided to cover teacher absences with parent volunteers. The funds those schools haven't had to spend on salaries for substitute teachers can be used elsewhere in the school.

The concept, called "shared governance," came to Salt Lake City in 1973, as part of the agreements Don Thomas obtained when he was engaged as superintendent. The school district enrollment had dropped from 42,000 in 1958 to slightly more than 29,000. Partly because of the school closing decisions necessitated by that decrease, partly because of strong value differences over curricula and material, Salt Lake City was considered a "high conflict" school district. "The parents were angry, the teachers were upset, the board of education was swamped with so many issues they couldn't do much long-range planning," explains Dr. Thomas. So he instituted "shared governance," negotiated it into the master contract with the teachers, and trained the teachers in the concept in the first year and the parents in the second year, with special attention to such skills as "option exploration" and "conflict mediation." Gradually the parents, teachers, and administrators began to accept and use well the principle of parity — the concept of equal position of the parties. "It takes five years," says Dr. Thomas, who is helping to establish shared governance in school systems in other states.

The results? "School regulations," says Dr. Stanley Morgan, head of the school district's research office, "are now the considered judgment of a group of interested and concerned professionals and parents and as such have their support." Parents who feel they are losing control over experiences they believe to be critical in the development of their children have a place, a process, and people to work with to reestablish their active protective role in the lives of their children.

None of the other parent advocacy leaders I interviewed knew about FOCAL, or about shared governance in the Salt Lake City schools. But they should, for in every part of the country parent advocates are struggling to transform schools, hospitals, and social services into something which the small rural day-care centers and the Utah school system exemplify: children's services where parents and staff establish a partnership to fight for and achieve a better, safer future for children. These two examples contrast directly with the one that opened this book: that of a terrified eighteen-month-old separated by hospital authorities from her parents, who stand helplessly by. For the children of the nation, and the millions of adults whose lives are connected to their care, it matters profoundly which of these becomes the central example in the next few decades. The scholars and social critics who warn of the demise of parental authority are in one sense right. As school systems, hospitals, and social service agencies become larger, more complex, and more specialized, it's easy for an individual parent to feel smaller, weaker, and less significant. And as scientific research deepens our knowledge about child development and sharpens our society's desire for "ideal child-rearing," it's easy for individual parents to feel increasingly guilty, inadequate, and incompetent.

If this is the way we're going as a society, it is entirely the wrong way. Our human destinies are profoundly dependent upon the power of millions of parents to nurture their children, to stave off harm and to fight for their children. Our policies, institutions, agencies, and government ought to be vibrant with respect for the power of parents — power both personal and social.

This is an attainable goal. Professionals serving children and families are changing. Among school superintendents implementing the Education for All Handicapped Children Act or pediatricians caring for sick babies in hospitals, there is a new respect for the rights of parents as partners. Over the past decade, in different levels of government, new policies and laws have been designed to ensure that parents play decisive roles in the services their children need. These programs do not yet form a national policy of parent responsiveness in children's services. But over time, they could.

Most important, in the grass-roots organizations that exist now and will be organized in the future, parents have both the opportunity and the ability to establish power and claim a decisive role as a natural right. Reflecting on the many things I have heard from parent advocates, I propose five recommendations for directions in programs, policies, and parent actions.

1. *Schools, hospitals, and social agencies should develop a greater emphasis on parent responsiveness.*

The natural ambition of pediatric wards, special-education

programs, and children's protective services is and ought to be continually improved capacity for meeting the needs of children. But that struggle too often takes place within an organizational framework that shuts parents out. And too often it is sluggish and uninspired, with far too much acceptance of either the risk or the reality of serious harm to children.

Services to help children must be designed and organized to be enormously open to parents. Flexibility, easy-going sharing, and humor are features of self-help that professionally organized services would do well to adopt. But openness requires parent access to information, explanations, data, and real opportunities to influence the policies and standard operating practices of services. It also requires respect for parents' needs for both physical and psychological proximity to their children. Parent responsiveness means that children's services will be conceptualized in consultation with parents, and that the design includes deliberate emphasis on parent choice and parent influence over decision making in the guiding policies. Finally, it means that mechanisms such as access to and influence over the economic resources that are the life-blood of the institution will be established to keep those services open and responsive to parent advocacy.

Since the 1960s, some new services to children have been organized and operated in this way. The Head Start program, once a pilot demonstration and now a model national comprehensive child-development program, is an example. Any advocate of greater institutional responsiveness to parents should examine the model it offers to other children's services. Day-care services like the ones sponsored by FOCAL often furnish other, very creative strategies for parent responsiveness. In addition, fundamental organizational changes aimed at introducing greater openness to parents have been made in some of the older, more established services during the 1970s. Childbirth, pediatric hospitalization, some educational services, and institutionalized care for severely retarded and mentally ill children have in many cases been transformed by sustained advocacy. Authorities now ask rather than just tell parents what choices can be made for a baby's birth, promote rather than flatly prohibit parents' rooming in with a hospitalized child, support rather than suppress the rights of a retarded or handicapped child to a full, equal educational opportunity — and the rights of parents to fight for the realization of those opportunities.

My recommendations in this area are strongest when the children reached by government or professional help are either preschool and preadolescent children or adolescents with serious intellectual or emotional impairments. As children enter and move through adolescence, of course, they need gradually to assume more responsibility for their own lives. They need gradually to acquire a stronger voice in shaping policies and programs. Professionals need to accord adolescents an even larger role in decisions about their own health, education, and well-being. The triad of parent-professional-adolescent is among the most difficult for institutions to be responsive to; it is perhaps the most challenging, sensitive situation in the helping services. But it is also one that the Candlelighters routinely face when their teenaged children are undergoing treatment; that parents of moderately retarded or mildly autistic adolescents deal with when decisions are made about employment or independent living; that mothers and fathers in divorce confront when choices have to be made about custody. Some interesting and innovative proposals for opening up institutions to both parents and teens are in development within parent advocacy organizations. Here I recommend strongly that professionals seek out parent groups and look for creative ways to delicately balance the triads which occur during adolescence.

Critics of the emphasis on openness point out that many parents do not exercise the rights they have now. Many parents, they say, do not care to influence and shape the services their children receive. That may be so. But services to children should still be designed so that parents have the right to do so, when they decide it matters. All Americans have the right to free assembly, but not everyone organizes public meetings or marches. And if the right to vote were contingent on 90 percent participation in each election year, we would all have lost it years ago. As this book clearly shows, many parents are ready to exercise those rights, and to work with parent-responsive services. To achieve that goal, they spend their days in persistent struggle. They shouldn't have to.

2. *Relationships between parent and professionals should be reestablished around assumptions of equality and tolerance.* Stripped of all the rhetoric, the relationship between a parent and a teacher, social worker, or physician is simply between two adult human beings who happen to be drawn together by a child. It would help enormously if most parents and most professionals saw it that way rather than as some over-mystified and convoluted relationship. A general acceptance that most adults raising and caring for children make mistakes would also benefit us all. The tolerance, empathy, and honesty that parents show to one another within self-help groups will probably never fully characterize parent-professional relationships. But some fresh, liberating winds are blowing us in that direction, and we ought to move with them enthusiastically.

How to get from here to there? Parents need to continue doing just what this book describes: depending on ourselves, making demands on the system, fighting for our children. When this occurs, parents feel more equal and more confident. Eventually we begin behaving as if we are equal partners, whether the professional dealing with us thinks so or not (eventually many do). Parents should avoid the pitfall of blaming professionals for what really is a system-wide problem. As one activist pointed out to me, "Lots of teachers have their own children. That makes them parents too. And they face the same problems when they go to their children's schools."

For their part, professionals ought to listen to what parents are really expressing when we denounce a program's failures, confront professionals, or bring lawsuits. Our anger is motivated by the extraordinarily powerful responsibility parents feel for children. It makes no sense to bemoan the diminishing sense of responsibility among parents, on the one hand, and then upbraid those parents whose sense of responsibility has propelled them into what too many professionals like to call "neurotic pushiness." If professionals really want to encourage strong bonding between parent and child, as they often claim, they need to tolerate and even encourage parental "neurotic pushiness."

Better training for professionals is crucial. Increasingly, teachers and health professionals are trained to be sensitive to a child's needs. But very few teacher or pediatric training programs try to broaden the students' understanding that parents also have needs, that teachers, doctors, and nurses sometimes relate to parents in ways that diminish parents' sense of worth, and that other, healthier ways of collaborating are possible. Parent self-help and advocacy groups provide a resource for the planners of this kind of training. Beyond that, both parents and professionals need training to understand the new partnership roles that are emerging for parents in the human service professions: co-evaluator and member of the educational team developing the Individual Education Program (IEP); consultant to the treatment team in pediatric cancer services; co-signer to contracts designed to improve the safety and well-being of the child in child-welfare services; member of parent policy or advisory councils with responsibility for approving budgets, grant applications, and personnel decisions; co-leader of parent education courses; co-therapist in groups of parents struggling with severe stress. These new partnerships are scattered now across the country, more strongly within some services than in others. They have the potential of becoming a much more dominant feature of children's services in the 1980s.

3. *The relationship between parents and government should be seen as complex and sensitive, but also quite positive.*

Parent self-help and advocacy is both a rejection and an affirmation of government. Lincoln's description of the purpose of government, "to do for a community of people whatever they need to have done, but cannot do at all in their separate and individual capacities," has strong concurrence from parent advocates. Their affirmation of this objective is infused by an understanding of government as an expression of the will of the people.

Government is frequently painted as an opponent of the rights of parents. In balancing child rights and parent rights, say some critics, government too often throws its weight toward the child, inevitably increasing the distance between parents and their children. At the extremes of this view, government looms like some powerful monster, scaring parents into submission. The parents I listened to have, for the most part, a different attitude. They are not frightened. They are clearly not submissive. Most feel strongly that government should function for the well-being of the people and that parents *can* make government function for them.

At the same time, parent activists are refusing to accept government that doesn't work well either for children or for themselves. Self-help itself is a turning aside from more impersonal government-funded services to create warm and caring communities. Of course, government funds, as in the case of Parents Anonymous, can be a modest support to the increased emergence of self-help groups in many communities around the nation. Beyond self-help, the resolute advocacy of parent activists, their mastery of legislative process, their acquisition of the skills needed to negotiate bureaucratic agreements, and their widescale networks reflect an unwillingness to put up with ineffective government.

Government can do its part to support a positive relationship with parents. First, government can listen in many ways. Consulting with organized groups of parents at critical points in the development of public policy is one. Sponsoring surveys to ask individual parents their views on policy issues and incorporating the results of those studies into policy formulation is another.

Government policy makers can also structure laws and regulations so that they strengthen the rights of parents in services delivered to children. Specifically, this means inserting into laws and regulations language that strengthens the rights of (1) parental access to children, and to information collected about them; (2) direct, regular personal interaction between parents and the professionals involved with their children; (3) parental involvement in making the decisions that affect children; and (4) parental oversight of the policies and administrative practices that ultimately shape those services.

Governmental support for the rights of parents must be exercised, however, with a view to assuring the well-being of all citizens. The constitutional rights of some parents should not be pushed aside in order to enhance the rights of others. And government cannot violate some fundamental rights of the child — the right to protection from physical abuse, for example — simply to strengthen parental authority. Here, at the intersection of competing values, the relationship between parents and government becomes sensitive, sometimes painful. At this intersection, advice from parent self-help and advocacy groups can profitably be sought. Effective reconciliation of child rights with parent rights, after all, is a major, daily task of parenting.

4. *Parent activists ought to consider greater coalescence in advocating public policies that benefit children.*

For the diverse parent groups working to make government more responsive to them, connectedness with each other matters tremendously. Coalitions among different groups of parents of handicapped children have proven their worth. Other such coalitions should be considered. Policies affecting children often involve the interests of many of the parent groups described in this book, but parent activists seem not to recognize this. Take, for example, the Adoption Assistance and Child Welfare Act, passed in 1980 by the United States Congress. Designed to stimulate reform of the foster-care and adoption systems, this bill — even with the strong advocacy of committed congressional supporters like Representative George Miller — took over four years to reach the point of final approval. The lack of a broad-based active constituency to demand this legislation in every congressional district slowed its progress considerably. Yet almost every parent group discussed here could have mobilized to support the new policies it represents. Of course, adoptive parents' groups did work hard to support this law, which reemphasizes preventive services over foster-care placements and adoption over lengthy, multiple foster-care arrangements. But since the current response to child abuse is often immediate separation of the child and placement in foster care, Parents Anonymous also had a stake in the successful passage of the act. Many of the children waiting for adoption are handicapped and therefore judged as "unadoptable" by some child-placing agencies. Some of these children are not receiving the services rightfully theirs under the Education for All Handicapped Children Act. In fact, they cannot even be found counted in state censuses of handicapped children.

Since each state's count affects the appropriations for the Education for All Handicapped Children program, parents of handicapped children could claim an interest in this bill, which mandates a nationwide count of children in foster care. The Sisterhood of Black Single Mothers was also affected, for black children of single mothers disproportionately end up in foster care. Fathers United for Equal Justice can also support reform of the foster-care system, for there have been instances when judges, faced with mothers unable to assume custody of their children, place children with foster others rather than with their biological fathers. Finally, Title I parents find that when children are returned to the community from institutionalized foster care, they often end up in Title I schools. The Adoption Assistance and Child Welfare Act was a legislative excursion outside the concentration of most Title I parents in the educational system. But it's an excursion that matters.

Similar opportunities for effective parent coalescence exist in policy issues related to effective and accessible preventive child health services, better day-care opportunities, and improved tax policies affecting families. The possibilities are inviting, and they can be realized in the 1980s if parents choose to do so.

5. *Individual parents ought to make themselves aware of the very real choices and alternatives offered by parent self-help and advocacy organizations.*

I hope that parents who read this book will decide that they no longer have to accept intolerable or inadequate situations for their children.

This doesn't mean that all parents should see organized self-help or advocacy as another mandatory responsibility of parenting. Many parents now mobilize personal or family resources in order to protect and nurture their children and find that this suffices. I would be saddened if individual parents who choose not to involve themselves in the kind of activism described in this book felt guilty or less adequate as a consequence of that choice.

The great value of self-help and advocacy organizations, for us as individual parents, is simply that these groups are there. Most of us raising children may not now need a group like

Children in Hospitals, or the Association for Children with Learning Disabilities, or the National Federation of Parents for Drug-Free Youth. But none of us can ever be sure that we won't need the support that such groups offer at some point in our lives as parents. I hope it heartens parents to know that these organizations do exist.

Most of all, if truly helpful resources do not exist now in our communities, we can organize our own. The clearest message of the parents I listened to was this: When we need help and it's not there, we can organize our own.

Appendix
Parent Self-Help
and Advocacy Organizations

Notes

Bibiliography

Index

Appendix
Parent Self-Help and Advocacy Organizations

Note: These are local, state, or national organizations whose membership is primarily made up of parents, and/or whose board of directors or steering committees are chiefly parents. Those national or state organizations that have local units and chapters are marked with an asterisk (*). Those groups discussed in this book are marked with a cross (+).

+ * ASSOCIATION OF CHILDREN WITH LEARNING DISABILITIES (ACLD)

   4156 Library Road
   Pittsburgh, Pennsylvania 15234
   412-341-1515

   ACLD is a "nonprofit organization whose purpose is to advance the education and general welfare of children of normal or potentially normal intelligence who have learning disabilities of a perceptual, conceptual or coordinative nature."

+ BLACK PARENTS FOR QUALITY EDUCATION

   Detroit, Michigan
   313-934-7721

   Black Parents for Quality Education is a citywide organization dedicated to improving the quality of Detroit's educational system.

+ * CANDLELIGHTERS

   123 C Street, S.E.
   Washington, D.C. 20003
   202-544-1696

   A national organization of parents of children with cancer,

Candlelighters includes other family members as well, and provides for mutual support and legislative action designed to improve research and treatment of childhood cancer.

+ CHILDREN IN HOSPITALS, INC. (CIH)
31 Wilshire Park
Needham, Massachusetts 02192

An organization that seeks to educate the public about the needs of children and parents for "continued and ample contact" when either is hospitalized, and encourages hospitals to adopt flexible visiting policies and provide live-in accommodations whenever possible.

* COMPASSIONATE FRIENDS, INC.
P.O. Box 1347
Oak Brook, Illinois 60521

A self-help and mutual-support group for bereaved parents.

FAMILIES ANONYMOUS
P.O. Box 344
Torrance, California 90501
213-775-3211

A mutual-support group for families of juveniles with behavioral, drug, or alcohol-related problems.

+ * FATHERS UNITED FOR EQUAL JUSTICE
339 Auburn Street
Auburndale (Newton), Massachusetts 02156
617-965-5460

FUEJ is an organization that provides guidance and mutual support to fathers before, during, and after divorce and custody proceedings. FUEJ also works for reform of divorce laws and legislative and court actions that promote joint child custody arrangements.

Many similar groups operate under different names in numerous communities in the country.

+ * FEDERATION FOR CHILDREN WITH SPECIAL NEEDS
Suite 347
120 Boylston Street
Boston, Massachusetts 02116
617-482-2915

An association of Massachusetts parent organizations representing children with various disabilities, which "offers help to individual parents and also strengthens the 'Parent Power' of the member groups."

* INTERNATIONAL ASSOCIATION OF PARENTS OF THE DEAF (IAPD)

   814 Thayer Avenue
   Silver Springs, Maryland 20910
   301-585-5400

   An international organization that helps put parents of deaf children in touch with each other, encourages mutual support among parents, and works for legislative and other changes in public policy that favor the participation of deaf children in educational services, TV captioning, TT-Y telephone communications, and other opportunities.

* LA LECHE LEAGUE INTERNATIONAL

   9616 Minneapolis Avenue
   Franklin Park, Illinois 60131
   312-455-7730

   An international organization of parents who provide information and support to mothers who are breast-feeding their babies.

+* MOTHERS AGAINST DRUNK DRIVERS (MADD)

   P.O. Box HC
   Fair Oaks, California 95628
   916-966-7433

   MADD is directed primarily by parents whose children have been killed or injured in alcohol-related car crashes; however, it is also a citizen's organization whose membership comprises both other relatives of victims and a variety of individuals concerned about drunk driving. MADD works for stronger anti-drunk-driving laws at the federal, state, and local levels, and educates the public about driving under the influence of alcohol. Many local groups help bereaved parents with practical support and referrals to mutual-help organizations and counseling services.

+* MOTHERS' CENTER DEVELOPMENT PROJECT

   129 Jackson Street
   Hempstead, New York 11550
   516-486-6614 in New York State
   800-645-3828 elsewhere

   This project disseminates information nationally about the

Mothers' Center described in this book and helps parents form "a community program where women/mothers, in conjunction with members of the professional community, provide services, research and advocacy on mothering, pregnancy, childbirth and health care."

+* NATIONAL COALITION OF ESEA TITLE I PARENTS
The Parent Center, Suite 520
1341 G Street, N.W.
Washington, D.C. 20005
202-638-5466

The National Coalition provides a voice at federal, state, and local levels for parents of children eligible for federally funded educational services for economically disadvantaged children. The Coalition also brings parents together for workshops and training conferences and distributes information which helps parents in local communities design and carry out an advisory role.

+* NATIONAL FEDERATION OF PARENTS FOR DRUG-FREE YOUTH (NFP)
P.O. Box 722
Silver Spring, Maryland 20901
301-649-7100

NFP is a national association of several thousand local parent groups dedicated to preventing drug use in young people and freeing adolescents from dependency on drugs. It works for stronger antidrug laws at the federal and state levels and supports the formation of parent peer groups (and combined parent-community leadership action) at the local level. Many local groups offer parent-to-parent mutual support around issues related to adolescence and drugs.

* NATIONAL ORGANIZATION OF MOTHERS OF TWINS CLUBS
5402 Amberwood Lane
Rockville, Maryland 20853
301-460-9108

An organization that provides information and encourages mutual support among mothers of twins.

+* NATIONAL SOCIETY FOR AUTISTIC CHILDREN (NSAC)
Suite 1017
1234 Massachusetts Avenue, N.W.
Washington, D.C. 20005
202-783-0125

NSAC is "an organization of parents, professionals and other interested citizens working together to bring into being programs of legislation, education and research for the benefit of all children with severe behavior disorders." Organized primarily by parents, NSAC's membership at present is primarily comprised of parents, and its board of directors is totally made up of parents of autistic children.

+ * NORTH AMERICAN COUNCIL ON ADOPTABLE CHILDREN (NACAC)

Suite 229
1346 Connecticut Avenue, N.W.
Washington, D.C. 20036
202-466-7570

NACAC is a national federation of local and state citizens' groups that serves "as a voice for waiting children and adoptive families." NACAC works for legislative and other activities that ensure legal adoptive placement of every child eligible for adoption, provides information and support during the adoption process and after placement, and speaks for the rights of children in foster care to permanent homes.

+ * PARENTS ANONYMOUS (PA)

Suite 208
22330 Hawthorne Boulevard
Torrance, California 90505
213-371-3501
Toll-free: 800-421-0353
California toll-free: 800-352-0386

A self-help group for persons with child-abuse problems, which strongly encourages mutual support and provides a toll-free telephone service for parents seeking information or help.

+ * PARENTS' CAMPAIGN FOR HANDICAPPED CHILDREN AND YOUTH

Box 1492
Washington, D.C. 20013

The Parents' Campaign for Handicapped Children and Youth is an "organization of parents dedicated to working for the right of handicapped individuals to be full participants in the mainstream of society." The Parents' Campaign distributes information about education for handicapped children under federal and state law and about other rights to equal opportunity.

Parents Concerned for Hospitalized Children (PCHC), an organization described in this book, was organized in 1972 and worked actively for changes in the hospital practices regarding pediatric stays. In May 1980, owing to expanding commitments of its founding parents to employment and graduate school, PCHC was dissolved.

+ * THE PARENTS' NETWORK

National Committee for Citizens in Education (NCCE)
410 Wilde Lake Village Green
Columbia, Maryland 21044
301-997-9300
Toll-free: 800-NETWORK

The Parents' Network is a project of the National Committee for Citizens in Education (NCCE) which links together and provides information to state and local parent-citizen groups working to improve public schools.

+ PARENTS' UNION FOR PUBLIC SCHOOLS

Room 704
401 N. Broad Street
Philadelphia, Pennsylvania 19108
215-574-0337

Parents' Union is a "city-wide independent organization *of, by* and *for* parents" which focuses on school system-wide issues such as the budget, desegregation, discipline, special education, and reading.

* PARENTS WITHOUT PARTNERS INTERNATIONAL (PWP)

7910 Woodmont Avenue
Bethesda, Maryland 20014
301-654-8850

A self-help group for single parents. Encourages mutual support and practical assistance among single parents.

+ SISTERHOOD OF BLACK SINGLE MOTHERS

1360 Fulton Street (Room 423)
Brooklyn, New York 11216
212-638-0413

The Sisterhood is a "self-help organization comprised of Black Women who are raising their children alone." Encourages mutual support and practical assistance among Black single mothers.

* SUDDEN INFANT DEATH SYNDROME FOUNDATION

310 S. Michigan Avenue
Chicago, Illinois 60604
312-663-0650

A national organization that provides information and mutual support to parents whose infants have died unexpectedly and apparently without cause, a disease diagnosed as "sudden infant death syndrome."

Notes

1: THE SHARED EXPERIENCE

1. "From Colorado," *Frontiers,* Winter 1975.
2. Schuchard, Marsha Keith, "The Family Versus the Drug Culture." Presentation given to the Southeast Drug Conference, May 25, 1978.
3. Newsletter of Children in Hospitals, Winter 1976, p. 5.
4. Dr. Mary Jo Bane cogently makes this point in *Here to Stay: American Families in the Twentieth Century* (New York: Basic Books, 1976), p. 50.
5. "The Net Spreads Out," Newsletter of the National Society for Autistic Children, September 1978.
6. "Happy Ending Dept.," ACLD Newsbriefs, Spring 1980, p. 8.
7. Manatt, Marsha, *Parents, Peers and Pot* (Rockville, Maryland: National Institute on Drug Abuse, 1981), p. 8.
8. Roos, Philip, "Parents of Mentally Retarded Children — Misunderstood and Mistreated," in Turnbull, Ann, and Turnbull, H. Rutherford, *Parents Speak Out: Growing With a Handicapped Child* (Columbus, Ohio: Charles E. Merrill, 1978), p. 13.
9. International Childbirth Education Association, *Father Participation Guide* (Milwaukee, Wisconsin: ICEA, 1975), pp. 1–12.
10. Personal conversation with James Levine, co-director, The Fatherhood Project, Bank Street College of Education, New York, New York, December 1981.
11. Yarrow, Leah, "When My Baby Was Born," *Parents,* Vol. 57, No. 8, August 1982, pp. 43–48.
12. Children's Defense Fund, *Children Out of School in America* (Washington, D.C.: Children's Defense Fund, 1974), p. 93.
13. Gliedman, John, and Roth, William, *The Unexpected Minority: Handicapped Children in America* (New York: Harcourt, Brace, Jovanovich, 1980), p. 181.

14. *Better Health For Our Children: A National Strategy,* the report of the Select Panel for the Promotion of Child Health, Vol. 2, p. 72.
15. "Characteristics of State Adoption Assistance Programs," unpublished data prepared by CSR-Creative Associates, January 1982.
16. Ibid.
17. Newsletter of Children in Hospitals, Spring 1978.
18. O'Leary, Elizabeth, "Survey of Psychosocial Policies and Programs in Hospitals," Association for the Care of Children's Health, 1982.
19. "Highlights for Student Drug Use in America, 1974-1981" (Washington, D.C.: National Institute on Drug Abuse, 1981).
20. "The War Against Drunk Drivers," *Newsweek,* September 13, 1982, pp. 34-39.

2: A HISTORY OF PARENT ACTIVISM

1. Ravitch, Diane, *The Great School Wars: New York City, 1805-1973* (New York: Basic Books, 1974), p. 217. See also Tyack, David, *The One Best System: A History of American Urban Education* (Cambridge: Harvard University Press, 1974), p. 250; and Rothman, Sheila, *Women's Proper Place* (New York: Basic Books, 1978), pp. 165-170, for good descriptions of parent activism and the Gary Plan.
2. Ravitch, *Great School Wars,* p. 139.
3. *60 Years of Parent Involvement* (New York: United Parents' Associations of New York City, Inc., 1977).
4. Ibid.
5. Billingsley, Andrew, and Giovanni, Jeanne, *Children of the Storm* (New York: Harcourt, Brace, Jovanovich, 1972), and Lightfoot, Sara Lawrence, *Worlds Apart: The Relationships Between Families and Schools* (New York: Basic Books, 1978). See also Aptheker, Herbert, *A Documentary History of the Negro People in the United States* (New Jersey: Citadel Press, 1973) for numerous examples of Black parents' efforts to secure education for their children before the Civil War. Bremner, Robert, *Children and Youth in America: A Documentary History* (Cambridge: Harvard University Press, 1970-74) also offers examples of Black-established schools as early as the beginning of the nineteenth century.

6. Lightfoot, *Worlds Apart*, pp. 149-151.
7. Until the twentieth century, fathers were presumed to have the primary right to custody.
8. See Rothman, Sheila, *Woman's Proper Place*, Chapter 3, "The Ideology of Educated Motherhood," and Chapter 4, "The Politics of Protection," as well as Schlossman, Steven, "Before Home Start: Notes Toward a History of Parent Education in America, 1897-1929," *Harvard Educational Review*, Vol. 46, No. 3, August 1976.
9. Adams, Margaret. "Mental Retardation, The Historical Background to Services," in Wortis, Joseph, *Mental Retardation*, Vols. 1-4. (New York: Grune and Stratton, 1972). I am also grateful here to Elizabeth Boggs, one of the founders of the National Association for Retarded Citizens, who gave me hours of personal interviews and much literature helpful to understanding the history of organizing by parents of retarded children.
10. United States Public Health Service, "Two Hundred Years of Child Health in America," in Grotberg, Edith, *200 Years of Children* (Washington, D.C.: Department of Health, Education and Welfare, 1976), p. 107. See also Boggs, Elizabeth, "Federal Legislation Affecting the Mentally Retarded, 1955-67: An Historical Overview," in Wortis, *Mental Retardation*, Vol. 3, and "Federal Legislation, 1966-71," in Vol. 4.
11. Good, H. G., *A History of American Education* (New York: MacMillan, 1962), p. 581.
12. See Gliedman, John, and Roth, William, *The Unexpected Minority: Handicapped Children in America* (New York: Harcourt, Brace, Jovanovich, 1980), and Friedman, Paul, *The Rights of Mentally Retarded Persons* (New York: Avon Books, 1976) for a fuller discussion of these precedent-setting lawsuits. I am also grateful to Elizabeth Boggs for sharing with me her observations on this period of activity in advocacy for the retarded.
13. Geer, William, "New Era for Special Education," in Grotberg, E., *200 Years of Child Health*, Chapter 10 (Washington, D.C.: U.S. Superintendent of Documents, 1976), p. 204.
14. Moore, Emily, *Women and Health: United States 1980*. Supplement to September-October 1980 issue, *Public Health Reports*, p. 57.
15. Klingberg, Marcus A., Avaramovici, Armand, and Chemke, Jan, *Drugs and Fetal Development* (New York: Plenum Press, 1972). See also Chamberlain, Geoffrey, *The Safety of the Unborn Child* (New York: Penguin, 1970).
16. See, for example, Karmel, Marjorie, *Thank You, Dr. Lamaze*

(New York: Doubleday, 1965). The La Leche League was founded in 1958 as a self-help and mutual-support group. Despite the protestation in its literature of willingness to obey doctors' instructions and repeated exhortations to mothers to "check with the doctor," the La Leche League and the movement toward breast-feeding was very much parent-dominated. A few pediatricians publicly endorsed breast-feeding and the work of the La Leche League during its early years, but the intent of the founders was to establish groups where mothers could teach each other the skills and the practical tips needed to breast-feed successfully. Pediatricians were typically ignorant about these tips, which in societies less hostile to breast-feeding were passed on from mother to daughter. The La Leche League also intended mothers to offer each other encouragement and support (again, something which was often not forthcoming, particularly in La Leche's early years, from either professionals or immediate family). However, the organization appears to have been almost entirely devoted to self-help and mutual aid, eschewing advocacy for institutional change or even case advocacy. Some of the mothers interviewed for this book referred to the La Leche League as the place where they had "gotten started" in respecting their own judgment, even when their own "mother wit" did not enjoy the support of professional opinion. Although breast-feeding became more of an activist issue with the well-publicized lawsuit brought by Linda Eaton, the firefighter who was dismissed for breast-feeding her infant while on duty, the rights of nursing mothers to sustain both employment and lactation have not been sought through organized activity sponsored by the La Leche League. Because of its concentration on self-help and mutual aid, the League as it functions today was not explored in depth in this book. Neither was the leadership of childbirth education organizations. These organizations support parental influence over hospital childbirth policies and practices, and advocate careful choices by consumers of both physicians and hospitals. The newsletters of the International Childbirth Education Association also describe lawsuits and other activist measures designed to speed up hospitals' progress toward fathers' participation in labor and delivery, or the right of mothers and infants to be kept together immediately after birth. But the major purpose of ICEA is educational, and its leadership includes both professionals and parents. The leaders of ICEA, when I first asked to interview them, claimed that the organization had been founded by and represented combined professional and parent effort. Consequently, it fell outside the scope of this book.

17. Klaus, Marshall, and Kennell, John, "Labor, Birth and Bonding," in Klaus and Kennell, *Parent-Infant Bonding* (St. Louis: C. V. Mosby, 1982), p. 22.
18. Ibid.
19. "Aroused Parents Declare War on the System," *U.S. News and World Report,* September 10, 1979.
20. "SAT Scores and College Plans of High School Seniors," in National Center for Education Statistics, *Digest of Education Statistics, 1980* (Washington, D.C.: Government Printing Office, 1980), p. 67.
21. "Average scores of students on international achievement tests, by field of study: United States and selected foreign countries, 1970," in National Center for Education Statistics, *Digest,* p. 217.
22. "Estimated expenditures of educational institutions, by source of funds: United States, 1969-70 to 1979-80," in National Center for Education Statistics, *Digest,* p. 21.
23. "Estimated average annual salary of classroom teachers in public elementary and secondary schools: United States, 1955-56 to 1978-79," in National Center for Education Statistics, *Digest,* p. 56.
24. "Selected characteristics of public school teachers, by level and by sex, United States, 1975-76," in National Center for Education Statistics, *Digest,* p. 55.
25. Breneman, David, and Nelson, Susan, "Education and Training," in Pechman, Joseph (ed.), *Setting National Priorities: Agenda for the 1980s* (Washington, D.C.: Brookings Institution, 1980), pp. 205-247.
26. Jones, Philip, and Jones, Susan, *Parents Unite! The Complete Guide for Shaking Up Your Children's School* (Ridgefield, Connecticut: Wyden Books, 1976), p. 81.
27. "Number and Size of Public School Systems," in National Center for Education Statistics, *Digest,* p. 61.
28. Ibid.
29. Fernandez, Happy, "Empowering Parents," Part 1, *The Urban Review: Issues and Ideas in Public Education,* Vol. II, No. 2, Summer 1979. Ms. Fernandez cites Guthrie, J. W., Thomason, D. K., and Craig, P. A., "The Erosion of Lay Control," *Public Testimony on Public Schools* (Columbia, Maryland: National Committee for Citizens in Education, 1976), pp. 92-94.
30. "The People Look at Their School Boards," report of a Gallup Poll conducted for the National School Boards Association, cited in Jones, *Parents Unite!,* p. 31.
31. "Results of public school bond elections: United States, 1957-58

to 1976-77," in National Center for Education Statistics, *Digest,* p. 72.
32. "Amid Discontent, Private Schools Are Booming," *U.S. News and World Report,* September 10, 1979, p. 40.
33. Jones, *Parents Unite!,* p. 7.
34. Davies, Don, *Schools Where Parents Make a Difference* (Boston: Institute for Responsive Education, 1976), p. 8.
35. Ibid, p. 8.
36. Rioux, William, et al., *You Can Improve Your Child's School* (New York: Simon and Schuster, 1980), p. 108.

3: IMAGES OF PARENTS

1. See Clark, Kenneth, *Dark Ghetto* (New York: Harper and Row, 1965), and Friedan, Betty, *The Feminine Mystique* (New York: Norton, 1963), for two examples of this kind of literature.
2. Handlin, Oscar and Mary, *Facing Life: Youth and Family in American History* (Boston: Little, Brown, 1971); Mencher, S., *Poor Law to Poverty Program* (Pittsburgh: University of Pittsburgh Press, 1967); Platt, Anthony, *The Child Savers* (Chicago: University of Chicago Press, 1961).
3. Bourne, William O., *History of the Public School Society of New York* (New York, 1870), excerpted in Bremner, Robert, *Children and Youth in America: A Documentary History,* Vol. 1 (Cambridge: Harvard University Press, 1970-74), p. 254.
4. Address of DeWitt Clinton, first president of the Public School Society, 1805, excerpted in Bremner, *Children and Youth,* Vol. 1, p. 257.
5. Educating Black children up until the Civil War was in some areas of the country a legally punishable offense. After Emancipation, particularly in the late nineteenth century, attitudes changed, and although segregated education was the primary form of public schooling advocated for Black and Native American children, advocacy even for this was at times built on images of Incompetent Parents that are much more florid than the images applied to other impoverished parents, such as immigrants. Native American children, for example, were considered educable. However, the incompetence of Native American parents was judged so utterly "irredeemable" that boarding schools were instituted as an absolute necessity to save Indian children from their "savage parents." Consider the words of an Indian school superintendent in 1885, arguing for boarding-school education: "The barbarian child of barbarian parents spends a possible six of the twenty-four hours

of the day in the school room. Here he is taught the rudiments of the books, varied perhaps by fragmentary lessons in the good manners of the superior race to which his teacher belongs. He returns at the close of his day-school to eat and play and sleep after the savage fashion of his race." (Oberly, John H., "Report of the Indian School Superintendent, 1885," in "Annual Report of the Commissioner of Indian Affairs for 1885," Washington, D.C., 1885, pp. cxi-cxiii; excerpted in Bremner, *Children and Youth,* Vol. 2, p. 1352.) See also Tyack, David, *The One Best System: A History of American Urban Education* (Cambridge: Harvard University Press, 1974), pp. 109–125, for a discussion of the exclusion of Blacks from white schools and of the white perception of universal public education as a right of childhood.
6. "Memorial to the Legislature of New York...on the subject of erecting a House of Refuge," New York Society for the Reformation of Juvenile Delinquents, 1824, excerpted in Bremner, *Children and Youth,* Vol. 1, p. 679.
7. See, for example, Billingsley, Andrew, and Giovanni, Jeanne, *Children of the Storm: Black Children and American Child Welfare* (New York: Harcourt, Brace, Jovanovich, 1972) for further analyses of the exclusion of Black children from nineteenth-century established child-welfare services.
8. Handlin, *Facing Life.* See also Goodman, L. V., "Tending the Melting Pot," in Grotberg, Edith, *200 Years of Children,* Chapter 4 (Washington, D.C.: United States Department of Health, Education and Welfare, 1976).
9. Goodman, "Tending the Melting Pot," p. 175.
10. *New York Daily Times,* June 28, 1853, excerpted in Bremner, *Children and Youth,* Vol. 1, page 417. See also Platt, Anthony, *The Child Savers: The Invention of Delinquency* (Chicago: University of Chicago Press, 1969) for a well-documented study of the middle-class discovery of the urban slums during this period in American history, and the subsequent "child-saving" movement.
11. United States Public Health Service, "Two Hundred Years of Child Health," in Grotberg, *200 Years of Children,* p. 79.
12. Baker, Josephine, *Fighting for Life* (New York: MacMillan, 1938), cited in Bremner, *Children and Youth,* Vol. 2, p. 16.
13. Philopedos, pseud. (An Ex Dispensary Doctor), "A Few Remarks About Sick Children in New York, and the Necessity of a Hospital For Them," New York, 1852. Children's Hospital of Philadelphia, *Constitution and By-laws,* Philadelphia, 1856. Both references are excerpted in Bremner, Vol. 1, pp. 797–799.
14. Palmer, Alice Freeman, *Why Go To College* (Boston, 1897), p. 23, cited in Rothman, Sheila, *Woman's Proper Place* (New York: Basic Books, 1978), p. 108.

15. United States Public Health Service, "Two Hundred Years of Child Health," pp. 83-85. See also Rothman, *Woman's Proper Place,* pp. 151-53, for a discussion of Sheppard-Towner.
16. Boone, Mary Stanley, "The Kindergarten from a Mother's Point of View," *Education,* Vol. 25, November 1904, p. 143, cited in Rothman, *Woman's Proper Place,* p. 97.
17. Schlossman, Steven, "Before Home Start: Notes Toward a History of Parent Education in America, 1897-1929," *Harvard Educational Review,* Vol. 46, No. 3, August 1976.
18. See Rothman, *Woman's Proper Place.*
19. Ross, Catherine J., "Early Skirmishes with Poverty: The Historical Roots of Head Start," in Zigler, Edward, and Valentine, Jeanette, *Project Head Start: A Legacy of the War on Poverty* (New York: Free Press, 1979), p. 27.
20. Report of the New York State Commission on Relief for Widowed Mothers Transmitted to the Legislature, March 27, 1914, in Abbott, Grace, *The Child and the State,* Vol. 3 (Chicago: University of Chicago Press, 1938), pp. 251-254.
21. "The Special Committee on Widows' Pensions of the New York Neighborhood Workers' Association," in Abbott, *Child and State,* p. 253.
22. Abbott, p. 230.
23. Abbott, pp. 249-261.
24. U.S. Public Health Service, "Two Hundred Years of Child Health," p. 86.
25. Ibid., p. 87.
26. Ibid., p. 96.
27. "Parental Rights and the Amendment According to the Manufacturers Records," taken from the *Manufacturers Record* (September 11, 1924), excerpted in Abbott, *The Child and the State,* Vol. 1, pp. 231-234.
28. Ibid.; also, U.S. Public Health Service, "Two Hundred Years of Child Health," pp. 83-84.
29. Kilpatrick, James, "Another Family Squabble," *Washington Post,* March 11, 1980.
30. *Los Angeles Times,* February 1980.
31. Lasch, Christopher, *The Culture of Narcissism* (New York: W. W. Norton, 1979), p. 291.
32. Keniston, Kenneth, and the Carnegie Council on Children, *All Our Children: The American Family Under Pressure* (New York: Harcourt, Brace, Jovanovich, 1977), pp. 17-18.
33. Snapper, Kurt, "The American Legacy," in Grotberg, *Two Hundred Years of Children,* p. 26.
34. Goodman, L. V., "Tending the Melting Pot" in Grotberg, *Two*

Hundred Years of Children, p. 175. See also Tyack, *The One Best System,* for an interesting discussion of the urban schools' attempts to deal with multilingual realities in some typical classrooms, including some early attempts at bilingual education.
35. "Illiteracy of the population, by State: 1900 to 1970," in National Center for Education Statistics, *Digest,* p. 19.
36. Tyler, Ralph, "Tomorrow's Education," in Grotberg, *Two Hundred Years of Children,* p. 207.
37. Howell, Mary, *Helping Ourselves: Families and the Human Network* (Boston: Beacon Press, 1975), pp. 92-93.
38. Lightfoot, Sara Lawrence, *Worlds Apart: Relationships Between Families and Schools* (New York: Basic Books, 1978).
39. I am indebted to Gil Steiner for this phrase.
40. Lieberman, Jethro, *The Tyranny of Experts* (New York: Walker, 1970). For an excellent discussion of professionalization, see also Becker, Howard (ed.), *Sociological Work* (Chicago: Aldine, 1970), and Friedson, Eliot, *Profession of Medicine* (New York: Dodd, Mead, 1970).
41. Lieberman, *The Tyranny of Experts.*
42. Radl, Shirley, *Mother's Day Is Over* (New York: Charter House, 1973), p. 125.
43. Lasch, *Culture of Narcissism,* p. 291.
44. Cited in Boggs, Elizabeth, "Who is Putting Whose Head in the Sand or in the Clouds?" in Turnbull and Turnbull, *Parents Speak Out,* p. 60.
45. Beck, Rochelle, and Butler, John, "An Interview with Marian Wright Edelman." *Harvard Educational Review,* Vol. 44, February 1974, p. 72.
46. Hill, Robert, *The Strengths of Black Families* (New York: Emerson Hall, 1972), p. 2.

4: WHAT PARENT GROUPS PROVIDE

1. U.S. Department of Health and Human Services, *Better Health for Our Children: A National Strategy,* the report of the Select Panel for the Promotion of Child Health to the United States Congress and the Secretary of Health and Human Services, Vol. 1 (Washington, D.C.: DHHS, 1981), p. 291.
2. Kingsley, David, "The American Family in Relation to Demographic Change," in Westoff, Charles R., and Parke, Robert Jr., eds., *Demographic and Social Aspects of Population Growth,* Vol. 1, Commission on Population Growth and the American Future (Washington, D.C.: Government Printing Office, 1972); cited in Keniston, Kenneth, *All Our Children* (New York: Harcourt, Brace, Jovanovich, 1977), p. 4.

3. Children's Defense Fund, "America's Children and Their Families: Basic Facts" (Washington, D.C.: Children's Defense Fund, 1979), p. 5.
4. Keniston, *All Our Children,* p. 229.
5. "Who's for Children?" Address of Marian Wright Edelman, president, Children's Defense Fund, to the National Conference on Social Welfare, May 1980.
6. Troup, Phil and Sara, "One Family's Experience: Sibling Adoption," *COAC Newsletter,* New York Council on Adoptable Children, Spring 1977.
7. Caplan, Gerald, and Kililea, Marie, *Support Systems and Mutual Help* (New York: Grune and Stratton, 1976); see Chapter 1, "The Family as a Support System."
8. Roos, Philip, "Parents of Mentally Retarded People," *International Journal of Mental Health,* Vol. 6, No. 1, pp. 96–119.
9. McBridge, Angela Barron, *The Growth and Development of Mothers* (New York: Harper and Row, 1974), p. 69.
10. *Child Abuse Prevention and Treatment Act,* Hearings before the Subcommittee on Children and Youth, Committee on Labor and Public Welfare, United States Senate, March 1973.
11. "The Mothers' Center: A Self-Descriptive Paper," November 1977.
12. Zimmerman, Hope, et al., "The Mothers' Center," *Children Today,* March/April 1977, p. 13.
13. Manatt, Marsha, *Parents, Peers, and Pot* (Rockville, Maryland: National Institute on Drug Abuse, 1979), p. 19.
14. Ibid., p. 20.
15. Monaco, Grace, "Family Support Groups" (Washington, D.C.: Candlelighters, 1977).
16. Rioux, William, et al., *You Can Improve Your Child's School* (New York: Simon and Schuster, 1980).
17. Manatt, *Parents, Peers, and Pot,* p. 13.

5: SHAKING UP INSTITUTIONS

1. "America's Children and Their Families" (Washington, D.C.: Children's Defense Fund, 1979), p. 9.
2. Ibid., p. 8.
3. deLone, Richard, *Small Futures* (New York: Harcourt, Brace, Jovanovich, 1979), p. 107.
4. "Selected statistics in the 60 largest local public school systems: United States 1979-80," in National Center for Education Statistics, *Digest of Education Statistics 1981,* p. 41.
5. Hentoff, Nat, "Look for the Parents' Union Label," *Village Voice,* Vol. 25, No. 34, August 20-26, 1980.

6. New York City Comptroller Harrison J. Goldin, testimony concerning foster-care legislation before the United States Senate, Committee on Finance, Subcommittee on Public Assistance, July 18, 1977.
7. Mnookin, Robert, "Child Custody Adjudication," in Duke University School of Law, *Law and Contemporary Problems,* Vol. 39, No. 3, Summer 1975, p. 274.
8. Goldin, testimony concerning foster-care legislation.
9. O'Leary, Elizabeth, "Survey of Psychosocial Policies and Programs in Hospitals," Association for the Care of Children's Health, 1982.
10. "A Summary of Statistics Related to the National Drunk Driving Problem," fact sheet distributed by Representative Michael Barnes, House of Representatives, U.S. Congress, 1982.
11. Kahn, Alfred, *Child Advocacy: Report of a National Baseline Study* (Washington, D.C.: U.S. Department of Health, Education and Welfare, 1973), p. 65.
12. Davies, Don (ed.), *Schools Where Parents Make a Difference* (Boston: Institute for Responsive Education, 1976), p. 7.
13. *60 Years of Parent Involvement* (New York: United Parents Associations of New York City, Inc., 1977).
14. Fernandez, Happy, *Parents Organizing to Improve Schools* (Columbia, Maryland: National Committee for Citizens in Education, 1976).
15. "Courtwatching," Newsletter of the National Federation of Parents for Drug-Free Youth, Summer 1982.
16. Steinberg, Lois, "How Suburban Parents Cope With Educational Bureaucrats," *Citizen Action in Education,* Vol. 4, No. 1, Fall 1976.
17. Friedman, Paul, *The Rights of Mentally Retarded Persons* (New York: Avon Books, 1976), p. 57.
18. Ibid., p. 58.
19. Ibid., p. 59.

6: WORKING FOR LAWS THAT WORK FOR CHILDREN

1. Will, George, "For Drunk Drivers, Fearsome Penalties," *Washington Post,* May 2, 1982.
2. Remarks of Representative Shirley Chisholm before the Conference of the National Coalition of ESEA Title I Parents, October 8, 1977.
3. I am indebted to Gil Steiner for personal conversations that enriched my understanding of the relationship of "acts of God" and "acts of will" to the legislative process.
4. Senate Report No. 95-167, Child Abuse Prevention and Treatment and Adoption Reform Act of 1978, p. 46.
5. Report from Closer Look, Summer 1976.

7: PARENT GROUPS

1. Newsletter of Children in Hospitals, Spring 1975.
2. "Anger and Action After the Tears," *Washington Post,* October 17, 1982.
3. Fernandez, Happy, *Parents Organizing to Improve Schools* (Columbia, Maryland: National Committee for Citizens in Education, 1976).
4. *Adoptalk,* Newsletter of the North American Council on Adoptable Children, Summer 1978.
5. Kuykendall, Crystal, *Developing Leadership for Parent/Citizen Groups* (Columbia, Maryland: National Committee for Citizens in Education, 1976), p. 39.
6. "Chapter Development Manual" (Redondo Beach, California: Parents Anonymous, 1974), p. 3.
7. Des Jardins, Charlotte, "How to Organize an Effective Parent Group and Move Bureaucracies" (Chicago, Illinois: Coordinating Council for Handicapped Children, 1971).
8. Ibid., p. 40.
9. I am indebted here to Dr. T. Berry Brazelton, who first proposed to me that professionals working with children will inevitably be inclined to some competitive feelings toward parents, as a natural part of the bonding process.
10. Katz, A. H., "Self-Help Organizations and Volunteer Participation in Social Welfare," *Social Work,* Vol. 15, 1970, pp. 51-60.
11. Lasch, Christopher, *Haven in a Heartless World: The Family Besieged* (New York: Basic Books, 1977); see chapters on "Social Pathologists and the Socialization of Reproduction" and "Doctors to a Sick Society."
12. Marcus, Lee, "Patterns of Coping in Families of Psychotic Children," *American Journal of Orthopsychiatry,* Vol. 47, No. 3, July 1977.

8: A LOOK TOWARD THE FUTURE

1. "Percent of the population 3 to 34 years old enrolled in school, by age and by State: Spring 1970," in National Center for Education Statistics, *Digest of Education Statistics 1980,* p. 10.
2. "Direct expenditures of State and local governments for all functions and for education, by per capita amount and percent of per capita income: 1976-77," in National Center for Education Statistics, *Digest,* p. 25.
3. "Median school years completed by persons 25 years old and over, by sex, race and State: 1970," in National Center for Education Statistics, *Digest,* p. 18.

4. "Expenditures per pupil in average daily attendance in public elementary and secondary schools, by State: 1978-79," in National Center for Education Statistics, *Digest 1981,* p. 81.

Bibliography

Nearly all the parent self-help and advocacy organizations listed in the appendix distribute literature. Many will send a list of publications upon request. The following are additional materials that the reader might find helpful. An asterisk (*) means that this organization distributes a number of publications and should be contacted for more information.

Abbott, Grace. *The Child and the State.* Chicago: University of Chicago Press, 1938.
Adams, Margaret. *Mental Retardation and Its Social Dimensions.* New York: Columbia University Press, 1971.
Annas, George. *The Rights of Hospitalized Patients.* New York: Avon Books, 1975.
Aptheker, Herbert. *A Documentary History of the Negro People in the United States.* Secaucus, N.J.: Citadel Press, 1973.
Arms, Suzanne. *Immaculate Deception: A New Look at Women and Childbirth in America.* Boston: Houghton Mifflin, 1975.
Bane, Mary Jo. *Here to Stay: The American Family in the Twentieth Century.* New York: Basic Books, 1977.
Barber, Virginia, and Skaggs, Merrill. *The Mother Person.* New York: Bobbs-Merrill, 1975.
Berger, Peter, and Neuhaus, Richard. *To Empower People: The Role of Mediating Structures in Public Policy.* Washington, D.C.: American Enterprise Institute for Public Policy Research, 1977.
Bilken, Douglas. *Let Our Children Go.* Syracuse, N.Y.: Human Policy Press, 1976.
Billingsley, Andrew, and Giovanni, Jeanne. *Children of the Storm: Black Children and American Child Welfare.* New York: Harcourt Brace Jovanovich, 1972.
Boggs, Elizabeth. "Relations of Parent Groups and Professional Persons in Community Situations." *American Journal of Mental Deficiency* 571, 1 (1952): 109-115.
Boston Women's Health Book Collective. *Our Bodies, Ourselves.* New York: Simon and Schuster, 1971.
──────. *Ourselves and Our Children.* New York: Random House, 1978.

Bremner, Robert. *Children and Youth in America: A Documentary History.* Cambridge, Massachusetts: Harvard University Press, 1970-74.
Callahan, Sidney. *Parenting: Principles and Politics of Parenthood.* Baltimore, Md.: Penguin Books, 1974.
Caplan, Frank (ed.). *Parents' Yellow Pages.* New York: Anchor Books, 1978.
Caplan, Gerald, and Kililea, Marie. *Support Systems and Mutual Help.* New York: Grune and Stratton, 1976.
*Children's Defense Fund. *Children Without Homes.* Published by the Children's Defense Fund, 1520 New Hampshire Avenue, N.W., Washington, D.C. 20036. 1979.
*Collins, Alice, and Pancoast, Diane. *Natural Helping Networks.* Published by the National Association of Social Workers, 1425 H Street, N.W., Washington, D.C. 20005.
*Council for Exceptional Children. *State Law and Education of Handicapped Children.* Published by the Council for Exceptional Children, 1920 Association Drive, Reston, Virginia 22091.
*Davies, Don (ed.). *Schools Where Parents Make a Difference.* Published by the Institute for Responsive Education, 704 Commonwealth Avenue, Boston, Massachusetts 02215.
deLone, Richard. *Small Futures: Children, Inequality and the Limits of Liberal Reform.* New York: Harcourt Brace Jovanovich, 1979.
Evans, Glen. *The Family Circle Guide to Self-Help.* New York: Ballantine Books, 1979.
Friedman, Paul. *The Rights of Mentally Retarded Persons.* New York: Avon Books, 1976.
Friedson, Eliot. *Patients' View of Medical Care.* New York: Russell Sage, 1961.
_____. *Profession of Medicine.* New York: Dodd, Mead, 1970.
_____. *Professional Dominance: The Social Structure of Medical Care.* New York: Atherton, 1970.
Goldstein, Joseph, Freud, Anna, and Solnit, Albert. *Beyond the Best Interests of the Child.* New York: Free Press, 1973.
_____. *Before the Best Interests of the Child.* New York: Free Press, 1979.
Good, H. G. *A History of American Education.* New York: Macmillan, 1962.
Greenfield, Josh. *A Place for Noah.* New York: Pocket Books, 1978.
Grotberg, Edith (ed.). *200 Years of Children.* Washington, D.C.: Superintendent of Documents, Government Printing Office, 1976.
Handlin, Oscar, and Handlin, Mary. *Facing Life: Youth and Family in American History.* Boston: Little, Brown, 1971.

Hargrove, Carol, and Dawson, Rosemary. *Parents and Children in the Hospital.* Boston: Little, Brown, 1972.

Hill, Robert. *The Strengths of Black Families.* New York: Emerson Hall, 1972.

Hope, Karol, and Young, Nancy. *Momma.* New York: Merton, Plume and Meridian Books, 1976.

Howell, Mary. *Helping Ourselves: Families and the Human Network.* Boston: Beacon Press, 1975.

*International Childbirth Education Association. *The Pregnant Patients' Bill of Rights — The Pregnant Patients' Responsibilities.* Available from ICEA Publication/Distribution Center, Post Office Box 9316, Midtown Plaza, Rochester, New York 14604.

Joffe, Carole. *Friendly Intruders.* Berkeley: University of California Press, 1977.

Jones, Philip, and Jones, Susan. *Parents Unite! The Complete Guide For Shaking Up Your Children's School.* Ridgefield, Ct.: Wyden Books, 1976.

Kahn, Alfred, et al. *Child Advocacy: Report of a National Baseline Study.* Washington, D.C.: Superintendent of Documents, Government Printing Office, 1973.

Katz, Sanford. *When Parents Fail: The Law's Response to Family Breakdown.* Boston: Beacon Press, 1971.

Keniston, Kenneth, and The Carnegie Council on Children. *All Our Children: The American Family Under Pressure.* New York: Harcourt Brace Jovanovich, 1977.

Klaus, Marshall, and Kennell, John. *Maternal-Infant Bonding.* St. Louis, Mo.: C. V. Mosby, 1976.

Klein, Carole. *The Single Parent Experience.* New York: Walker, 1973.

*Kuykendall, Crystal. "Developing Leadership for Parent/Citizen Groups." Columbia, Md.: National Committee for Citizens in Education, 1976.

Ladner, Joyce. *Mixed Families: Adopting Across Racial Boundaries.* New York: Anchor Books, 1978.

Lasch, Christopher. *The Culture of Narcissism: American Life in an Age of Diminishing Expectations.* New York: W. W. Norton, 1979.

_____. *Haven in a Heartless World: The Family Besieged.* New York: Basic Books, 1977.

Lazarre, Jane. *The Mother Knot.* New York: Dell, 1976.

Lightfoot, Sara Lawrence. *Worlds Apart: Relationships Between Families and Schools.* New York: Basic Books, 1978.

Levine, James. *Who Will Raise the Children? New Options for Fathers (and Mothers).* New York: J. B. Lippincott, 1976.

McBride, Angela Barron. *The Growth and Development of Mothers.* New York: Harper and Row, 1973.

Mencher, S. *Poor Law to Poverty Program.* Pittsburgh: University of Pittsburgh Press, 1967.

Mnookin, Robert. "Foster Care — In Whose Best Interest?" *Harvard Educational Review* 43 (1973): 467–479.

*National Association for Retarded Citizens. *Monitoring the Rights to Education.* Published by the National Association for Retarded Citizens, Post Office Box 6109, Arlington, Texas 76011.

National Commission on Children in Need of Parents. *Who Knows? Who Cares? Forgotten Children in Foster Care.* New York: The National Commission on Children in Need of Parents, 1979. Available through the Child Welfare League of America.

*National Committee for Children in Education. *Network.* Published periodically by the National Committee for Citizens in Education, Suite 410, Wilde Lake Village Green, Columbia, Maryland 21044.

*National Self-Help Clearinghouse. *Self-Help Reporter.* Published periodically by the National Self-Help Clearinghouse. Graduate School and University Center/CUNY, 33 West 42nd Street, Room 1227, New York, New York 10036.

Platt, Anthony. *The Child Savers.* Chicago: University of Chicago Press, 1961.

Radl, Shirley. *Mother's Day Is Over.* New York: Charterhouse, 1973.

Rich, Adrienne. *Of Woman Born: Motherhood as Experience and Institution.* New York: W. W. Norton, 1976.

Rioux, William, et al. *You Can Improve Your Child's School.* New York: Simon and Schuster, 1980.

Rivera, Geraldo. *Willowbrook: A Report on How It Is and Why It Doesn't Have to Be That Way.* New York: Random House, 1972.

Roman, Mel, and Hadad, William. *The Disposable Parent: The Case for Joint Custody.* New York: Penguin Books, 1979.

Rothman, Sheila. *Woman's Proper Place: A History of Changing Ideals and Practices, 1870 to the Present.* New York: Basic Books, 1978.

*Schimmel, David, and Fischer, Louis. *The Rights of Parents in the Education of Their Children.* Columbia, Maryland: National Committee for Citizens in Education, 1977.

Steiner, Gilbert Y. *The Children's Cause.* Washington, D.C.: Brookings Institution, 1976.

———. *The State of Welfare.* Washington, D.C.: Brookings Institution, 1971.

Tyack, David. *The One Best System: A History of American Urban Education.* Cambridge: Harvard University Press, 1974.

United States Department of Health, Education and Welfare. *Mental Retardation: Century of Decision.* Washington, D.C.: Superintendent of Documents, Government Printing Office, 1976.

———. *A Reader's Guide for Parents of Children with Mental, Physical*

or Emotional Disabilities. Washington, D.C.: Superintendent of Documents, Government Printing Office, 1976.
Weiss, Robert. "Helping Relationships: Relationships of Clients With Physicians, Social Workers, Priests and Others." *Social Problems* 20,43 (1973): 319-328.
Wortis, Joseph (ed.). *Mental Retardation.* (Vols. 1-4). New York: Grune and Stratton, 1972.
Zigler, Edward, and Valentine, Jeanette. *Project Head Start.* New York: Free Press, 1979.

Index

Abbott, Grace, 57
Abusive parents, 16, 22, 28, 76, 80, 152
   benefits to, from self-help groups, 90-91
   literature on, from Parents Anonymous, 102
   testimony of, before House of Representatives, 79
   See also Parents Anonymous
Accessibility, concern for, of self-help groups, 96
ACLD Newsbriefs, 22
Activists, sixties, 46-47
Adcock, Gerald, 135, 139-140, 142
Addams, Jane, 56
Adoptalk, 156, 163
Adoption Assistance and Child Welfare Act (1980), 15, 140, 142, 149, 189-190
Adoption(s), 14-15, 22-23, 26, 27, 84
   and alternative services, 172
   assistance, financial, 31
   groups discussing concerns on, 95-96
   international, 16
   older, minority, or handicapped, 30
   reform, legislation concerned with, 146, 189, 190
   subsidies, 131, 141-142
   transracial, 114
   See also North American Council on Adoptable Children (NACAC)
Adoptive parents, 22-23, 26, 28, 83, 84, 114
   and alternative services, 172
   grass-roots lobbying by, 135
   impact of, on funds for foster care, 123
   and lawsuit on behalf of five black children in foster care, 126-127
   legislation enacted by, 146, 189, 190
   organizations helping, 14-15
   social events planned by, 100-101

Advocacy, alternative services vs., 172-173
   See also Case advocacy
African Methodist Episcopal Church, 34
Akerley, Mary, 75, 81-82, 115, 138, 139, 141
   on alternative services vs. advocacy, 172
   and recruitment of parents, 152
   on relationship between parents and professionals, 168
Alcoholics Anonymous, 7, 17, 38-39, 87, 88
Alcoholism, 38
Almshouse, development of, 51
Alternative services, vs. advocacy, 172-173
American Academy of Pediatrics, 155
American Cancer Society, 140
American Journal of Orthopsychiatry, The, 175
Anderson, Bill, 145
Anti-Gary Leagues, 33
Aphasia, 5
Appropriation committees, congressional, 138
Assistance, practical, and mutual support among parents, 93-98
Association for Children with Learning Disabilities (ACLD), 16, 136-137, 147, 156, 191
   expansion of, 159
   funding of, 157
   Newsbriefs, 22
Atlanta, children slain in, 18
Autistic children, 14, 23, 74-76, 81, 110-111
   literature on parents of, 102, 165
   See also National Society for Autistic Children (NSAC)

Baker, Josephine E., 53, 54, 57
Barnes, Rep. Michael, 133, 135

Baumgartner, Leona, 58-59
Birney, Alice, 35
Black(s)
  cultural deprivation theories about, 55
  families, strengths of, 73
  victories for, 34, 36-37, 38
Black Parents for Quality Education, 117, 153, 154, 159, 160
  and case vs. class advocacy, 170, 171
  and coalition politics, 169
  growth of, 82
Blind children, 38
Block grants, parent groups' opposition to, 149
Bonding, parent-child, 4, 19-21, 23-24, 165-166
Brace, Charles Loring, 52
Bradley, Robert A., 41
Brazelton, T. Berry, 166
Brodie, Elayne, 147
Bunin, Sherry, 116
Bureau of Charities, 57
Busby, Daphne, 13, 24, 28, 76, 96, 160
  on case advocacy, 98
  on telephone counseling, 97
  on welfare mothers, 101-102

Cancer, children with, 12-13, 23, 76, 99-100, 132-133
  public sympathy for, 141
  See also Candlelighters
Cancer Act, 135
Candlelighters, 23, 71, 76, 85, 88, 185
  emotional restraint of, 141, 154
  expansion of, 159
  founding of, 12, 151
  Good News Column in newsletter of, 99-100
  legislative handbook drafted by, 134-135
  newsletter of, 12-13, 99-100
  professional parents in, 156
  role of, in enactment of legislation, 131, 132, 134, 140
  setting for meetings of, 164
  telephone counseling at, 97
Cannabis, 93
Caplan, Gerald, *Support Systems and Mutual Help* (with M. Kililea), 85-87

Carnegie Corporation of New York, 2
Carnegie Council on Children, *All Our Children,* report of, 60; *Small Futures* study for, 104-105
Case advocacy, 98, 115, 147-148
  vs. class advocacy, 170-171
Cerebral palsy, children with, 38
Chapter 766 (Massachusetts Special Education Law), 38, 140, 145-146
Chemotherapy, 13, 23
Chestor, Gerri, 74-75
Child abuse, 22, 28
  See also Abusive parents
Child Abuse, Prevention, and Treatment Act, 79, 90
Child Abuse Prevention, Treatment and Adoption Reform Act (1978), 146
Child and Family Services Act (1975), 59-60
Childbirth, 28-29, 30, 39, 64-65
  fathers' participation in, 30, 120
  at home, 120
  practices, sweeping changes in, 40-41, 62
  sharing experience of, 13
  See also Mothers' Center
Childbirth Education Association, 30, 152
  International, 8
Child development, explosion in knowledge about, 39-40
Children in Hospitals, 70, 77, 82, 102, 120, 191
  attitudes toward professionals of, 166, 168-169
  and Boston Children's Hospital, 164
  and case vs. class advocacy, 170, 171
  expansion of, 160, 162
  organization of, 12
  recruiting parents for, 151
  survey of, on hospital policies on overnight stays by parents, 117, 121, 174
Children's Aid Society, 52, 53
Children's Bureau, U.S., 5, 36, 57, 58, 59
Children's Defense Fund, 8, 72
Children's Hospital Medical Center (Boston), 121, 164

Index 225

Children's-rights movement, 72
Children Today, 91
Child-snatching, 16
Child vs. *Beame,* 126-127
Child-welfare legislation, 131
Chisholm, Shirley, 134
Chronically ill children, 26, 30
"Citizen Action in Education," 123-124
Civil-rights movement, 37, 47, 72, 88
Class advocacy, case vs., 170-171
Clinton, DeWitt, 51
Closer Look, 143, 147-148
Coalition(s), 140
　need for, in public policies for children, 189-190
　politics, 169-170
College Board, SAT of, 42
Communities, parents' self-help groups as new, 82-89
Congressional Record, 59-60
Consciousness, releasing, 90-93
Consumer pressure, institutional reform and, 119-122
Controversy, impact on issues of absence of, 141-142
Counseling, parent-to-parent group and individual, 95-96
　telephone, 96-98
Court watching, 118
Cultural deprivation, theories about, 55

Davies, Don, 116
　ed., *Schools Where Parents Make a Difference,* 108
Day care, 60, 177-179
Deaf children, 15, 38
Dean, Dorothy, 143
Desegregation, 36-37
Dick-Read, Grantly, 41
Discussion groups, 95-96
Divorce rate, increases in, 83
Down's syndrome, 165
Drug use, 10-11, 15, 26, 28, 172-173
　self-help groups for, 39, 94-95
　See also National Federation of Parents for Drug-Free Youth (NFP)
Drunk drivers, 17, 27, 31, 118, 128-129, 152
　and coalition politics, 170
　and incentive grants to states, 131
　judicial tolerance for, 106
　legislation to deter, 130, 131, 133-134, 135, 140
　See also Mothers Against Drunk Drivers (MADD)

Economic incentives, mobilizing, for institutional reform, 122-127
Edelman, Marian Wright, 72
Education, 63
　exclusion of parents from, 64, 65
　of immigrant children, 62-63
　parent activism in, 33-34, 42-46
　See also Black Parents for Quality Education; National Committee for Citizens in Education (NCCE); School(s)
Educational Bill of Rights for the Retarded Child, 72
Education for All Handicapped Children Act (EHA, PL 94-142), 15, 30-31, 38, 131, 133, 175
　analysis of passage of, 141
　appropriations for, 189-190
　implementation of, 143-145, 183
　importance of coalitions to passage of, 140
　proposed consolidation of, with Title I, 149
　regulations developed for, 139
Elementary and Secondary Education Act, 140
　Title I of, 149
Enactment, legislative, 131-134
　coalitions, 140
　getting regulations, 138-139
　grass-roots lobbying, 134-137
　personal lobbying, 137-138
　piggybacking, 140
　uncontroversial issues, 141-142
　using media, 139-140
Executive branch of government, 122

Facts, getting, for institutional reform, 114-117
Families, extended, 85-86, 88
Family Educational Rights and

226 Parent to Parent

Privacy Act (1974), 45
Fathers
  child custody decisions faced by, 83
  divorced, 76, 95
  and divorce reform, 116
  participation of, in childbirth, 30, 120
Fathers United for Equal Justice, 76, 95, 96, 116, 190
Federal Register, 139
Federation for Children with Special Needs (Boston), 98–99, 146, 147, 148
Federation of Community Controlled Child Care Centers of Alabama (FOCAL), 177–179, 182, 184
Federation of Parents' Organizations for the New York State Mental Institutions, 104, 114, 124–125, 153, 170
  Long Island Regional Council of, 81, 96, 171
Fernandez, Happy, 81, 115, 153, 155
Fetal monitoring, 40
Foster care, 27, 52, 84, 105–106, 116
  impact of adoptive parents on funds for, 123
  lawsuit brought on behalf of five black children in, 126–127
  New York City comptroller's audit of, 118–119
  reform of, 189, 190
Friedman, Paul, 127
Frontiers, 71, 85
Funding, of parent groups, 157–159

Gamblers Anonymous, 87
Gary Plan, 33
Golden, Harrison, 105–106
"Good Morning America," 82
Government, relationship between parents and, 187–189
Grass-roots lobbying, 134–137
Great Depression, 58
Great Society, 36
Groups, *see* Organization(s)
Grove, Judy, 155, 160–161

Handicapped children, 25, 26, 28, 30, 83, 149
  conference on early intervention with, 102
  organizations helping parents of, 15, 74, 98
  public education for, 15, 30–31, 37, 38
  reaction of parents with, 89
  role of parents in getting services for, 143–146
  victories for, 35–36, 37–38
  See also Parents' Campaign for Handicapped Children and Youth
Harper, Gordon, 166
Harris, Sophia, 177–178
Hartwell, Lynn, 101
Harvard Education Review, 56
Hayward, Mary, 152
Head Start, 5, 8, 184
Health, parental activism in, 38–41
  See also Hospitals
Health, Education and Welfare, Department of, 125
Hearst, Phoebe, 5
Hill, Robert, *The Strength of Black Families,* 73
Home-birth movement, 120
Hospitals
  consumer pressure on, 121–122
  development of emphasis on parent responsiveness by, 183–186
  policies of, on parental presence during child's stay, 30, 31, 106, 109, 117–118, 120, 183
  See also Children in Hospitals; Parents Concerned for Hospitalized Children (PCHC)
House of Representatives, U.S., 79, 133, 134, 146, 149
  drunk-driving bills introduced in, 130, 135
House Public Works and Transportation Committee, 135
Howard, Rep. James J., 135
Howard-Barnes bill, 130
Howell, Mary, 65
Hunter, Robert, 56

Image, projecting serious, 153–156
Immigrants
  children of, 62–63

Index 227

flood of, 52–53
Implementation, legislative, 142–146
  and case advocacy, 147–148
  and education for professionals, 147
Individual Education Program (IEP), 143–144, 147–148, 187
Insiders, information about institutions provided by, 114
Institute for Responsive Education (IRE), 45, 116
Institutions
  identified, 107–108
  involving parents in reform of, 108–113
  parents viewed by, 64–69
  parents' views of, 61–64
  personal pain and reform of, 104–108
  strategies for reform of, 113
    consumer pressure, 119–122
    getting facts, 114–117
    mobilizing economic incentives, 122–127
    public exposure, 117–119
Integration, racial, 34, 36–37
International Association of Parents of the Deaf, 15
International Childbirth Education Association, 8
Iran, hostages in, 18
Isolation, breaking out of parental, 81, 82

Joint Commission on Accreditation of Hospitals, 112, 124
Jolly K, 76, 90–91, 161

Kahn, Al, 107–108
Katz, Al, *The Strength in Us,* 167
Katzman, Al, 147
Kelley, Florence, 56
Kennell, John, 41
Keniston, Kenneth, *All Our Children,* 60
Kennedy family, mental retardation and, 36
Kidnapping, 16
Kililea, Marie, 87–88
  Support Systems and Mutual Help (with G. Caplan), 85–87

Kilpatrick, James, 60
Klaus, Marshall, 41
Ku Klux Klan, 36
Kuykendall, Crystal, 159–160

Ladies' Home Journal, 81, 151
La Leche League, 8, 41, 152
Lamaze, Fernand, 41
Lapicki, Lee, 79–80, 85, 96–97, 151–152, 157, 175
  on professional sponsors, 166, 168
Lasch, Christopher, 69, 167–168
  Culture of Narcissism, 60
  Haven in a Heartless World, 60, 168
Lawsuits, use of, by parent activists, 125–127
Learning disabled children, 16, 22, 26, 38
  organization of national parent network for, 136–137
  research about, 94
  See also Association for Children with Learning Disabilities (ACLD)
Le Clair, Bob, 76
Legislation, *see* Enactment; Implementation
Legislative branch of government, 122
Legislative committees, congressional, 135, 137
Leukemia, 12
Lightfoot, Sara Lawrence, 65
Lightner, Cari, 106
Lightner, Cindy, 106
Lobbying
  grass-roots, 134–137
  personal, 137–138
Loneliness, parental, 24–25

McBride, Angela Barron, *Growth and Development of Mothers,* 90
McLean, Agnes, 171
McNamara, Joan, 163
Mainstreaming, 83
Make Today Count, 17
Manatt, Marsh, 100
Marcus, Lee, 175
Marijuana, 26, 31, 85, 93
Media, use of, to get legislation passed, 139–140

Medicaid/Medicare, 124
Mental illness, 17, 38, 112
  children with, 81
Mental institutions, publicly funded, 103–104, 112
Mentally retarded children, 29, 35–36
  abuses of, 103–104, 107, 112
  lawsuit brought on behalf of, 125–126
  parents of, 72
  research about, 94
Miller, Rep. George, 189
Mills vs. *Board of Education for the District of Columbia,* 37
MOMMA, 101
Monaco, Grace, 13, 94, 97, 100, 158, 163
  on emotional restraint of Candlelighters, 141
  on founding of Candlelighters, 151
  on grass-roots and personal lobbying, 135, 137
  on institutional change, 111
  on legislative proposal formulated by Candlelighters, 132–133
  on professionals, 168
  on prolonged commitment of parents to Candlelighters, 85
  on use of media, 140
Mondale, Walter, 90
Montessori, Maria, 54
Moore, Helen, 117, 154, 160
Morgan, Stanley, 182
Mortality, infant and maternal, 62
Mothers, early activism on behalf of, 34–35
Mothers Against Drunk Drivers (MADD), 17, 31, 106, 129, 149
  and coalition politics, 170
  recruiting members for, 152
  role of, in enactment of legislation, 130, 131, 133–134, 140
Mothers' Center, 10, 68, 70, 76, 161–162
  and alternative services, 173
  consciousness-releasing at, 90, 91
  emphasis on equality at, 99
  expansion of, 163
  founding of, 13, 150
  growth of, 82
  on health professionals, 27, 28–29
  impact of, on hospitals, 120
  staffing of, 157
Mothers' Clubs, 54

National Assessment of Educational Progress, 42
National Association for Mental Health, 140
National Association for Retarded Children, 72
National Association for Retarded Citizens, 8, 36, 89
National Association of Manufacturers, 59
National Cancer Institute (NCI), 94, 135
National Coalition of ESEA Title I Parents, 14, 42, 45, 145
  role of, in enactment of legislation, 131, 134, 140
National Committee for Citizens in Education (NCCE), 45, 74, 97–98
  "Who Controls the Schools?," 116
  You Can Improve Your Child's School, 98
National Congress of Mothers, 35
National Federation of Parents for Drug-Free Youth (NFP), 11, 15, 82, 93, 94–95, 191
  and alternative services, 172–173
  court watching by, 118
  on professionals, 167
National Parents' Center, 14
National Safety Council, 140
National Self-Help Clearinghouse, 17
National Society for Autistic Children (NSAC), 23, 70, 75–76, 138, 140
  anger at professionals at, 165
  and article on autism in *Ladies' Home Journal,* 81–82, 151
  founding of, 14, 150–151
  funding of, 157
  literature of, on parents of autistic children, 102
  professional parents in, 156
  recruiting parents for, 152
National Urban League, 73

Networks, national parents, 136-137
  grass-roots lobbying by, 134-137
Newsletters, of parent groups, 136
New York City Council on Adoptable Children (COAC), 95-96, 116, 118, 126, 172
  founding of, 150
  recruiting parents for, 152
New York Public School Society, 51
New York Society for the Reformation of Juvenile Delinquents, 52
New York State Association for Retarded Children, Inc. vs. *Carey,* 125-126
North American Council on Adoptable Children (NACAC), 14-15, 22, 116, 131, 142, 163, 170
  "Citizen Action Manual," 116
  home base of, 156
  role of, in enactment of legislation, 131, 139

Obesity, self-help groups for, 17, 39, 87
Oppenheim, Rosalyn, 151
Opportunities for Adoption Act (1978), 15, 135, 139
Organization(s)
  choices and alternatives offered by, 190-191
  expansion of, to statewide or national organization, 159-169
  funding of, 157-159
  home base of, 156-157
  of parent self-help and advocacy groups, 150-153
  projecting image of, 153-156
  sustaining commitment in, 173-174
"Organized Motherhood," 34-35
Our Bodies, Our Selves, 39
OURS, 16
Overeaters Anonymous, 17

PARC case (*Pennsylvania Association for the Retarded* vs. *Commonwealth of Pennsylvania*), 37
Parent Advisory Council (PAC), 134
Parental Kidnapping Prevention Act, 16
Parent Representatives on Better Education, 45
Parents
  images of, 48-50
    consequences of negative, 61-69
    incompetent, 49, 50-56, 65, 67, 69, 176
    resourceful, 49, 50, 69-78
    victimized, 49-50, 56-60, 67, 69, 76
  recruiting, 151-153
  relationship between government and, 187-189
  relationship between professionals and, 27-30, 65-67, 174-176, 186-187
  single, 16, 83 (*see also* Parents Without Partners)
    Black, 13, 24, 28, 76 (*see also* Sisterhood of Black Single Mothers)
Parents' Action Network, 45
Parents Anonymous, 7, 22, 76, 85, 100, 175
  and Adoption Assistance and Child Welfare Act, 189
  "Chapter Development Manual" of, 161, 164
  expansion of, 159
  first meeting of Baltimore parents at, 80
  founding of, 16
  Frontiers, 71, 85
  funding of, 157, 188
  growth of, 16, 82
  "guidelines for achievement" of, 88
  literature put out by, on abusive parents, 102
  professional sponsor to, 166, 168
  recruiting parents for, 151-152
  testimony of, before House of Representatives, 79
Parents' Campaign for Handicapped Children and Youth, 15, 74, 143, 144, 147
Parents Concerned for Hospitalized Children (PCHC), 117, 121, 153, 154, 155, 160-161
  and case vs. class advocacy, 170
Parents Magazine, 30

Parents' Network, 45
Parents' Union for Public Schools, 45, 81, 92-93, 153, 163-164
  budget of, 105
  on case advocacy, 98
  founding of, 14
  image of, 154-155
  lawsuit filed by, 125
  membership size of, 82
  "Parents' Rights' Card" of, 94
  "Two-Year Plan" of, 173-174
Parents United for Full Funding, 45
Parents Without Partners (PWP), 16
Parent-Teachers Association (PTA), 35, 44-45, 152
Pediatric medicine, 67
Pell, Claiborne, 133
Perkins, Frances, 58
Pilgrim state hospital (New York), 124-125
Pinckney, Judge, 57-58
Planned Parenthood Association, 181
Poverty, association of incompetence and, 50-51, 55-56
"Pro-family movement," 60
Professionals(s)
  anger at, 165-169
  burnout, 168-169
  education for, 147
  parent, in advocacy groups, 156
  parental relationships with, 27-30, 65-67, 174-176, 186-187
Progressive era reforms, 34, 53-54, 56, 58
Psychological proximity, 20-21
Proximity, physical, 20-21
Proximity, psychological, 20-21
Ptosis, 5
Publication services, 119
Public exposure, and institutional reform, 117-119

Radl, Shirley, 68
Reach to Recovery, 17, 39
Reagan, Ronald, 145, 149
Reardon, Mary Ellen, 154
Recovery, Inc., 87
Regulations, getting federal, 138-139

Retarded, see Mentally retarded children
Rimland, Bernard, 81, 151
Roos, Philip, 29, 89
Ross, Catherine, 57
Rothman, Sheila, 54
Russell, Robert, 137

Salt Lake City school system, 179-182
  School Community Council of, 180-181
Schlossman, Steven, 56
Schneier, Max, 103, 124-125, 153
Scholastic Aptitude Test (SAT), 42
Schools
  development of emphasis on parent responsiveness by, 183-186
  parent activism in, 42-46
  reform, 29, 112
  See also Education; Parents' Network; Parents' Union for Public Schools
Scopolamine, 64-65
Segregation, 34
Self-images, parents', 48-49, 68-69
  increase in, from self-help groups, 89
  by practical assistance, 93-98
  by releasing consciousness, 90-93
  by renewing spirit, 98-102
Senate, U.S., 130, 133, 146, 149
Senate Finance Committee, 105
Services, inadequate, 25-27
Sex education, 42
Sexton, Dot, 128-129
Sexton, Tom, 128, 129
Sexton, Tommy, 129
Shared governance, 182
Sheppard-Towner Act (1921), 54
Sisterhood of Black Single Mothers, 13, 24, 70, 76, 96, 160
  and Adoption Assistance and Child Welfare Act, 190
  motivation behind formation of, 28
  social events sponsored by, 100
Smoking, cigarette, self-help groups for, 39
Social agencies, development of emphasis on parent responsiveness by, 183-186

Social legislation, support for, 56–57
Social Security, 63
Spirit, renewing, with mutual support, 98–102
Stereotypes, negative, 76–77
Stress, parental, 21–24, 32
  and inadequate services, 25–27
  and loneliness, 24–25
  and relationships with professionals, 27–30
Support system functions, 85–87
Supreme Court, U.S., 36–37

Teacher unions, 116–117
Telephone counseling, 96–98
Thomas, Donald, 181, 182
Title I, 144, 145, 147, 149, 190

Unions, labor, 56–57
United Parents' Associations of Greater New York Schools (later United Parents' Associations of New York City, UPA), 33–34, 92, 96, 112

Vietnam War, 47

Washington Post, 130, 152
Wellesley College, 53
Wheat, Patte, 71
Will, George, 130
Willowbrook state hospital (New York), 27, 103–104, 114, 118
  lawsuit brought against, 125–126, 127
  parents' march on, 103, 108, 112
Women's movement, 39, 47, 88
Workhouse, development of, 51
World War II, 58

Zimmerman, Hope, 76, 91

Peggy Pizzo has been active in children's services for more than fifteen years. As a former member of the White House staff, she has worked on Head Start, day care, adoption assistance, and child abuse programs. Currently an affiliate faculty member in the Bush Center at Yale, Pizzo lives with her husband and two children in Maryland.